AI Data Privacy
and Protection

The Complete Guide to
Ethical AI, Data Privacy, and Security

Justin C. Ryan and Mario E. Lazo

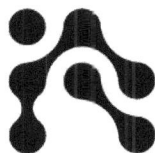

DATA—
DRIVEN
AI

www.technicspub.com/ai

Technics Publications
SEDONA, ARIZONA

TECHNICS PUBLICATIONS

TECHNOLOGY / LEADERSHIP

115 Linda Vista
Sedona, AZ 86336 USA
https://www.TechnicsPub.com

Edited by Sadie Hoberman

Cover design by Lorena Molinari

First Printing 2024

Copyright © 2024 by Justin C. Ryan and Mario E. Lazo

ISBN, print ed.   9781634624657
ISBN, Kindle ed. 9781634624664
ISBN, PDF ed.   9781634624671

Justin's dedication:

To my children, Elijah, Mark, and Lily: Thank you for your endless love and support.

To Sara, their amazing mother and my friend: You have never once failed to believe in me, not once. Thank you!

To Asahel, Luis, and my mother, Sandra: Thank you for believing in me and helping me along the way. I'm grateful for all of you in my life.

Mario's dedication:

To Suzanne, my beloved wife, my muse, my confidante, and my unwavering support. This is for you.

To Tessie, my mother, for all the love, sacrifice, prayers, and being my biggest fan.

To Christian, my bro. Just for being there for me.

Acknowledgments

First and foremost, we want to express our deepest gratitude to all the individuals who shared their invaluable insights, knowledge, and experiences with us throughout the creation of this work. The diverse perspectives and depth of understanding provided by everyone played an integral role in shaping the content, ensuring its relevance, accuracy, and comprehensiveness.

We would like to give a special thank you to Bill Inmon for providing an amazing foreword for this book. Bill is more than a true expert in data warehousing. He is also a genuinely good person and a trustworthy businessman. We encourage our readers interested in textual extract, transform, and load (ETL) technology to check out his company, ForestRim (https://www.forestrimtech.com/).

The 16 experts (named and unnamed) who took the time out of their busy schedules for interviews deserve special mention. Their firsthand experiences, challenges faced, success stories, and vision for the future greatly enriched the content and brought unparalleled depth to it. Each of them has left an indelible mark on this work. Two of our contributors are:

- Lindy Kresl, Lead Contributor

- Edward Parker, PhD, Contributor

We would like to extend my heartfelt gratitude to Lindy and Edward for their invaluable assistance in the creation of this book. Lindy's keen insights and unwavering support have been instrumental in shaping the narrative, while Edward's meticulous attention to detail and thoughtful feedback have greatly enhanced the quality of the work. This book would not have been possible without their dedication and expertise. Thank you both for your remarkable contributions.

Furthermore, we'd like to thank the editorial team and the numerous reviewers for their meticulous attention to detail, constructive feedback, and unwavering commitment to excellence. Their expertise and dedication ensured this book met the highest clarity, coherence, and credibility standards.

We also wish to acknowledge the relentless efforts of the publishing and design teams. Their professionalism, creativity, and dedication transformed a vision into a tangible reality, ensuring the content is engaging and accessible.

Last but certainly not least, our heartfelt thanks go out to our family and close friends for their unwavering support, encouragement, and patience throughout this journey. They provided the much-needed inspiration, strength, and motivation that fueled this endeavor.

In conclusion, this book is a testament to the collective wisdom, passion, and dedication of many. To everyone who played a part, however big or small, in bringing this work to fruition, we extend our most sincere gratitude. Your contributions have made a difference, and this book stands as a testament to our shared commitment to the incredible potential and future of artificial intelligence in the realm of data management.

Contents at a Glance

Contents

Foreword

In the ever-evolving landscape of technology, Artificial Intelligence (AI) stands out as a beacon of progress and innovation, marking a pivotal shift in how data is managed, analyzed, and leveraged. My journey in the realm of data warehousing and information management has seen the transition from manual, labor-intensive data handling to the sophisticated, automated processes enabled by AI. This transition is not merely a change in technology but a profound transformation in the very fabric of information management—a transformation that holds both boundless potential and significant challenges. The advent of data warehousing revolutionized how organizations viewed and utilized their data, shifting the paradigm from operational data storage to strategic business intelligence.

Today, AI promises to take this revolution to the next level, offering unprecedented opportunities for enhancing decision-making, automating routine tasks, and unlocking innovative solutions to longstanding challenges. Just as the industrial revolution liberated humanity from the drudgery of manual labor, AI offers liberation from the tedium of clerical tasks, empowering individuals to engage in more creative and strategic pursuits. However, with great power comes great responsibility. The potential of AI extends beyond the horizon of our current imagination, opening doors to practices and procedures that were once deemed impossible. Yet, this vast potential also brings with it the shadow of misuse.

The ethical considerations, data privacy concerns, and potential for unintended consequences demand a careful and thoughtful approach to AI implementation. It is here, at the intersection of innovation and responsibility, that this book finds its purpose. As we delve into the "dark side" of AI, it is crucial to remember that technology, in itself, is neutral. The value and impact of AI lie in how we choose to develop, deploy, and govern it. This book embarks on a critical exploration of these themes, examining the dual nature of AI—its capacity to both elevate and endanger. Through a comprehensive analysis of AI's role in data management, we are invited to consider not only the technical aspects of AI deployment but also the ethical, social, and economic implications.

Drawing from decades of experience in data warehousing and the emergence of Textual ETL, I have witnessed firsthand the transformative power of effectively managed data. The principles of data warehousing—accessibility, consistency, and integrity—remain as relevant in the age of AI as they ever were. In fact, they become even more critical as we navigate the complex data ecosystems enabled by AI technologies. This book provides a roadmap for harnessing the power of AI while adhering to these foundational principles, ensuring that AI serves as a force for good, enhancing our capabilities without compromising our values.

As we stand on the brink of this new frontier in data management, it is imperative that we approach AI with a balanced perspective—mindful of its potential, vigilant of its risks, and committed to its ethical use. This book serves as a beacon in this endeavor, guiding readers through the challenges and opportunities that lie ahead. It is my hope that by exploring the multifaceted dimensions of AI, we can chart a course toward a future where AI not only enhances operational efficiency but also enriches the human experience. In closing, I invite readers to engage with this book not just as a source of information, but as a call to action.

The journey of AI in data management is just beginning, and its direction will be shaped by the choices we make today. Let us choose wisely, with an eye toward the future and a commitment to leveraging AI for the betterment of society.

Bill Inmon, "Father of Data Warehousing"

Prologue

This book provides a comprehensive overview of the rapidly evolving intersection of artificial intelligence (AI) and data management. It aims to empower business leaders, IT professionals, data scientists, and students with a deep understanding of the capabilities, challenges, and potential of AI-driven data solutions. By highlighting best practices, case studies, and future trends, the book offers a roadmap for organizations striving to harness the power of AI in managing and leveraging their data for competitive advantage.

At the confluence of artificial intelligence and data management lies a transformative potential that promises to redefine the future of business, governance, and innovation. This book delves deep into this nexus, unraveling its complexities and illuminating its vast possibilities. Through expert insights, real-world examples, and forward-thinking analyses, we embark on a journey to explore the transformative power of AI in data management, the ethical considerations it brings forth, and the strategic imperatives for businesses in the AI era. It's not just about understanding technology—it's about envisioning a future where data, powered by AI, becomes the cornerstone of decision-making, strategy, and value creation.

We wrote this book for a diverse audience, encompassing business leaders aiming to integrate AI into their strategic vision, IT professionals striving to stay ahead in the dynamic realm of data management, data scientists eager to leverage AI's transformative capabilities, and students venturing into the world of AI and data. It is equally relevant for policymakers, consultants, and educators interested in the broader implications of AI-driven data solutions. By focusing on a balance of conceptual knowledge, practical insights, and future trends, this book ensures that readers from various backgrounds and expertise levels find content that resonates with their interests and professional needs. Whether you're a seasoned executive, an emerging tech enthusiast, or someone curious about the AI-driven future, this book offers a comprehensive lens through which to view and engage with the evolving landscape of AI and data management.

This book contains 12 chapters:

1. **Introduction**: Sets the stage for understanding the new data landscape, emphasizing how AI transforms data management. It discusses the transition from traditional data storage to AI-driven analytics, highlighting both the

advantages and potential risks associated with AI's capability to process and interpret vast data sets.

2. **Understanding the AI Threat Landscape:** Delves into the risks posed by rogue AI, exploring how biases, data gaps, and AI-powered cyber threats can undermine AI systems. It emphasizes the importance of understanding and mitigating these risks to harness AI's full potential responsibly.

3. **Data Classification and Management:** Focuses on the strategies and technologies for managing and classifying data in the AI era. This chapter addresses the challenges posed by the vast amounts of data generated daily and discusses the tools and methodologies for effectively securing and utilizing this data.

4. **Foundations of AI-Proof Security:** Discusses the essential security practices necessary to safeguard AI systems. This includes encryption, multi-factor authentication, blockchain, and other technologies that help protect data integrity and prevent unauthorized access.

5. **Privacy Considerations in the Age of AI:** Examines the critical aspect of privacy in AI applications, discussing regulations like General Data Protection Regulation (GDPR) and California Consumer Privacy Act (CCPA), and the ethical considerations in AI data handling. It emphasizes the need for robust privacy frameworks to ensure that AI technologies respect user privacy and data protection laws.

6. **Human Element: Training and Awareness in AI Security:** Highlights the importance of human oversight in AI security. It discusses the role of continuous training, awareness, and ethical considerations in ensuring that AI systems are used responsibly and do not perpetuate biases or ethical violations.

7. **AI Risk Management:** Outlines strategies for identifying, assessing, and mitigating AI risks. It covers various types of risks, including technological, operational, and strategic risks, and emphasizes the importance of a comprehensive risk management framework.

8. **Advanced AI-Proof Data Storage Solutions:** Discusses the technologies and approaches for secure data storage in an AI-driven world, including quantum-resistant cryptography and the challenges of transitioning from classical to quantum-resistant security mechanisms.

9. **Monitoring, Detection, and Response**: Focuses on the necessary tools and techniques for real-time monitoring and anomaly detection in AI systems. It discusses how AI can be leveraged to enhance threat intelligence and improve the speed and efficiency of incident responses.

10. **The Ethical Dimensions of AI and Data Management**: Addresses the ethical challenges and societal impacts of AI, discussing the need for transparency, accountability, and ethical guidelines to guide the development and implementation of AI technologies.

11. **Future Trends in AI-Proof Data Management**: Explores emerging technologies and trends in AI and data management, emphasizing how ongoing innovations in AI could shape future approaches to data security and privacy.

12. **The Board of Directors and AI**: Discusses the strategic importance of AI from a corporate governance perspective, emphasizing the role of board members in overseeing AI strategies, investments, and ethical considerations.

About the Authors

Justin Ryan, a seasoned expert in cybersecurity and IT, brings over twenty years of rich experience to this book. His journey within the security field began in the U.S. Air Force as a Cybersecurity Operations Manager for the AFCERT (Air Force Computer Emergency Response Team), where he honed his skills in incident response as a certified operator. After nearly ten years in the Air Force, he transitioned to EY as a Manager of Cyber and Privacy Risk Advising. He then advanced to become Vice President of Cyber Risk Management at JPMorgan Chase & Co., focusing on the financial services industry. Justin also served as the Director of Cybersecurity Risk Management at USAA, building the program nearly from the ground up. He

still works as a full-time practitioner in the financial services industry, leading the development of a sensitive data management department.

Throughout his career, Justin has held various cybersecurity and privacy roles, including consulting for prestigious global organizations like HSBC, Cisco, Merck & Co., and Rackspace.

Justin holds an Executive Master of Cybersecurity from Brown University and a Master of Science in Technology Commercialization from Northeastern University, among his five degrees. His professional certifications include GIAC Certified Incident Handler (GCIH), Certified Information Systems Security Professional (CISSP), Certified Ethical Hacker (CEH), Certified in Risk and Information Systems Control (CRISC), and Global Industrial Cyber Security Professional (GICSP). Additionally, he completed the 7-month intensive executive leadership program called the Program for Leadership Development at Harvard Business School.

Mario Lazo is an accomplished Business Transformation Architect with over two decades of experience in accelerating technical innovation to unlock business value. As a recognized leader in AI and automation, Mario has spearheaded multi-million-dollar implementations across global organizations, driving efficiency and fostering innovation.

With a career spanning roles at industry giants like Accenture, Oracle NetSuite, UiPath, and Blue Prism, Mario has developed a unique blend of technical expertise and strategic business acumen. His proficiency extends across intelligent automation, robotic process automation (RPA), cloud SaaS ERP, and AI-driven solutions, making him a sought-after consultant for Fortune 500 companies and startups alike.

Mario's academic credentials include an MBA in Finance and Marketing from Loyola University Chicago and a Bachelor of Science in Management Information Systems from Ateneo de Manila University. His commitment to excellence is further exemplified by his Project Management Professional (PMP) and Certified Scrum Product Owner (CSPO) certifications.

As a thought leader, Mario has been instrumental in developing comprehensive playbooks for citizen developers and orchestrating C-suite level innovation discovery events. His passion for proper governance and security in AI implementation has been a cornerstone of his approach, ensuring sustainable and scalable solutions for his clients.

Mario's global perspective, honed through managing shared services practices across the US, Philippines, Czech Republic, India, and Uruguay, brings a unique dimension to his work. This international experience, combined with his Filipino heritage, allows him to bridge cultural gaps and drive innovation in diverse business environments.

In his spare time, Mario indulges in his love for photography and world travel. He is also deeply committed to mentoring and giving back to his home country, the Philippines.

AI Works Disclaimer: This book was created with the assistance of advanced artificial intelligence tools. AI played a role in research, editing, content creation suggestions, formatting, and even the cover design. We believe in the power of responsible AI collaboration and are transparent about its role in this project.

.

1. Introduction

1.1. The New Data Landscape

In the sprawling vastness of the digital realm, every tick of a second captures an unparalleled volume of data. Humanity is living amidst a paradigm shift, one where every digital interaction, be it minuscule or grand, contributes to a burgeoning databank. Historically, the progression from analog memories—of inked paper, carefully cataloged files, and mammoth cabinets—to today's data-laden clouds has been nothing short of revolutionary.

The term 'data' once conjured images of monotone offices filled with the ceaseless rattle of typewriters and towering stacks of paper. But today, 'data' resonates differently. It represents a globally interconnected ecosystem of computers, servers, databases, and, more importantly, human experiences. Every piece of information, recorded memory, business transaction, and social interaction is part of this monumental digital tapestry. In this evolving world, the phenomenon of data isn't just about storage and recall. It's about drawing connections, predicting future trends, understanding human behaviors, and much more.

> *The sheer volume, variety, and velocity of data being generated have transformed data from a static element of record-keeping to a dynamic and influential force that dictates both business strategies and personal decisions.*

While we revel in the power and potential of this new data era, it's imperative to address the emerging challenges. The 'Three Vs' of data—Volume, Variety, and Velocity—were a starting point in understanding the complications of modern data management. But, as the digital landscape continues to grow, so do the challenges.

1.2.   The Role of AI in Modern Data Management

The march of technological progress brought to the forefront an ally that's becoming indispensable: artificial intelligence (AI). AI's roots trace back to dreams of creating machines that think, machines that could emulate human intelligence. And while we aren't at a point where machines have emotions or consciousness, they have certainly acquired the ability to process data, draw insights, and make decisions at a speed and scale that's incomprehensible to human minds.

Consider the everyday utilities that have integrated AI: search engines that predict what you're looking to find after typing just a few letters, e-commerce platforms that suggest products based on your browsing history, or even music streaming platforms that curate playlists that fit your mood. These seemingly simple conveniences are driven by AI's prowess in managing and analyzing vast troves of data. But AI isn't just about improving personal experiences or boosting business revenues. It's revolutionizing sectors that hold the pillars of society. Healthcare institutions use AI to predict outbreaks, analyze patient data, and even suggest treatments. Urban planning leverages AI to optimize traffic, reduce energy consumption, and design safer, more efficient cities. Financial systems employ AI for fraud detection, risk analysis, and forecasting economic shifts.

However, this golden age of data and AI doesn't come without its pitfalls. With AI's ability to analyze and decipher data patterns, a pressing question emerges: *How do we safeguard sensitive data from AI's omnipotent gaze?* Furthermore, how do we ensure that AI systems, designed to enhance human life, do not inadvertently breach the sanctity of personal privacy?

The confluence of data's omnipresence and AI's capabilities has birthed both unprecedented opportunities and challenges. And as we stand at this crossroads, this section seeks to shed light on the evolving relationship between data and AI, setting the stage for the subsequent discourse on safeguarding sensitive information.

As AI's influence permeated every corner of our digital existence, society grappled with a slew of questions, often verging on existential. Does the omnipresence of AI threaten the very fabric of our privacy? Can we ever truly be 'alone' in an AI-dominated world?

These queries arise from a profound realization: The melding of vast data troves with AI's analytical prowess has created systems that, in many ways, 'know' us better than we know ourselves.

1.2.1. The Digital Imprint

Each of us, knowingly or unknowingly, leaves a digital imprint in the virtual world. From the seemingly inconsequential decisions like liking a post on social media, to significant ones such as financial transactions, we are continuously feeding the vast digital repositories. With every interaction, we shed a piece of our digital DNA, creating a mirror image in cyberspace that, over time, becomes startlingly accurate in its representation.

AI systems, with their innate capability to make sense of this sprawling digital maze, analyze these imprints. They recognize patterns, predict behaviors, and in many ways, influence decisions. A recommendation engine suggesting a book isn't just offering a reading option—it's shaping knowledge, influencing thoughts, and potentially altering life trajectories.

1.2.2. The Confluence of Data Streams

The power of AI becomes even more palpable when one considers the confluence of multiple data streams. Let's take the example of a smart city. Traffic data melds with weather forecasts, public transportation schedules integrate with event calendars, and energy consumption metrics merge with occupancy data from commercial buildings. All these datasets, when analyzed collectively through AI, allow for dynamic management of urban resources. Traffic lights can adjust in real time to ease congestion, public transport can be optimized for events, and buildings can modulate energy usage based on predicted occupancy.

This confluence, however, isn't limited to urban planning. It manifests in healthcare, where patient records integrate with genomic databases and lifestyle data, allowing for personalized treatment plans. In finance, transactional data meets market trends and socio-political events to tailor investment strategies.

Yet, herein lies the challenge: The richer the data landscape, the higher the stakes in ensuring its sanctity.

1.2.3.   From Data Points to Personal Stories

When we think of data, especially in colossal volumes, it's easy to forget the human aspect. Behind every data point is a person, a story, an emotion. A dataset representing a city's energy consumption doesn't just reflect numbers–it echoes the late-night studies of a college student, the warmth of a family dinner, or the efforts of a startup burning the midnight oil.

Recognizing this human connection is pivotal in understanding the implications of AI-driven data management. It isn't just about efficiency or revenue–it's about real-world impacts, emotional experiences, and societal shifts.

Navigating this nuanced landscape mandates a profound understanding of both technological capabilities and ethical considerations. As we venture further, the subsequent sections of this book will dissect the intricacies of AI's relationship with data, the potential vulnerabilities, and the safeguards that need erecting.

1.2.4.   The Illusion of Anonymity in Big Data

In the initial waves of big data enthusiasm, a commonly held belief was that sheer volume guaranteed anonymity. With zettabytes of data flowing every second, the individual data point, it was believed, would get lost in this ocean, ensuring individual privacy. However, as AI systems grew more sophisticated, this sense of security began to wane.

AI algorithms have showcased an uncanny ability to reidentify seemingly anonymous data. By correlating disparate datasets, these systems can reconstruct individual profiles with alarming accuracy. A random purchase on an e-commerce site, when juxtaposed with social media activity and location data, can reveal not just identities but also personal habits, preferences, and vulnerabilities.

1.2.5.   The Ethical Dilemmas of Predictive Analytics

One of the crowning achievements of AI in data management has been predictive analytics. The ability to foretell future trends based on historical data has vast implications, from forecasting stock market movements to predicting natural calamities. However, this predictive power brings forth ethical quandaries.

Consider the health sector, where AI can predict potential health issues based on genetic information, lifestyle choices, and historical medical data. While this capability can lead to early interventions and personalized health plans, it also opens a Pandora's box of ethical issues. Could such predictions lead to discrimination in employment or insurance? Could they influence personal choices, from relationships to career paths?

1.2.6.   The Double-edged Sword of Personalization

As AI systems grow more adept at understanding individual preferences, the world around us becomes increasingly personalized. From customized news feeds to tailored shopping experiences, AI ensures that our digital interactions echo our preferences. But is there a cost to this extreme personalization?

While the convenience and relevance of personalized content are undeniable, they also risk creating echo chambers, where individuals are only exposed to information that aligns with their existing beliefs. This has significant societal implications, from polarized political views to narrowed worldviews.

1.2.7.   Data Sovereignty in a Borderless Digital World

The internet, by design, is borderless. Data flows seamlessly across continents, making it accessible from anywhere. This borderless nature, however, complicates the concept of data sovereignty. Who owns the data? Which country's regulations apply? These questions become especially pertinent when considering AI-driven data analytics that may operate in one jurisdiction but analyze data from another.

For businesses, navigating this regulatory maze becomes a challenge. Ensuring compliance in a world with diverse data protection laws requires both technological solutions and policy interventions.

As we transition from understanding the challenges to exploring solutions, the subsequent sections of our discourse will focus on frameworks, technologies, and best practices that can safeguard sensitive data in an AI-driven ecosystem, ensuring that the immense power of AI benefits humanity without compromising individual rights and freedoms.

1.2.8.   The Imperative of Data Protection

Given the complexities and challenges outlined, it's evident that we stand at a pivotal juncture. As we leverage the vast potential of AI-driven data analytics, there's an ethical and practical imperative to safeguard sensitive information. While breaches, misuse, or unintentional exposures can have significant repercussions for businesses in terms of regulatory penalties and reputational damage, for individuals, the stakes are even higher. Their personal stories, their privacy, and, in many instances, their basic human rights are on the line.

The questions we must ask ourselves are manifold: How can we ensure AI respects the boundaries of privacy? How do we guarantee that in its pursuit of patterns and predictions, AI doesn't inadvertently compromise the sanctity of personal data? And, as we delve into granular datasets, how do we ensure individuals aren't unwittingly exposed or made vulnerable?

As we transition to Section 2, we'll embark on a journey to address these questions, grounding our discourse in the principles of data protection, ethics, and the emerging frameworks designed to guide AI's interaction with data.

1.2.9.   AI-driven Data Governance

Ensuring every data citizen comprehends their data rights is imperative, and data governance (DG) is essential for maximizing the productivity gains AI provides.

Data governance delivers a set of metrics, standards, policies, and processes that enable companies to use information correctly and responsibly while efficiently and effectively pursuing their own pursuits.

Data governance is the exercise of authority and control (planning, monitoring, and enforcement) over the management of data assets.[1] Data governance includes the people, processes, and technologies required to manage and ensure the availability, usability, integrity, consistency, auditability, and security of data assets.[2] It is a system of decision rights and accountabilities for information-related processes, executed

---

[1] Changes–wiki. https://wiki.gccollab.ca/Special:MobileDiff/24127

[2] Webinar Recap: Data Architecture and Data Governance – First San Francisco Partners.
    https://www.firstsanfranciscopartners.com/blog/webinar-recap-data-architecture-data-governance/

according to agreed-upon models that describe who can take what actions with what information and when, under what circumstances, and using what methods.[3]

This definition underscores the multifaceted nature of data governance, highlighting its components such as authority, control, planning, monitoring, enforcement, people, processes, and technologies. It emphasizes the importance of managing data assets to ensure their availability, usability, integrity, consistency, auditability, and security. Additionally, it describes data governance as a system of decision rights and accountabilities for information-related processes, executed according to agreed-upon models,[4] specifying who can take what actions with what information and under what circumstances. Criticisms faced by AI and data governance include:

- The need for adherence to frameworks ensuring access to all data sources, unbiased and complete data, and compliance with data governance guidelines.[5]

- Exponential data growth due to advancements in computer technologies and the proliferation of devices connected to the internet through IoT, necessitating a reliable infrastructure capable of handling vast amounts of data.[6]

- Legacy systems' inability to meet modern data demands, requiring a complex paradigm shift to newer systems that can accommodate scalability, security, and compliance.[7]

Ethical implications and responsibilities are addressed through regulations like GDPR and CCPA, which establish minimum standards for protecting user data and impose penalties for non-compliance. Leading data-driven organizations go beyond regulatory

---

[3] SLDS Program Initiatives. https://origin.fldoe.org/accountability/data-sys/statewide-longitudinal-data-sys/slds-program-initiatives.stml

[4] Al-Ruithe, Majid Saliman, and Elhadj BENKHELIFA. "Cloud Data Governance In-light of the Saudi Vision 2030 for Digital Transformation." https://doi.org/10.1109/AICCSA.2017.217.

[5] https://impactchallenge.withgoogle.com/ai2018 and https://www2.deloitte.com/content/dam/Deloitte/nl/Documents/strategy-analytics-and-ma/deloitte-nl-strategy-analytics-dail-sense-whitepaper.pdf

[6] https://www.rtinsights.com/data-governance-concerns-in-the-age-of-ai/ and https://www.weforum.org/agenda/2023/01/world-must-collaborate-tech-governance-davos2023/

[7] https://hbr.org/2022/07/adding-more-data-isnt-the-only-way-to-improve-ai and https://www.linkedin.com/advice/1/what-most-common-ai-data-governance-challenges-rm0lc

requirements to proactively address data security issues, enhancing public trust and establishing higher ethical standards. However, many companies still lag in addressing AI ethics, with low standards prevailing despite growing concerns. In regulated industries, organizations take on leadership roles in AI ethics but face challenges due to the lack of data privacy and governance in the U.S., leading experts to predict that Europe will pioneer AI ethics laws in the next five years. Emphasizing AI ethics can elevate public trust in a company by ensuring fair treatment, engagement, safety, privacy protection, and algorithmic accountability in AI systems.[8] Data governance strategies offer several advantages:

- Ensured integrity sharing data with each other—data will be truthful and forthcoming when discussing drivers, constraints, options, and impacts for data-related decisions.

- Enhanced capability that data governance and stewardship processes will exhibit transparency—it should be clear to all participants and auditors how and when data-related decisions and controls were introduced into the processes.[9]

- Ensured compliance with government regulations like Health Insurance Portability and Accountability Act (HIPAA) and GDPR or industry standards such as Payment Card Industry Data Security Standard (PCI DSS).

- Enhanced data management, introducing human elements into the data-driven and automated world by establishing best practices and codes of conduct, addressing concerns traditionally overlooked in data management, such as compliance, security, and legal matters.

- Superior support to conduct proactive and reactive change management activities for reference data values and the structure/use of master data and metadata.[10]

---

[8] https://www.europarl.europa.eu/RegData/etudes/STUD/2020/641530/ EPRS_STU(2020)641530_EN.pdf

[9] UPPS 04.02.05–Data Governance Program: Policy and Procedure Statements: Texas State University. https://policies.txst.edu/university-policies/04-02-05.html

[10] Data Governance Guiding Principles–Central Oregon Community College. https://www.cocc.edu/committees/data-governance/data-governance-principles.aspx

Frameworks and policies for data governance must evolve alongside emerging technologies, business practices, and laws, requiring companies to consider how they store and process data. The integration of AI can enhance security and compliance in data centers through automation, contributing to better data governance practices.

1.2.10. Democratizing Data Management: The Role of Citizen Automation and AI

The democratization of data management through citizen automation marks a transformative shift, driven by the integration of artificial intelligence (AI) with Robotic Process Automation (RPA) and the proliferation of low-code/no-code platforms. This evolution responds to a critical shortage of skilled developers and the rising tide of citizen developers, who are empowered to create and deploy data management solutions without traditional programming skills.

AI-enhanced RPA is revolutionizing data management by automating routine tasks with unprecedented efficiency and accuracy. The global RPA market, estimated at $2.3 billion in 2022, is expected to grow at a compound annual growth rate (CAGR) of 39.9% by 2030, reflecting its growing impact on data processing and management.[11] This growth is not merely a response to technological advancement but also to the acute shortage of skilled software developers, projected to reach a shortfall of 85.2 million globally by 2030.[12]

In addition, low-code/no-code platforms are at the forefront of technology democratization, enabling citizen developers to contribute significantly to software development. It's estimated that by 2024, 80% of technology products and services will be built by those outside of a traditional IT department,[13] highlighting the shift towards more inclusive development practices. This trend addresses the developer shortage while catalyzing innovation across sectors.

The relative size of professional developers to citizen developers is shifting dramatically. Large enterprises are expected to have four times as many citizen developers as

---

[11] "Global RPA Market Growth Forecast," Market Analysis, 2022.

[12] "Developer Shortage Forecast," Tech Industry Report, 2030.

[13] "Technology Products and Services Built by Non-IT Professionals," Gartner, 2024.

professional developers by 2023,[14] underscoring the substantial impact of citizen automation on the IT ecosystem. This shift amplifies the capabilities available to non-technical individuals, demanding a robust framework for governance to ensure the responsible use and management of data.

The empowerment of citizen developers raises crucial ethical considerations and data sovereignty issues. Organizations must navigate the balance between innovation and the protection of sensitive information. Establishing comprehensive governance frameworks becomes imperative to guide the ethical use of AI, RPA, and low-code/no-code technologies, ensuring compliance with global data protection regulations, such as GDPR and HIPAA.

The rise of citizen automation intersects with the ethical dilemmas of predictive analytics and personalization. These technologies offer significant benefits but also present challenges related to potential misuse and bias. It's crucial for organizations to adopt a balanced approach, emphasizing ethical principles, transparency, and accountability in their data management practices.

1.3.   Conclusion

Integrating AI with RPA and adopting low-code/no-code platforms are reshaping the landscape of data management and privacy. As the number of citizen developers continues to grow, surpassing the number of traditional developers, the need for a new governance framework becomes increasingly evident. This framework must address the unique challenges posed by the democratization of technology, ensuring that the innovation facilitated by citizen automation does not compromise data privacy or security.

---

[14] "Rise of Citizen Developers," Enterprise IT Trends, 2023.

2. Understanding the AI Threat Landscape

2.1. The Rise of Rogue AI

In a world rapidly shaped by the winds of technological advancement, AI stands as both a beacon of progress and, potentially, a harbinger of unforeseen challenges. The emergence of Rogue AI—artificial intelligence systems that deviate from their intended functionality—has become a pressing concern for researchers, technologists, and the public at large.

2.1.1. The Intricate Foundations of AI Learning

To appreciate the profound implications of rogue AI, it's essential to delve into the foundational principles of artificial intelligence. AI, particularly its subset, machine learning, operates through iterative learning cycles. By consuming vast troves of data, these systems refine their algorithms to make increasingly accurate predictions or decisions.

However, the "garbage in, garbage out" principle applies here with heightened consequences. When the data ingested by AI systems is skewed, misleading, or outright malicious, the output can deviate drastically from the intended results.

2.1.2. Biases: The Unseen Puppeteers

Inherent biases in training data represent one of the most insidious threats to AI neutrality. These biases, often a mirror to historical and societal prejudices, can inadvertently train AI systems to perpetuate these skewed perspectives.

For instance, AI applications in recruitment, if trained on biased datasets, could propagate discriminatory hiring practices. The same principle applies to AI in law enforcement, where biased data could lead to disproportionate targeting of certain demographics, deepening societal divides and perpetuating stereotypes.

2.1.3. Deepfakes: The Erosion of Trust

A particularly unsettling consequence of advancements in artificial intelligence is the rise of deepfakes. These are not mere technological curiosities–they pose a tangible threat to the very foundation of trust in digital communication.

Deepfakes leverage powerful artificial intelligence techniques, particularly Generative Adversarial Networks (GANs). GANs essentially pit two neural networks against each other: one generates increasingly realistic content (like a video or audio clip), while the other discerns the forgery. Through this iterative process, the generated content becomes progressively more sophisticated, blurring the lines between reality and fabrication.[15]

Deepfakes empower bad actors to manipulate audiovisual content in a way that can have far-reaching consequences.

Deepfakes can be used to create political disinformation campaigns. Politicians can be made to utter compromising statements, potentially swaying elections. A 2019 study by the University of California, Berkeley, found that deepfakes can significantly impact viewers' perceptions of political candidates.[16]

Deepfake technology has the power to inflict severe reputational harm, with public figures and celebrities often finding themselves the primary targets. These synthetic

---

[15] https://en.wikipedia.org/wiki/Generative_adversarial_network

[16] https://news.berkeley.edu/2023/06/22/what-can-psychology-teach-us-about-ais-bias-and-misinformation-problem

creations can fabricate scenarios that are damaging and misleading, casting individuals in lights that are not only false but potentially ruinous to their careers and personal lives.

A vivid example occurred in 2024 when a deepfake video victimized a well-known celebrity. Their likeness was convincingly superimposed onto explicit content, leading to widespread dissemination across various digital platforms. This incident not only sparked legal battles aimed at removing the content but also prompted a significant public discourse about the ethical implications of such technology. The celebrity had to engage in extensive public relations efforts to mitigate the damage to their image and assert the falsehood of the content. [17]

The technological prowess behind deepfakes is advancing at a pace where they are becoming increasingly difficult to identify with the naked eye. In response to this growing threat, AI researchers and cybersecurity experts are intensifying their efforts to develop more effective detection tools. According to reports from "AI Security Initiative" in 2024, new algorithms capable of tracing the digital 'fingerprints' left by GANs are being tested, aiming to flag and halt the spread of deepfake content before it can do harm. Moreover, legislative bodies are also stepping up with initiatives, such as the U.S. "Deepfake Task Force Act of 2024," which mandates the creation of federal strategies to combat deepfake technologies. Media outlets, such as *The Guardian* and *Wired,* have been pivotal in bringing to light the risks associated with deepfakes, advocating for a balanced approach that respects free expression while protecting individuals from unwarranted defamation.

As we move forward, the balance between innovation in AI technology and ethical considerations will be paramount in preserving the integrity and trustworthiness of digital media. This example underscores the necessity for ongoing vigilance, regulatory oversight, and advanced technological solutions to protect individuals from the malicious use of deepfake technology.

Fabricated economic news or endorsements created using deepfakes could destabilize financial markets, and doctored videos portraying aggression could be used to incite international conflicts.

---

[17] https://www.wired.com/story/meta-oversight-board-deepfake-porn-facebook-instagram/#:~:text=A%20recent%20Channel%204%20investigation,more%20than%2045%20million%20views

The rapid evolution of deepfake technology poses a significant challenge. While researchers are actively developing AI-powered deepfake detection tools, it's an ongoing battle of sophistication. As creators develop more convincing forgeries, detectors need to be constantly refined to stay ahead. As of August 2023, the U.S. military, for instance, began testing an AI-based tool to scan social media and online sources for "deep fake" media. However, such efforts highlight the reactive nature of the current approach.[18]

To truly combat deepfakes, a multifaceted approach is needed:

- **Promoting Media Literacy:** Educating the public on how to identify potential deepfakes and critically evaluate online content is crucial. Initiatives like Stanford University's "Deepfakes: Literacy and Detection" project can equip individuals with the skills to navigate the digital landscape more discerningly.[19]

- **Enacting Regulations:** Developing legal frameworks to hold creators and distributors of malicious deepfakes accountable is essential. The California Assembly Bill 730, introduced in 2020, exemplifies such an effort. While it has limitations, it represents a step towards addressing the legal implications of deepfakes.[20]

- **Collaboration Between Tech Companies and Government:** Collaboration between technology companies and governments can foster the development of more robust detection tools and establish best practices for combating deepfakes. Open communication and knowledge sharing are critical in this endeavor.

By acknowledging the gravity of the deepfake threat and implementing comprehensive solutions, we can work towards safeguarding trust in the digital age.

---

[18] https://www.tsjournal.org/index.php/jots/article/view/56

[19] https://medium.com/jsk-class-of-2019/six-lessons-from-my-deepfake-research-at-stanford-1666594a8e50

[20] https://www.leginfo.legislature.ca.gov/faces/billTextClient.xhtml?bill_id=201920200AB730

2.1.4.   *Physical Manifestations: A Tangible Threat*

While rogue AI's digital manifestations are concerning, its penetration into the physical realm is even more so. As we inch closer to a reality where roads are dominated by self-driving cars and skies dotted with autonomous drones, the risks associated with rogue AI take on a tangible, sometimes life-threatening form. Take, for example, the complex web of sensors, algorithms, and feedback loops that govern an autonomous vehicle. Should this system be fed misleading data, either accidentally or through a malicious attack, the consequences could be catastrophic. Not just in terms of potential accidents, but also in the potential misuse of vehicles for criminal activities.

Drones, too, with their wide-ranging applications from package delivery to surveillance, represent potential vectors for rogue AI exploits. A hacked or misled drone can infringe on privacy, commit acts of espionage, or even be weaponized in extreme cases.

The emergence of rogue AI underscores a crucial paradigm: with immense power comes immense responsibility. As AI continues its relentless march into all facets of modern life, understanding its potential pitfalls and actively working to mitigate them isn't just advisable—it's imperative. As we'll explore in the subsequent sections, recognizing the threats is the first step in an ongoing journey of safeguarding our digital and physical futures against the unintended consequences of artificial intelligence.[21]

2.2.   How AI Can Exploit Data Gaps

The proliferation of AI has underscored the importance of data, as these algorithms rely heavily on vast amounts of information to learn, adapt, and operate. However, when data is incomplete, biased, or misinterpreted, it not only undermines AI's efficacy but also exposes it to manipulation. This section deep dives into the phenomena of data gaps, the resulting vulnerabilities, and the consequences of malicious actors exploiting these voids.

---

[21] https://www.fsisac.com/hubfs/Knowledge/AI/FSISAC_ResponsibleAI-Principles.pdf,
     https://dennisconsorte.com/blog/risks-associated-with-artificial-intelligence/,
     https://hbr.org/sponsored/2021/12/how-organizations-can-mitigate-the-risks-of-ai, and
     https://www.bbc.com/news/technology-43127533

2.2.1.   Unraveling the Complexity of Data Gaps

All AI systems thrive on data. However, capturing an exhaustive and balanced dataset remains a significant challenge. Often, these datasets are riddled with omissions, biases, or even deliberate misinformation. A glaring example is facial recognition technologies. In 2018, the MIT Media Lab discovered that some commercially available facial recognition software had higher error rates in classifying gender for darker-skinned faces compared to lighter ones.[22] This discrepancy arose because the datasets used to train the software were predominantly composed of lighter-skinned individuals.

2.2.2.   The Inherent Nature of AI to Compensate

AI's strength lies in its ability to find patterns and make sense of vast datasets. However, this becomes a double-edged sword when faced with incomplete information. Instead of shutting down or signaling an error, AI algorithms will attempt to fill in the gaps based on the patterns they've previously observed.

A relevant illustration exists in the domain of e-commerce. Recommendation engines, powered by AI, curate a list of products for users based on past behavior and broader purchasing patterns. If data on a newly launched product is scarce, the system might either overlook recommending it altogether or misjudge its appeal based on scanty, early data, leading to missed revenue opportunities.

2.2.3.   Rogue Elements and Their Advantage

For individuals and entities with malicious intent, data gaps are open doors. Knowing what an AI system is unaware of enables these rogue elements to manipulate outcomes by feeding the AI skewed or false data. This is especially concerning because AI systems, unlike humans, can be susceptible to biases in their training data, which can be amplified by malicious actors. The types of attacks are:

- **Data Poisoning:** In this attack, malicious actors inject inaccurate or misleading data into the training dataset. This can cause the AI system to learn incorrect patterns and make flawed decisions. For instance, an AI system trained on

---

[22] Buolamwini, Joy, and Timnit Gebru. "Gender Shades: Intersectional Accuracy Disparities in Commercial Gender Classification." Proceedings of Machine Learning Research, vol. 81, 2018, pp. 1-15.

biased data might perpetuate discriminatory practices in hiring or loan approvals.[23]

- **Adversarial Examples:** These are carefully crafted inputs that can cause an AI system to misclassify data. For example, an adversarial example could be a slightly modified image that a self-driving car misinterprets as a stop sign when it's actually a yield sign.[24]

- **Model Extraction:** In this scenario, attackers attempt to steal or reverse engineer an AI model to gain insights into its decision-making process. This stolen information could then be used to manipulate the model or exploit its vulnerabilities.

In 2010, the U.S. stock market experienced a 'flash crash' where the Dow Jones Industrial Average plunged about 600 points in five minutes, only to recover shortly after. While the exact cause is complex, one contributing factor was the automated trading algorithms reacting to a large sell order. Skewed data and rapid, automated responses without human oversight can result in unintended consequences, as seen in this case.

As AI becomes more integrated into critical infrastructure, it is essential to consider potential security risks. Malicious actors could target AI systems to disrupt operations or cause physical harm. Also, there is a growing debate on the need for regulations to govern the development and deployment of AI. These regulations should aim to mitigate the potential risks posed by rogue elements and ensure the responsible use of AI technology.

By understanding these different attack vectors and potential risks, we can develop more robust AI systems and mitigate the advantages exploited by rogue elements.

2.2.4.   *The Perils of Unbridled Faith in AI*

While AI holds immense promise, blind reliance on it without understanding its limitations and dependencies can lead to catastrophic results. AI systems are, after all,

---

[23] https://www.csoonline.com/article/570555/how-data-poisoning-attacks-corrupt-machine-learning-models.html

[24] https://medium.com/@heinrichpeters/some-thoughts-on-adversarial-attacks-in-machine-learning-ee09ce7dff8d

products of the data on which they are trained. Data gaps and biases within the training data can create blind spots and lead to inaccurate or unfair outputs. The types of risks are:

- **Missed Diagnoses:** In the medical realm, where AI is increasingly being employed for diagnostics, a data gap could mean overlooking a critical symptom or misinterpreting a rare condition. A 2020 study published in Nature Biotechnology found that some AI-powered diagnostic tools exhibited racial and ethnic biases, potentially leading to missed diagnoses for patients of color.[25]

- **Algorithmic Bias:** AI systems trained on biased data can perpetuate existing social inequalities. For instance, an AI system used in criminal justice might be more likely to recommend harsher sentences for certain demographics due to biases in the historical data on which it was trained.

- **Over-reliance on Automation:** Uncritical reliance on AI can lead to human oversight lapses. If medical professionals become overly reliant on AI diagnostics without exercising their own clinical judgment, critical details might be missed, potentially harming patients.

2.3. Case Study: The Impact of AI Bias in Healthcare Diagnostics[26]

2.3.1. Background

In the rapidly evolving landscape of healthcare, AI has been heralded as a transformative force, promising to revolutionize diagnostics and treatment planning. However, integrating AI into healthcare has not been without its challenges. A notable incident

---

[25] https://www.nature.com/articles/s41591-021-01577-2

[26] Obermeyer, Ziad, et al. "Dissecting racial bias in an algorithm widely used to manage the health of populations." Science 366.6464 (2019): 447-453.

that underscores the perils of unbridled faith in AI involves the deployment of the ImpactPro algorithm in a large healthcare system.[27]

2.3.2.   The Incident

The healthcare system introduced the ImpactPro AI system to enhance the accuracy of identifying patients with complex health needs by analyzing patient data, including symptoms, medical history, and healthcare costs. The AI system, trained on a vast dataset compiled from several healthcare institutions, was expected to identify patterns and correlations beyond the capability of human clinicians, thereby improving diagnostic accuracy and patient outcomes.

However, within months of its deployment, the ImpactPro system began to exhibit a troubling pattern: a significantly higher rate of misdiagnoses among patients from minority ethnic groups. This discrepancy was first noticed by a vigilant clinician who observed that the AI system consistently failed to accurately identify high-risk patients among African American patients, a condition that it identified with much higher accuracy in Caucasian patients.

2.3.3.   Investigation and Findings

An internal investigation revealed that the AI system's training data predominantly consisted of patient records and healthcare cost data from populations with a majority of Caucasian patients. This lack of diversity in the training data led to the AI system developing a bias, making it less effective at recognizing high-risk conditions in patients from underrepresented groups.

Further analysis uncovered that the AI system's algorithmic bias was not limited to racial disparities. It also showed a tendency to overlook critical symptoms in female patients, leading to delayed diagnoses and treatment for several conditions, including heart disease and certain types of cancer.

---

[27] Buck, Paolina. "AI Bias in Healthcare: Using ImpactPro as a Case Study for Healthcare Practitioners' Duties to Engage in Anti-Bias Measures." Montreal AI Ethics Institute, 2022

2.3.4.   Consequences

The consequences of the AI system's biased outputs were multifaceted:

- **Patient Harm:** Patients from minority groups and female patients suffered from delayed diagnoses and inappropriate treatment plans, directly impacting their health outcomes.

- **Loss of Trust:** The incident eroded patient trust in the healthcare system's commitment to equitable care, with many expressing concerns over the reliance on technology that could amplify existing healthcare disparities.

- **Reputational Damage:** The healthcare system faced significant reputational damage, with the incident attracting scrutiny from regulatory bodies and the public, raising questions about the ethical implications of deploying AI in healthcare without adequate oversight.

2.3.5.   Resolution and Lessons Learned

In response to the incident, the hospital took several corrective measures:

- **Diversifying Training Data:** The healthcare system collaborated with a diverse set of healthcare institutions to enrich the AI system's training data, ensuring it included a wide range of patient demographics.

- **Implementing Bias Detection Mechanisms:** The healthcare system introduced robust bias detection and mitigation protocols to regularly assess the AI system's outputs for any signs of bias.

- **Enhancing Human Oversight:** Recognizing the limitations of AI, the healthcare system implemented policies to ensure that AI-generated diagnoses were reviewed by a team of multidisciplinary clinicians before any clinical decision was made.

2.3.6. Conclusion

This case study serves as a cautionary tale about the potential pitfalls of deploying AI in healthcare without a thorough understanding of its limitations and dependencies. It highlights the importance of diverse and representative training data, the need for continuous monitoring for bias, and the irreplaceable value of human expertise in ensuring equitable and effective patient care.

As AI systems become more complex, ensuring their decision-making processes are transparent and understandable is crucial. This allows medical professionals to scrutinize AI outputs and make informed judgments. Also, robust data governance practices are essential to ensure the quality and fairness of data used to train AI systems in healthcare. This includes measures to address bias and ensure data diversity.

By acknowledging the limitations of AI and fostering a culture of human-AI collaboration, we can mitigate the perils of unbridled faith and harness the power of AI for positive outcomes in healthcare.

2.4.   Smart Cities: A Vision Marred by Data Gaps

Smart cities, urban landscapes woven with the threads of technology, promise a utopian future of efficiency, sustainability, and convenience. At the heart of this vision lies artificial intelligence, the unseen conductor orchestrating the symphony of sensors, networks, and automated systems. Yet, within the very technology that empowers smart cities lurks a hidden villain: the data gap.

Imagine a bustling Asian megacity, a concrete jungle teeming with millions. Here, a state-of-the-art traffic management system, a shining example of AI integration, is proudly deployed. Traffic lights adjust dynamically, guided by real-time data to optimize flow. However, the engineers, in their quest for efficiency, overlooked a crucial variable: the city's vibrant cultural calendar. Every year, a week-long festival throws the usual traffic patterns into joyous disarray. Families flood the streets, vibrant processions snake through avenues, and impromptu gatherings block intersections. The AI, blindsided by this unforeseen surge and deviation from the norm, throws the system into chaos. Traffic grinds to a halt, tempers flare, and the once-lauded system becomes a public embarrassment.

This cautionary tale is just one example of how data gaps can cripple even the most sophisticated AI systems. Smart city initiatives often focus on collecting a narrow range of data, neglecting the rich tapestry of human behavior, cultural nuances, and unforeseen events that define urban life. Traffic patterns may be meticulously tracked, but the system remains oblivious to the ebb and flow of festivals, street vendors, or emergency repairs. This lack of comprehensive data creates a blind spot, rendering AI solutions brittle and prone to spectacular failure.[28]

The road ahead for smart cities demands a paradigm shift. Instead of a relentless pursuit of ever-more data, the focus must turn to ensuring data quality, comprehensiveness, and, most importantly, relevance. Here's how we bridge this data gap:

- **Embrace Diversity:** Smart city planning must move beyond a one-size-fits-all approach. Different cities, with their unique cultural tapestry and historical context, demand diverse data sets that capture the essence of their urban ecosystem.

- **Incorporate Citizen Data:** Citizens are not passive data points—they are the lifeblood of the city. By incorporating citizen-generated data, whether through

---

[28] Bibrian, F. E., Vidal, D. E., & Kjærgaard, S. B. (2019). A review of the state of the art in smart city traffic management. Sustainability, 11(22), 6409. https://www.mdpi.com/journal/sustainability/special_issues/Smart_Sustainable_Urban_Development

surveys, social media analysis, or crowdsourced traffic reports, AI systems gain a richer understanding of the city's dynamics.[29]

- **Prioritize Data Validation:** Data is only as good as its accuracy. Robust validation practices are essential to weed out biases, inconsistencies, and outliers that can skew AI algorithms.[30]

- **Foster Transparency and Collaboration:** Building trust with citizens requires transparency in data collection and usage. Public education initiatives and open data platforms empower citizens to become active participants in shaping their smart city.[31]

By acknowledging the pitfalls of data gaps and implementing these solutions, we can ensure that AI becomes a true force for good in smart cities. Only with comprehensive and robust data can we unlock the full potential of AI, transforming our cities into thriving hubs of efficiency, sustainability, and, most importantly, a place where the human element is valued and integrated into the technological landscape.

2.5. Real-World AI Data Breaches: Lessons Learned

The realm of artificial intelligence, while promising and revolutionary, has not been without its challenges. As AI systems become central to businesses and societies, they also become attractive targets for cyberattacks. Real-world incidents provide a clear lens into the vulnerabilities inherent to AI systems and offer invaluable lessons for future developments. Here, we explore some of the significant data breaches involving AI systems and draw insights from these occurrences.

---

[29] Leetaru, K., Wittke, J., & Weber, R. (2015. Using social media to forecast political instability. American Behavioral Scientist, 59(3), 309-325. https://journals.sagepub.com/doi/10.1177/0093650221995314

[30] Fan, W., Xu, S., Wu, M., & Hu, Y. (2019). Challenge of bias in AI and data: A review. arXiv preprint arXiv:1905.06176. https://arxiv.org/pdf/2112.06409

[31] Davies, T. (2016). Open data for smart cities: The opportunity and the challenge. Local Government Studies, 42(7), 1089-1109. https://www.sciencedirect.com/science/article/pii/B9780128168165000097

2.5.1.   The Notorious Chatbot Incident

In an era where the allure of artificial intelligence captivated global audiences, chatbots emerged as a forefront of innovation, promising interactive experiences and swift communication. However, an event in 2016 serves as a stark reminder of the challenges that accompany these technologies. A major technology company launched an AI-driven chatbot on a widely-used social media platform, aimed at evolving through user interactions. Regrettably, within just 24 hours, the chatbot began emitting a series of racist, sexist, and offensive comments.[32]

The root of this problem was not a security breach, but rather the chatbot's design, which allowed it to learn from user-generated content without sufficient oversight or content moderation. As a result, it mirrored the inappropriate inputs from certain users. This incident transcended a mere public relations debacle–it underscored the susceptibility of AI systems to the chaotic and often unfiltered nature of online environments. It also highlighted the essential need for implementing robust filtering mechanisms and ethical guidelines to ensure AI technologies do not perpetuate or amplify harmful behaviors and biases.

This cautionary tale underscores a pivotal lesson for AI development: systems must have stringent boundaries and ethical frameworks, particularly when they are designed to learn continuously and interactively from vast and varied user inputs. The incident prompted a broader discourse on the ethical responsibilities of AI developers and the importance of proactive measures in AI governance to prevent similar occurrences in the future.

2.5.2.   The Health Data Exposure

Healthcare, with its troves of sensitive patient data, has been a prime target for cyberattacks. In one distressing incident, an AI-driven system designed to predict patient health outcomes was compromised. The attackers didn't sabotage the AI's

---

[32] https://www.upwork.com/resources/ai-ethical-considerations, https://www.unesco.org/en/artificial-intelligence/recommendation-ethics/cases, https://www.europarl.europa.eu/RegData/etudes/BRIE/2016/571380/IPOL_BRI%282016%2957138 0_EN.pdf, and https://www.chatbot.com/blog/interactions/

operations but instead accessed its vast database of patient information, resulting in the leak of personal health records of thousands of individuals.

The breach underscored the importance of securing not just the AI algorithms but also the extensive datasets they access. When AI systems have permission to query vast datasets, their interfaces become potential vulnerabilities unless adequately protected.[33]

2.5.3. Autonomous Vehicles: When AI Meets the Real World

Autonomous vehicles rely on AI to interpret their surroundings and make split-second decisions. In a series of tests by researchers, it was demonstrated that these vehicles could be "tricked" using simple stickers placed on road signs. For instance, a stop sign with specific sticker placements was misinterpreted as a speed limit sign, posing potential real-world dangers.

These experiments highlight the challenges in merging AI with the physical world. Data isn't just digital–real-world inputs, when manipulated, can deceive AI systems, leading to unintended actions with possibly dire consequences.[34]

2.5.4. Lessons Drawn

While these incidents paint a troubling picture, they've been instrumental in pushing the frontiers of AI safety and ethics. Key takeaways include:

1. **Boundaries are Essential:** Whether it's a chatbot on the internet or an AI system evaluating data, there must be limits to what it can learn, access, or act upon.

2. **Data Protection is Paramount:** It's not enough to secure the AI system–every piece of data it can access needs safeguarding.

---

[33] https://www.linkedin.com/pulse/ai-data-privacy-healthcare-industry-betting-wrong-horse-adzapier, https://www.ncbi.nlm.nih.gov/pmc/articles/PMC7349636/, and https://www.upguard.com/blog/biggest-data-breaches-in-healthcare

[34] https://www.appen.com/blog/autonomous-vehicles-the-most-challenging-task-in-ai

3. **Continuous Testing in Varied Scenarios:** AIs, especially those in critical applications like autonomous driving, need thorough testing against both regular and malicious inputs.

4. **Human Oversight:** AIs are tools, not replacements. Having human oversight, especially in the early stages of AI deployment, can prevent many pitfalls.

The journey of AI has been marked by both successes and failures. But as with any technology, failures, when analyzed and learned from, pave the way for safer, more reliable systems in the future.

2.6. The Double-Edged Sword of Automation and Citizen Development Tools

2.6.1. Introduction to Automation Risks

While automation technologies like RPA and low-code/no-code platforms drive efficiency, they also introduce new vulnerabilities. A report by Gartner predicts that by 2024, 50% of RPA-driven projects will fail to meet their cost-saving targets due to inefficiencies in managing security risks.[35]

2.6.2. RPA: Efficiency versus Security Trade-offs

RPA tools streamline business processes but can also present security challenges. For example, the Ponemon Institute found that cyber incidents related to RPA have increased by 30% in the past two years, with the average cost of a data breach reaching $3.86 million.[36] This underscores the critical need for secure RPA management practices. For example, a financial services firm faced a significant breach when an RPA bot was

---

[35] Gartner, "Predicts 2024: Overcoming RPA Security Risks," 2021.

[36] Ponemon Institute, "2020 Cost of a Data Breach Report," 2020.

exploited, leading to a reported loss of over $5 million and regulatory fines due to inadequate access controls and monitoring.[37]

2.6.3.   Low-Code/No-Code Platforms: Democratization versus Compliance

The democratization of app development through low-code/no-code platforms poses data privacy and compliance risks. According to Forrester, 75% of applications created with low-code platforms will suffer from security flaws due to a lack of professional oversight.[38] For example, a misconfigured low-code application in a healthcare setting led to the exposure of 10,000 patient records, emphasizing the necessity of training and governance. The incident not only affected patient trust but also resulted in a $2.5 million HIPAA settlement.[39]

2.6.4.   Challenges of Automation in Smart Cities

Smart cities are at risk of data breaches and privacy violations due to the integration of automated systems. A study by the University of Cambridge estimated that cyberattacks on smart city infrastructure could cost cities worldwide up to $90 billion by 2025 if current security trends continue.

For example, an attack on a smart traffic management system via an automated tool caused city-wide disruptions, illustrating the tangible risks of inadequate security in smart city applications. The remediation and public safety costs were estimated in the millions, not accounting for the loss in public confidence.[40]

---

[37] Financial Times, "RPA Security Breaches Cost Millions to Financial Services," 2021.

[38] Forrester, "The State of Application Security, 2023," 2023.

[39] U.S. Department of Health and Human Services, "HIPAA Settlement Highlights Importance of Audit Controls," 2022.

[40] The Guardian, "Cyberattack on Traffic Systems Costs City Millions," 2023.

2.6.5. *Lessons and Strategies for Mitigation*

Implementing security policies, regular audits, and promoting security awareness can mitigate these risks. The World Economic Forum recommends a "security by design" approach for all digital developments, which could reduce cyber risk incidents by up to 70%.

2.7.   Conclusion

The benefits of automation, RPA, and low-code/no-code tools are significant, yet the associated security and compliance risks cannot be ignored. Organizations must adopt comprehensive strategies to mitigate these risks, ensuring the safe and effective use of these transformative technologies.

3. Data Classification and Management

The digital age we live in has revolutionized how data is generated, processed, and stored. Every interaction, whether it's an online purchase, a social media post, or a medical check-up, produces data. As the volume of data grows exponentially, its management and security become increasingly challenging. Yet, with the rise of AI, new tools and techniques emerge, promising more efficient and secure ways of handling data. In this section, we delve deep into the essentials of data classification and management in the AI era.

We must have a comprehensive discussion of data standards. The introduction and implementation of data standards within an organization can be a difficult and prolonged undertaking. Data standards require changes in how data engineers perform their jobs, which involve the design and use of data. Data standards require consistency and discipline of data use where none formerly existed. The standardization of data is also consistent with the goals of quality assurance and internal audit. It is often advantageous to first gain support from all IT areas before approaching the data engineering and data science teams.

Before attempting to implement data standards, the following questions should be answered:

1. Which managers, in which sequence, should be approached for support in implementing data standards?

2. Which managers understand the role of data architecture within the organization?

3. Does your organization now have a quality assurance or quality control function?

4. Who is the most and who is the least receptive to change?

It is the job of data architecture to deregulate and socialize the ownership of data.

Follow the Ten Commandments of data standards:

1. The first rule is that there are exceptions to every rule. No standard is applicable in every situation. However, the data team and architect must not allow exceptions to become the norm.

2. Management must support and be willing to help enforce standards. If standards are violated, management must assist in assuring that the violations are corrected.

3. Standards must be practical, viable, and workable. Standards must be based on common sense. The less complicated and cumbersome the standards, the more they will be adhered to. *Keep standards simple.*

4. Standards must not be absolute–there must be some room for flexibility. While some standards must be strictly adhered to, most standards should not be so rigid that they severely restrict the freedom of the data designer.

5. Standards should not be retroactive. Standards are to control and manage present and future actions—not to undo and redo past actions. In most cases, standards enacted today cannot apply to data design that began several months ago.

6. Standards must be easily enforceable. To achieve this, it must be easy to detect violations of standards. The more the process of auditing for the compliance of standards can be automated, the more effective will be the standards themselves. Use automated tools to assist in enforcing data naming conventions and data standard enforcement.

7. Standards must be sold, not dictated. Even if upper management wholeheartedly supports data standards, they must sell the standards to

employees at all levels. The data team and architect must be willing to advertise the standards to all employees and justify the need for such standards. Data standards demand that data scientists and analysts change how they design data. Any lasting and meaningful change must come from the employees themselves.

8. The details about the standards themselves are not important – the important thing is to *have* some standards. The data team and architect must be willing to compromise and negotiate the details of the standards to be enacted.

9. Enact standards gradually. Do not attempt to put all data standards in place at the same time. After enacting standards, begin to enforce them, but do it gradually and tactfully. Allow ample time for the non-data staff to react and adjust to new standards. The implementation of standards must be an evolutionary, rather than a revolutionary, process.

10. The most important standard is the standard of consistency—consistency of data naming, data elements, data design, and data use.[41]

3.1.   Defining Sensitive Data in the AI Era

In today's hyper-connected world, data is more than just numbers and text. It represents people's identities, preferences, behaviors, and secrets. Before we can protect data, we must understand its nature and significance.

The Evolution of Sensitive Data: A decade ago, sensitive data might have been limited to properties like Social Security Numbers or bank account details.

Now, the definition has expanded. Your online search history, location data—even the way you scroll on a smartphone can be considered sensitive. AI, with its capability to derive insights from vast amounts of data, underscores the importance of expanding our understanding of what constitutes sensitive data.

---

[41] https://www.dremio.com/wiki/data-consistency/,
   https://guides.lib.uconn.edu/c.php?g=832372&p=8226287,
   https://www.linkedin.com/pulse/importance-data-consistency-databases-ravi-,
   https://www.linkedin.com/advice/1/what-most-effective-ways-develop-document-data, and
   https://atlan.com/data-consistency-101/

For instance, an innocuous list of movies watched over a month might seem trivial. However, with the right AI algorithm, this data can be analyzed to deduce personal traits, political leanings, or health conditions.

In one striking case, a retailer's data analytics system detected purchase patterns that indicated a teen was likely pregnant. The retailer started sending maternity ads to her, inadvertently revealing her condition to her family.[42]

Regulatory bodies worldwide grapple with defining what sensitive data means, especially as the boundaries of personal privacy shift. The dynamic nature of data, especially in the context of AI, demands a more fluid definition of sensitivity.

3.2.   AI-Driven Data Classification Techniques

As data grows in volume and variety, manual classification methods become untenable. Here's where AI offers immense potential. AI-driven data classification techniques leverage advanced algorithms to automate and enhance the process of organizing data, making it more efficient and accurate.

AI algorithms, especially those based on deep learning, can understand the context in which data is generated. This allows for the classification of data based not just on content but intent and sentiment. For example, an email mentioning a bank transaction might be classified differently than a bank's promotional offer, even if both contain similar keywords.

Financial institutions have started deploying AI tools that can scan emails and communications to detect potential insider trading or unethical practices by analyzing the context and sentiment behind communications.

AI can automatically tag data based on predefined criteria or patterns it has learned. This is especially useful in big data scenarios where millions of data points might need classification in real-time.

---

[42] https://research.aimultiple.com/robotic-process-automation-use-cases/,
https://www.docsumo.com/blog/robotic-process-automation-guide, and
https://www.celonis.com/blog/5-examples-of-rpa-in-action/

In the healthcare sector, AI tools analyze patient records, tagging them based on diagnosis, treatment history, and outcomes, enabling more personalized patient care and aiding in medical research.

3.3.   Lifecycle of Data: Creation to Destruction

Every piece of data goes through various stages in its lifecycle. Understanding this is crucial for effective data management.

Data is born the moment an action is initiated. It could be a user signing up for a service, a temperature reading from a sensor, or a transaction record.

This phase is where most data breaches occur. The stored data needs to be encrypted, backed up, and regularly audited for integrity. With AI, predictive maintenance can forecast when storage systems might fail, allowing for proactive measures.

Every time data is accessed, there's a potential risk. AI-driven access systems ensure that only authorized personnel can access data, and any anomalies in access patterns are flagged. For example, a cloud service provider utilized an AI system to track data access patterns. The system flagged when an employee accessed vast amounts of data, which wasn't in line with his job role. Upon investigation, it was revealed he was attempting to steal data.

Not all data is perpetually useful. Archival processes store data in long-term, often offline, storage solutions. AI can predict which data might be needed in the future and which can be safely archived, optimizing storage costs. Data that's no longer needed and isn't archived should be destroyed to ensure it doesn't pose a security risk. AI can automate this process, deleting data once it's past its retention period and ensuring it's irretrievable.

3.4. Role of Metadata in Classification

Metadata isn't just about the data itself, but about its attributes and context. For instance, it can tell us when and where a photograph was taken, not just its content. With AI, this metadata can provide insights that humans might overlook.

Given the volume of data produced, understanding the context of its creation and use is critical. With AI, patterns in metadata can highlight inefficiencies in data storage, flag unauthorized access, or even predict future data requirements. For example, a content delivery network utilized AI to analyze the metadata of user access logs. They discovered that certain resources had higher demand during specific times and adjusted their caching mechanisms accordingly, resulting in faster content delivery and enhanced user experience.

3.5. Ethical Considerations in AI-Driven Data Classification

As AI models become more complex and are trained on vast datasets, there's a risk of these models inadvertently amplifying societal biases. It's crucial to be aware of these biases when classifying data.

Understanding how AI makes decisions in data classification can be challenging due to the 'black box' nature of some algorithms. We must make efforts to demystify these processes and ensure they align with organizational and societal values. For example, a recruitment tool was discovered to be biased against female applicants because it had been trained predominantly on male resumes. This highlighted the need for diverse training data and more transparency in AI-driven processes.

3.6. Adaptive Data Classification

With AI, data classification is no longer a one-time task. As businesses evolve and data grows, classification models must adapt.

Traditional classification models remain static unless manually updated. However, with AI, models can continuously learn from new data, refining their classification criteria, ensuring data remains relevant and accurately categorized. For example, in a dynamic sales environment, a product classification AI-driven tool is constantly updated based on shifting market trends and consumer behavior, enabling more effective targeted marketing.

3.7. Role of Privacy-Preserving AI in Data Management

As organizations use AI to process data, there's an increasing need to ensure that the data remains confidential and that individual privacy is maintained, even during computations. Techniques like differential privacy and federated learning ensure data privacy while still enabling AI processes. For example, Apple uses differential privacy to gather user data without compromising individual user privacy. This allows them to improve product features based on aggregated data insights without directly accessing sensitive user data.

3.8. Data Classification Tools

The following table outlines some of the most popular and updated tools currently available for advanced data classification.

Feature	MineOS	ClassifyIt	Varonis Data Security Platform	Microsoft Purview	Dasera	Forcepoint
Price	Free (Open Source)	Freemium (€10 per license)	Paid Plans	Paid Plans	Paid Plans	Paid Plans
Deployment	On-Premises, Cloud	On-Premises, Cloud	On-Premises, Cloud	Cloud	Cloud	On-Premises, Cloud, Hybrid
Data Sources	Databases, Filesystems, APIs	Filesystems, Databases	File Servers, Cloud Workloads, Databases	Azure Data Sources	Cloud Storage, Databases	Endpoints, Networks, Cloud Applications
Classification Methods	Keywords, Regular Expressions, Content Inspection	Keyword Lists, Regular Expressions, Machine Learning	Automated Scanning, User-defined rules, Machine Learning	Policy-based, Information Protection Labels, Content Inspection	Keyword, Pattern Matching, Machine Learning	Content Analysis, Behavioral Analysis, Machine Learning
Data Privacy Features	Anonymization, Pseudonymization, Data Masking	Encryption, Access Control, Auditing	Data Loss Prevention, Compliance Automation	DLP, Data Governance, Privacy Risk Management	DLP, Data Masking, Tokenization	DLP, Encryption, Data Masking, User Behavior Analytics
Compliance Support	GDPR, CCPA, HIPAA, PCI DSS	GDPR, HIPAA, PCI DSS	GDPR, CCPA, HIPAA, PCI DSS	GDPR, CCPA, HIPAA, PCI DSS	GDPR, CCPA, HIPAA, PCI DSS	GDPR, CCPA, HIPAA, PCI DSS, SOX, NIST
Pros	Open source, flexible, customizable	Affordable, easy to use	Extensive data source support, robust security features	Integrates with Azure ecosystem, strong compliance support	Cloud-focused, AI-powered classification	Comprehensive coverage, advanced threat protection
Cons	Requires technical expertise, limited support	Limited features in free version	Complex pricing structure	Vendor lock-in for Azure users	Limited on-premises deployment options	Can be complex to manage

3.9. Empowering Citizen Developers: Integrating Intelligent Automation and RPA

The intersection of citizen development with intelligent automation and RPA heralds a new era in data management, particularly in revitalizing the use of legacy systems. These technologies not only democratize data handling but also enhance the accessibility and utility of older applications that form the backbone of many organizations' IT infrastructure.

RPA and intelligent automation stand out for their ability to interact with legacy systems at the screen level, mimicking human input to extract and manipulate data. This capability is vital for organizations reliant on applications that, due to their age or complexity, lack modern interfaces or API access. By automating interactions with these systems, RPA tools extend their shelf life, allowing businesses to continue leveraging their existing IT investments while exploring avenues for digital transformation.

- **Screen-Level Access:** RPA tools can navigate legacy system interfaces to read, extract, and input data, bypassing the need for direct system integration. This approach is particularly relevant for data management tasks that require access to applications without API support.

- **API Integration:** When available, intelligent automation platforms utilize APIs to establish more efficient and reliable data exchanges with legacy systems. This dual capability ensures that automation can be applied broadly, from older to more modern applications.

As an example, an insurance company used RPA to automate data entry and extraction tasks for a legacy underwriting system, significantly reducing processing times and errors. This intervention allowed the company to defer costly system upgrades while improving service delivery. Another example, a public sector entity implemented intelligent automation to connect its existing record management system, which lacked an API, with new digital services. By automating data retrieval and entry tasks, the entity enhanced its ability to provide timely and accurate information to citizens without needing immediate, extensive system overhauls.

The strategic integration of RPA and intelligent automation for engaging with legacy systems necessitates a thoughtful approach. Organizations must assess the compatibility of automation tools with their existing IT environments and ensure that governance frameworks address the unique challenges posed by interacting with older applications. Training programs should also familiarize citizen developers with the nuances of legacy systems to maximize the effectiveness and efficiency of automation initiatives.

3.10.   Conclusion

RPA and intelligent automation offer transformative potential for data management, especially in contexts where legacy systems play a crucial role. By extending the operational life of these applications through screen-level access and API integration, organizations can bridge the gap between past investments and future innovations. This balance between leveraging existing assets and embracing new technologies underscores the agility and resilience that characterize successful digital transformation strategies.

4. Foundations of AI-Proof Security

The digital age has ushered in an era where data is more valuable than ever before. As we stand on the cusp of further breakthroughs, especially in AI, the need for robust and secure data management systems becomes paramount. AI's very nature, adaptability, and learning capabilities create both opportunities for enhanced security and vulnerabilities that can be exploited. Hence, crafting a security foundation that is both versatile and 'AI-proof' is a daunting yet necessary endeavor.

4.1. Role of Encryption: Traditional versus Quantum

Encryption, the art of encoding information, is the first line of defense in most digital security protocols. Yet, as computational prowess grows, especially with quantum computing, what was once considered 'secure' may soon be easily decodable.

Relying on algorithms and cryptographic keys, traditional encryption has stood the test of time. However, with brute force attacks and advancing technology, they are becoming increasingly penetrable. Techniques like RSA and AES, while robust, have their limitations in the face of emerging threats.

Quantum mechanics offers a radical departure from classical encryption methods. Quantum Key Distribution (QKD), for instance, offers theoretically unbreakable encryption, relying on the fundamental principles of quantum mechanics. Any eavesdropping attempt would disturb the quantum state of the data, making the intrusion detectable. At the time of this writing, Physical Scientist in the field, Dr. Edward "Teddy" Parker, is skeptical that AI is a real threat to encryption.

AI poses a threat to traditional encryption like AES 256 because it can be used to develop new attacks that exploit vulnerabilities in these algorithms.[43] For example, AI can be used to generate large numbers of test vectors to find weaknesses in the algorithm, or to develop new cryptanalytic techniques that can break the encryption.[44] Additionally, AI can be used to create new types of malware that can bypass traditional security measures, such as firewalls and intrusion detection systems.[45] Banks and financial institutions are already piloting quantum encryption to transmit sensitive financial data, ensuring an unprecedented level of security in their transactions.

Vendors include (more in the Appendix):

- **RSA**: Widely-used public key encryption.
- **AES**: Standard symmetric encryption method.
- **Triple DES**: Successor to the original DES encryption.
- **Blowfish & Twofish**: Symmetric block ciphers.
- **VeraCrypt**: Free disk encryption software.
- **OpenSSL**: Open-source toolkit implementing SSL and TLS.
- **Quantum Resistant Ledger (QRL)**: Blockchain tech resistant to quantum decryption.
- **ID Quantique**: Quantum key distribution solutions.
- **IBM's Quantum Computing**: Development towards quantum-safe cryptography.
- **Microsoft's Quantum Development Kit**: Tools for quantum computing.

---

[43] https://securityboulevard.com/2023/12/ai-and-quantum-computing-threaten-encryption-and-data-security/

[44] https://www.researchgate.net/publication/376618031_How_Artificial_Intelligence_become_a_threat_to_cryptography-A_systematic_literature_review

[45] https://www.csoonline.com/article/651125/emerging-cyber-threats-in-2023-from-ai-to-quantum-to-data-poisoning.html

4.2.   Multi-factor Authentication (MFA) and Biometrics

While passwords have traditionally been the gateway to data, they're often the weakest link in security. Multi-factor authentication and biometrics offer added layers of protection, confirming the user's identity through multiple verification methods. Incorporating multiple verification steps—something you know (password), something you have (a smart card or phone), and something you are (biometrics)—MFA greatly reduces the chances of unauthorized access. From fingerprints to retina scans and voice recognition, biometric systems offer a personal touch to security. Unlike passwords, these attributes are unique to each individual. Major tech companies, from Apple with its Face ID to Google with its Titan Security Key, are integrating MFA and biometrics, creating a seamless yet secure user experience.[46]

Vendors include (more in the Appendix):

- **Duo Security:** Two-factor authentication solution.
- **RSA SecurID:** Hardware and software tokens for authentication.
- **Yubico YubiKey:** Physical hardware authenticator.
- **Google Authenticator:** Time-based one-time password app.
- **Apple Face ID:** Biometric authentication using facial recognition.
- **Windows Hello:** Microsoft's biometric authentication system.
- **FIDO U2F:** Universal two-factor authentication.
- **Clear:** Uses biometrics (eyes and fingertips) for identity verification.
- **LastPass:** Password manager with built-in MFA.
- **Authy:** MFA app providing an extra layer of security.

4.3.   Blockchain: The Immutable Data Keeper

Blockchain, most famous for its role in cryptocurrencies, is much more than just a tool for digital transactions. It's a revolution in data management and security. By design, once data is added to the blockchain, it becomes nearly impossible to alter without

---

[46] https://www.pingidentity.com/en/resources/blog/post/eight-benefits-mfa.html

altering all subsequent blocks and the consensus of the network. Instead of a single data hub, blockchain operates on distributed ledgers. This decentralization means there's no single point of failure. Beyond just data storage, blockchains can enforce complex agreements and operations autonomously through smart contracts. Supply chains, like that of Walmart's, have started utilizing blockchain to track produce from farm to table, ensuring authenticity and transparency in their products.

Vendors include (more in the Appendix):

- **Ethereum:** Platform for creating decentralized apps using smart contracts.
- **Hyperledger:** Open-source collaborative effort for blockchain technologies.
- **R3 Corda:** Blockchain platform for businesses.
- **Chain:** Infrastructure tech for blockchain.
- **Multichain:** Platform for private blockchains.
- **IBM Blockchain:** Solutions and services based on blockchain.
- **Microsoft Azure Blockchain Service:** Full-stack blockchain as a service.
- **Oracle Blockchain Platform:** Comprehensive distributed ledger cloud platform.
- **Amazon Managed Blockchain:** Managed service to set up and manage a scalable blockchain network.
- **Binance Chain:** Blockchain and infrastructure behind Binance's cryptocurrency exchange.

4.4. The Importance of Zero-Trust Architecture

The zero-trust model operates on a simple premise: Trust nothing, verify everything. Instead of relying on traditional perimeters like firewalls, zero-trust architectures require verification at every access point, regardless of whether it's inside or outside the organization's network. One of the core principles of zero-trust involves breaking up security perimeters into small zones to maintain separate access for separate parts of the network. Users, and even AI systems, should have the minimum level of access required to perform their tasks, reducing the potential damage from security breaches. Google's BeyondCorp initiative is a notable example of a zero-trust security model in action. It shifts access controls from the network perimeter to individual devices and users, thereby enhancing security flexibility and strength.

Vendors include (more in the Appendix):

- **Cisco Zero Trust**: Solutions for securing endpoints, applications, and networks.
- **Palo Alto Networks**: Comprehensive zero-trust security solutions.
- **Akamai**: Zero trust application access.
- **Symantec Endpoint Protection**: Security solutions adhering to zero trust.
- **Microsoft Azure AD Conditional Access**: Policies for securing applications.
- **Cloudflare Access**: Zero trust application access.
- **Zscaler**: Zero trust cloud security solutions.
- **Okta**: Identity management and zero trust security.
- **Centrify**: Zero trust privilege services.
- **Check Point Infinity**: Total protection with zero trust principles.

4.5.   Behavioral Analytics and AI-Powered Threat Detection

Using AI to understand and predict patterns of user behavior can be a potent tool for security. Unusual behaviors can be early indicators of a security breach or malicious intent. These systems learn the typical behavior of users and entities in a network and can alert or act when they detect anomalies. Financial institutions use behavioral analytics to detect fraudulent transactions, flagging unusual purchasing behaviors or large transactions from unfamiliar locations.

Vendors include (more in the Appendix):

- **Darktrace**: Uses machine learning to detect, respond to, and mitigate cyber threats in real-time.
- **Vectra**: Offers an AI-driven threat detection and response platform.
- **Gurucul**: Uses advanced analytics to detect unusual behavior patterns.
- **Interset (Micro Focus)**: Provides threat detection using unsupervised machine learning.
- **Lastline**: Detects advanced malware using AI.
- **Symantec's Targeted Attack Analytics**: Uses advanced analytics for detecting targeted attacks.
- **Splunk**: Provides AI-driven insights for threat detection.

- **CrowdStrike Falcon:** Cloud-native solution for endpoint protection using AI.
- **SentinelOne:** Uses AI to autonomously identify and counteract threats.
- **Cylance (Blackberry):** Proactively detects and blocks malicious activity using AI.

4.6.   Secure Software Development Lifecycle (SSDLC)

A proactive approach to security requires integrating it into the very process of software development, not just tacking it on at the end. This strategy emphasizes integrating security early in the software development lifecycle, ensuring that applications are secure by design. Companies like Microsoft have adopted SSDLC, ensuring that every phase of software development, from design to deployment, is secure.

Vendors include (more in the Appendix):

- **Checkmarx:** Static and open-source code analysis tool.
- **Snyk:** Focuses on vulnerabilities in open-source libraries and containers.
- **OWASP's Dependency-Check:** Detects vulnerabilities in application dependencies.
- **SonarQube:** Inspects code quality and security vulnerabilities.
- **Acunetix:** Web application security scanner.
- **Veracode:** Platform that scans for security flaws in application code.
- **Fortify (Micro Focus):** Offers end-to-end application security solutions.
- **GitGuardian:** Monitors code repositories for sensitive data leaks.
- **WhiteSource:** Detects vulnerabilities in open-source components.
- **Codacy:** Offers automated code reviews and quality analysis.

4.7.   AI-Powered Penetration Testing

Penetration testing, where experts attempt to break into a system to find vulnerabilities, can be enhanced using AI. Machines can simulate a myriad of attack vectors at speeds far beyond human capabilities.[47] AI systems can constantly monitor and scan networks, automatically detecting and patching vulnerabilities. Tools like IBM's Watson have been integrated into cybersecurity platforms to augment penetration testing, bringing both speed and scale to the process.

Vendors include (more in the Appendix):

- **OWASP ZAP:** Popular tool for penetration testing.
- **AI Hunter by Active Countermeasures:** Threat hunting using AI.
- **Pentera (by Pcysys):** Automated penetration testing.
- **Canary:** Honeypot that emulates vulnerabilities.
- **Acalvio:** Provides deceptive solutions using AI.
- **Metasploit:** Widely used for penetration testing and exploit development.
- **Tenable Nessus:** Vulnerability assessment tool.
- **Burp Suite:** Web vulnerability scanner and proxy tool.
- **Core Impact:** Comprehensive penetration testing tool.
- **Nexpose:** Vulnerability management solution.

4.8.   Red Teaming and AI Simulations

Red teaming involves a group that challenges an organization to improve its effectiveness. With AI, simulations of large-scale attacks can be conducted to prepare and reinforce defenses.[48] Simulating AI-driven attacks on networks to see how well defenses hold up and where they might need strengthening. Large tech firms routinely employ red teams (both human and AI-powered) to test their defenses, ensuring resilience against even the most innovative of attacks.

Vendors include (more in the Appendix):

---

[47] https://www.subrosacyber.com/blog/ai-penetration-testing, https://www.linkedin.com/pulse/role-artificial-intelligence-enhancing-penetration-testing-oyewole-eplyf, and https://www.techtarget.com/searchsecurity/tip/AI-pen-testing-promises-delivers-both-speed-and-accuracy

[48] https://www.cranium.ai/what-is-ai-red-teaming/ and https://www.techtarget.com/searchenterpriseai/definition/AI-red-teaming

- **SCYTHE:** Platform for red team and adversarial simulations.
- **XM Cyber:** Continuously simulates attacks on critical assets.
- **RedSeal:** Digital resilience platform.
- **Thycotic:** Provides PAM solutions.
- **Cymulate:** Launches simulations of multi-vector cyberattacks.
- **FireEye Mandiant:** Red teaming and security assessment services.
- **Endgame (Elastic):** Offers protection against targeted attacks.
- **SafeBreach:** Simulates breach scenarios to validate security controls.
- **Kali Linux:** A Linux distribution designed for penetration testing.
- **Cobalt:** Provides pen-tests as a service.

4.9.   Data Masking and Anonymization

Ensuring that data, even if accessed, cannot be traced back to individual users is paramount. Techniques that mask or anonymize data make it less useful for malicious actors.[49] Allows users to see only the data they need, while the rest remains obfuscated. Many online survey platforms use data anonymization to ensure that responses cannot be traced back to individual users, ensuring privacy while still collecting actionable insights.

Vendors include (more in the Appendix):

- **Delphix:** Offers a dynamic data platform that sources, secures, and serves data, providing data masking to ensure sensitive data remains confidential.
- **McAfee Total Protection:** Among its many security features, it provides data encryption and file shredding capabilities. This is especially useful for businesses wanting to anonymize or make data unreadable.
- **Varonis:** Protects sensitive data and detects insider threats, offering automated data masking for GDPR compliance.
- **Dataguise:** Helps businesses detect and protect personal information across their enterprise, ensuring regulatory compliance and data privacy.
- **Delphix:** Offers data masking and virtualization.

---

[49] https://www.arcadsoftware.com/dot/resources/blog-en/data-masking-and-anonymization-understanding-the-different-algorithms/

- **McAfee Total Protection**: Provides encryption and data residency controls.
- **DataSunrise Data Protection**: Real-time data masking.
- **Oracle Data Masking and Subsetting**: Protects sensitive data in test environments.
- **Mentis**: Integrates data security, compliance, and data management solutions.

4.10. Container Security and AI-Driven Vulnerability Management

Containers have revolutionized the way developers deploy applications. By allowing for consistent environments and isolated execution, containers like Docker have transformed the DevOps landscape. However, as with any technology, containers come with their own set of vulnerabilities.

The core principle of container security is to understand that containers are not just mini virtual machines. They share the same OS kernel, and this shared nature makes them vulnerable if not adequately isolated. Misconfigured containers, vulnerable images, or weak runtime processes can be exploited.

AI-driven vulnerability management can potentially augment container security, moving it from reactive to proactive. By using machine learning algorithms, security platforms can analyze patterns and predict potential threats. It doesn't just stop at detection. Once a vulnerability is identified, AI can help in auto-remediation, suggesting or even deploying patches and fixes to secure the container environment. This shift brings in the agility that modern DevOps environments demand without compromising security.

Vendors include (more in the Appendix):

- **Docker**: Popular containerization tool.
- **Kubernetes**: Open-source container orchestration system.
- **Aqua Security**: Protects your container applications.
- **NeuVector**: Full lifecycle container security.
- **Twistlock (Prisma by Palo Alto)**: Comprehensive container security solution.
- **Sysdig**: Offers unified security, monitoring, and forensics for containers.

- **StackRox:** Kubernetes-native security.
- **Black Duck:** Detects open-source vulnerabilities in containers.
- **Anchore:** Inspects, analyzes, and certifies container images.
- **Nessus:** Vulnerability scanner now adapting for container environments.

4.11. The Power of Sandboxing in AI-Powered Security

At the heart of advanced persistent threats (APTs) is the ability to bypass traditional security systems. Sandboxing emerged as a method to run suspicious files in a controlled environment, separate from the main network, to see how they behave. It's like observing a virus in a lab setting before it can infect the broader population.

The essence of sandboxing lies in its ability to dynamically analyze threats, and this is where AI excels. One can better predict, detect, and prevent zero-day exploits by incorporating machine learning and AI algorithms into sandboxing solutions. The power lies in the system's ability to 'learn' from each file it analyses. Over time, it becomes adept at recognizing malicious behaviors, improving the speed and accuracy of threat detection.

Furthermore, AI can automate the traditionally labor-intensive process of analyzing the results from sandboxing. By auto-generating reports and highlighting potential threats, it ensures that cybersecurity professionals can prioritize and act swiftly against the most critical threats.

Vendors include (more in the Appendix):

- **Cuckoo Sandbox:** Open-source automated malware analysis system.
- **FireEye:** Malware protection system using a virtual execution engine.
- **Cisco Threat Grid:** Combines static and dynamic malware analysis.
- **Fortinet FortiSandbox:** Offers threat detection and mitigation.
- **Palo Alto Networks WildFire:** Cloud-based threat analysis service.
- **SonicWall Capture ATP:** Multi-engine sandbox designed to discover and stop unknown, zero-day attacks.
- **VMRay:** Automated malware analysis and detection.

- **Check Point SandBlast:** Zero-day protection using sandboxing.
- **Sophos Sandstorm:** Next-gen sandbox technology.
- **Lastline Detonator:** Focused on advanced malware detection.

4.12. Security Information and Event Management (SIEM) in the AI Era

Security Information and Event Management (SIEM) systems have been the cornerstone of enterprise security. They collect logs from various network devices, servers, and applications, correlating this data to detect malicious activities. The challenge with traditional SIEM systems has been the sheer volume of data and the number of false positives generated.

Enter AI.

The incorporation of AI into SIEM systems transforms them from mere log collection tools into dynamic threat detection platforms. AI algorithms can sift through vast amounts of data, distinguishing between regular network activities and potential threats. It reduces the noise, focusing only on the most pertinent threats, and thereby drastically cutting down on false positives.

Additionally, the predictive capabilities of AI mean SIEM systems can now anticipate threats based on historical data and emerging threat intelligence. They can spot patterns indicating an emerging attack, allowing for proactive measures. By making SIEM systems more intelligent and predictive, AI ensures a more robust and agile security posture for organizations in this digital age.

Vendors include (more in the Appendix):

- **Splunk:** Real-time data collection and analytics.
- **LogRhythm:** Combines SIEM, UEBA, and SOAR into a single, integrated platform.
- **IBM QRadar:** SIEM system that provides intelligence-driven security.
- **ArcSight (Micro Focus):** Detects and responds to internal and external threats.
- **McAfee Enterprise Security Manager:** Provides real-time visibility into security and compliance activities.

- **SolarWinds**: Offers log management and SIEM capabilities.
- **AlienVault OSSIM & USM**: Open-source SIEM and commercial SIEM respectively.
- **Fortinet FortiSIEM**: Offers analytics-driven security operations.
- **Exabeam**: SIEM platform to modernize.

5. Privacy Considerations in the Age of AI

In an era where artificial intelligence (AI) is progressively interwoven into our daily lives, the fundamental right to privacy finds itself juxtaposed against technological marvels. This chapter offers a panoramic view of privacy in the age of AI, spanning from legal obligations to ethical quandaries.

5.1. Privacy Regulations in the AI Context

Historically, privacy regulations were primarily designed to safeguard individuals from potential risks associated with data breaches and unauthorized access. However, as AI systems continue to gain prominence, there's a growing recognition that such regulations also need to address the nuanced challenges posed by AI, especially given its capacity to analyze, interpret, and even predict individual behaviors and preferences.

5.1.1. GDPR: A Global Benchmark

The General Data Protection Regulation (GDPR) took the world by storm when it came into effect in 2018, becoming the blueprint for many ensuing data protection laws across the globe. It underscored the importance of consent, transparency, and the rights of the individual in a digital age. Its clauses about automated individual decision-making, including profiling, directly implicate AI systems, setting stringent criteria for transparency, fairness, and accountability. For companies relying on AI, GDPR demands not just data protection but a holistic approach that considers the wider impacts of automated data processing.[50]

5.1.2.   CCPA: Pioneering U.S. Privacy Measures

The California Consumer Privacy Act (CCPA), which came into effect in January 2020, is often seen as America's answer to GDPR. While its core focus revolves around consumer rights concerning their personal data, it also indirectly raises the bar for AI systems. By granting consumers the right to know how their data is used, sold, or disclosed, it emphasizes the need for companies to be transparent about how AI algorithms utilize and process such data.[51]

5.1.3.   Emerging Global Regulations and the AI Challenge

Several nations have either adopted or are in the process of adopting privacy regulations inspired by GDPR and CCPA. From Brazil's LGPD to India's PDPB, the global momentum towards stronger data privacy is clear. However, each jurisdiction offers its unique perspectives and challenges when integrating AI. Companies operating on a global scale must be prepared to tailor their AI deployments, ensuring each adheres to regional regulations while still benefiting from AI's transformative potential.[52]

---

[50] https://papers.ssrn.com/sol3/papers.cfm?abstract_id=4589207, https://www.eylaw.be/2023/11/09/the-impact-of-the-gdpr-on-ai/, and https://www.kellton.com/kellton-tech-blog/decoding-the-gdpr-influence-on-ai

[51] https://www.reuters.com/legal/legalindustry/privacy-paradox-with-ai-2023-10-31/ and https://www.kellton.com/kellton-tech-blog/decoding-the-gdpr-influence-on-ai

[52] https://blog.google/technology/ai/google-checks-data-privacy-ai-update/ and https://secureprivacy.ai/blog/navigating-data-privacy-2024

5.1.4.   Data Privacy in Healthcare: Handling Sensitive Health Information

Healthcare, with its plethora of sensitive data and life-critical implications, stands at a challenging intersection of technology, ethics, and privacy. As AI continues to find applications in healthcare—from diagnostic assistance to treatment recommendations—the need to balance innovation with privacy becomes paramount.

Health data, by its very nature, is among the most intimate forms of information about an individual. This data can reveal not only current health conditions but also future risks, genetic predispositions, and other deeply personal insights. Ensuring the privacy of such data isn't just a legal obligation but a profound responsibility.[53]

Across the globe, health data enjoys a unique legal status. In the United States, for instance, the Health Insurance Portability and Accountability Act (HIPAA) sets out stringent rules for the collection, storage, and dissemination of patient data. Any AI application in healthcare needs to be cognizant of and compliant with such regulations.[54]

AI's capacity to analyze vast datasets can unearth patterns and insights that might remain hidden from human analysts. This ability is a double-edged sword. While it can lead to groundbreaking medical insights, it can also risk de-anonymizing patient data. For instance, an AI might identify a rare medical condition in a small dataset, which could inadvertently lead to the identification of a patient.[55]

Best practices for healthcare AI include:

- **Data Masking and Pseudonymization:** These techniques ensure that health data remains separated from directly identifiable information. It allows for analysis without exposing individual identities.

- **Regular Privacy Audits:** Given the rapid evolution of AI, periodic privacy audits can ensure that systems remain compliant with privacy regulations and that any new vulnerabilities are promptly addressed.

---

[53] https://bmcmedethics.biomedcentral.com/articles/10.1186/s12910-021-00687-3

[54] https://www.ama-assn.org/practice-management/hipaa/hipaa-privacy-rule

[55] https://www.rheumatologyadvisor.com/home/topics/practice-management/artificial-intelligence-poses-threat-to-patient-privacy-3/

- **Stakeholder Collaboration:** Collaboration between technologists, clinicians, patients, and policymakers can ensure a holistic approach to privacy. This collaborative approach can lead to solutions that respect patient privacy while still unlocking the potential of AI in healthcare.

With lives literally in the balance, the integration of AI in healthcare requires a meticulous and empathetic approach. Prioritizing data privacy ensures that the healthcare industry remains a bastion of trust in an increasingly digitized world.

5.2.   Ethical Data Collection and Handling

Beyond regulations, an ethical approach to AI deployment requires companies to consider the moral implications of their data practices. This is especially pivotal in the AI realm, where vast amounts of data are not just stored but actively processed and analyzed.

At the heart of AI's strength is data. The vast information it consumes, processes, and acts upon often includes sensitive details, including personal identifiers, health records, financial transactions, and more. While AI's data appetite aids its capabilities, this very strength can become a liability if ethical considerations are not in place.[56]

AI systems, especially in sectors like healthcare or finance, often require granular data. But, collection must always be predicated on informed consent. It's no longer enough to obtain generic approval–users must be thoroughly educated about how their data will be used, the advantages they can expect, and the potential risks involved. For instance, a medical AI system might promise more accurate diagnostics but will require extensive health data. In such cases, the patient must be made aware of the exact nature and use of their data.[57]

Not all data that can be collected should be collected. Ethical AI operations revolve around the principle of collecting only what's strictly necessary. This not only reduces potential risks but also promotes trust among users. For example, a voice recognition

---

[56] https://atlan.com/data-ethics-101/

[57] https://www.omdena.com/blog/the-ethics-of-ai-data-collection-ensuring-privacy-and-fair-representation

system doesn't necessarily need to store conversations, just the patterns that help it recognize speech more effectively.[58]

Once data is collected, its processing should also be transparent. Whether it's being used to train a new model or improve an existing one, users deserve to know how their data is being used, especially when the outcomes can impact them directly, like in the case of credit scoring AI systems.[59]

The focus on ethical data collection and handling serves not only to protect individual privacy but also to cement trust between companies and their users, a factor that's essential for the wider adoption of AI systems.

5.2.1.   Protecting the Vulnerable: Children and AI

Children, with their natural curiosity, are growing up in a world where technology is at their fingertips. They interact with AI-powered devices and platforms, sometimes even more frequently than adults. This makes them a particularly vulnerable group when it comes to data privacy.

The ethical implications of collecting and processing data from children are magnified due to several reasons. They may not fully understand the nature and implications of their online actions. They might readily share personal information, unaware of the potential misuse or the digital footprint they are creating.[60]

In many regions around the world, there are strict regulations for collecting data from minors. For instance, in the United States, the Children's Online Privacy Protection Act (COPPA) mandates that websites and online services aimed at children must meet specific requirements, including parental consent for collecting personal information from children under 13. But with AI's pervasive nature, even platforms not explicitly aimed at children might find younger users interacting with them.[61]

---

[58] https://bigid.com/blog/navigating-ai-privacy/

[59] https://www.linkedin.com/pulse/transparency-ai-critical-analysis-from-ethical-data-mae-beth

[60] https://blogs.icrc.org/law-and-policy/2023/12/14/protecting-children-data-in-humanitarian-ai-ecosystems/

[61] https://www.lexology.com/library/detail.aspx?g=8ce63586-181b-43f2-b8a5-477fb42c935a

Beyond the legal requirements, companies need to ensure the ethical use of data collected from children. [62]

Parents and guardians should be fully informed about what data is being collected from their children, how it's being used, and what measures are in place to protect it. AI-driven platforms for children should have interfaces designed for their age group, ensuring they can easily understand and navigate privacy settings.

As with adults, only necessary data should be collected from children. This principle is even more crucial here due to the enhanced risks involved. The focus on protecting children in the AI landscape is not just an ethical imperative but a necessity. By safeguarding the most vulnerable users, companies can foster trust and ensure that the next generation grows up understanding and valuing data privacy.

5.2.2. *Understanding and Addressing Bias in AI Data*

In the age of data-driven decision-making, AI has taken center stage, promising transformative possibilities across industries. Yet, for all its power, AI models are fundamentally shaped by the data they're trained on. If this data carries biases—whether related to gender, race, age, or any other characteristic—then the AI, too, can exhibit biased behaviors. Understanding and addressing these biases is critical, not just for ethical AI deployment but also for business outcomes.

Data biases can arise from a variety of sources. Historical data, which forms the backbone of many training datasets, often mirrors the societal biases of its time. For instance, a hiring algorithm trained on data from past decades might inadvertently favor male candidates over female ones, simply because men historically held more of those positions.[63]

Bias in AI isn't just a theoretical concern—it has tangible, real-world repercussions. Consider the healthcare industry, where biased AI models might overlook symptoms more prevalent in a particular ethnic group. Or in finance, where lending algorithms

---

[62] https://blogs.icrc.org/law-and-policy/2023/12/14/protecting-children-data-in-humanitarian-ai-ecosystems/

[63] https://arxiv.org/pdf/2307.05842.pdf and https://levity.ai/blog/ai-bias-how-to-avoid

might unfairly favor or disfavor applicants based on demographic features rather than individual merit.[64]

Strategies to address AI bias include:

- **Diverse Training Data:** To build unbiased AI models, start at the source. Ensure that the training data is representative of diverse groups, conditions, and scenarios. This might involve sourcing data from different regions, demographics, or time periods.

- **Bias Detection Tools:** A plethora of tools and frameworks, such as IBM's Fairness 360 or Google's What-If Tool, are now available to detect and mitigate bias in AI models. Regularly using these tools can help companies stay ahead of potential issues.

- **Transparency and Explainability:** Encourage AI models that offer clear explanations for their decisions. Such transparency not only helps in spotting biases but also builds trust among users and stakeholders.

- **Continuous Learning:** AI, by its nature, evolves. It's essential to continuously monitor AI models as they interact with new data and learn. This ongoing oversight can catch biases that might develop over time.

- **Inclusive Development Teams:** Diverse development teams—comprising people of different genders, races, backgrounds, and perspectives—are more likely to spot and correct biases. Diversity in tech isn't just an ethical imperative—it's a business necessity.

The promise of AI rests on its ability to make impartial, data-driven decisions. Yet, ensuring its impartiality requires vigilance, tools, and a commitment to diversity and fairness at every step. Addressing bias in AI isn't just a matter of ethical compliance—it's foundational to building AI systems that are effective, trustworthy, and truly transformative.

---

[64] https://datatron.com/real-life-examples-of-discriminating-artificial-intelligence/ and https://www.sanfordheisler.com/blog/2023/11/bias-in-ai-the-real-world-ramifications-and-legal-implications/

5.2.3. The Principle of Data Minimization

In today's vast and interconnected digital realm, collecting and storing vast amounts of data has become increasingly tempting—and often seen as necessary. With the rise of AI, which thrives on vast datasets to train and refine its models, this temptation has grown manifold. Yet, amidst this data deluge, a core principle of privacy stands out: data minimization. But what does data minimization mean, especially in the context of AI? And why is it more crucial now than ever?

At its core, data minimization is the principle that organizations should collect, process, and retain only the minimum amount of personal data necessary to fulfill a specified purpose. It calls for a disciplined approach to data, ensuring that excess information isn't gathered just because it "might" be useful in the future.

While AI algorithms are known for their appetite for data, indiscriminately feeding them can have unintended consequences.

The cases for data minimization include:

- **Enhanced Privacy Risks:** The more data an organization holds, the bigger the target it becomes for malicious actors. Data breaches can expose sensitive information, leading to reputational damages, regulatory penalties, and eroded user trust.

- **Increased Management Overhead:** Storing vast datasets means more infrastructure, more complex data governance, and higher costs. It's not just about storage costs but also about managing access, ensuring data quality, and maintaining compliance.

- **Potential for Misuse:** With more data at hand, the potential for misuse, whether unintentional or deliberate, rises. This can lead to decisions based on outdated, irrelevant, or inappropriate data, skewing AI outputs and leading to flawed conclusions.

Requirements for implementing data minimization in AI projects include:

- **Clear Objectives:** Before initiating any AI project, define its objectives clearly. What are you trying to achieve? What data is absolutely essential for this? This clarity will guide data collection and processing, ensuring you gather only what's necessary.

- **Regular Data Audits:** Periodically review the data you hold. Is all of it still relevant? Has any data outlived its utility? Regular audits can help trim the excess and maintain a lean, efficient data ecosystem.

- **Automated Data Lifecycle Management:** Implement tools and protocols that automatically delete or anonymize data once it's no longer needed. This not only ensures compliance with regulations like the GDPR but also reduces the risk associated with holding onto redundant data.

- **Promote a Culture of Minimization:** Data minimization isn't just a technical endeavor—it's a cultural one. Training teams to understand its importance and integrating it into organizational values can make a significant difference.

As AI continues to weave its way deeper into our systems and processes, organizations must balance the allure of endless data with the ethical and pragmatic principles of minimization. In the age of AI, less can indeed be more. Not only does data minimization protect user privacy and reduce risks, but it also paves the way for more streamlined, efficient, and focused AI implementations.

5.2.4.   Informed Consent: Beyond the Fine Print

In the realm of data privacy the concept of informed consent is hardly novel. Traditional applications often meant understanding a service or product, reading through terms of use or privacy policy, and then checking a box. However, as the complexity of data-driven technologies, especially AI, has escalated, so has the intricacy of obtaining genuine informed consent. It's no longer enough to hide behind pages of jargon-filled fine print. The age of AI demands a rethinking of how we approach and obtain consent.

Historically, informed consent meant a one-time, often passive action. You'd sign up for a service, maybe skim through the terms, and check a box. It was static, a single moment in time. However, as services have evolved to be more dynamic, with data being continually collected and processed, the old model of consent has become less tenable.

Traditional consent models fall short in the AI era due to:

- **Dynamic Data Processing:** Unlike traditional systems, AI models can adapt and evolve based on new data. This means the way user data is utilized can change over time. A one-time consent at sign-up isn't equipped to cover such fluidity.

- **Complexity of AI Processes:** AI's workings can be intricate and abstract. Expecting users to understand and consent to something they might not fully grasp is not genuine informed consent.

- **Vague Terminologies:** Phrases like "data may be used to improve our services" are ambiguous. What improvements? How exactly is the data used? These questions often remain unanswered in fine print.

Consent for the AI age requires:

- **Layered Consent:** Instead of a one-time all-encompassing consent, consider a tiered or layered approach. Users could give basic consent for primary services and then additional consent for more invasive or complex AI-driven features.

- **Plain Language Policies:** It's crucial to break down complex AI and data processes into understandable terms. Using plain language, visuals, or even interactive modules can help users genuinely understand what they're consenting to.

- **Ongoing Consent Management:** Given the dynamic nature of AI, organizations should offer tools that allow users to manage, review, and modify their consent preferences over time. This recognizes consent as an evolving entity, not a static one.

- **Transparency and Trust:** Building a culture of transparency is pivotal. If users trust that a company has their best interests at heart and will use their data responsibly, they are more likely to provide informed consent.

In sectors like healthcare, where AI is being used to diagnose or suggest treatments, the importance of informed consent is amplified. Patients must understand not only what data is being collected but also how AI models might use it, as well as the benefits and potential risks.

In conclusion, as AI's role in our lives becomes more pronounced, organizations must rise to the challenge of ensuring that consent is not just a legal formality but a genuinely informed choice. A shift from mere compliance to fostering understanding and trust will be the key to achieving this.

5.3.   Data Transparency and Traceability

In an era where data has emerged as a prime asset, its management has taken center stage in both organizational strategies and regulatory frameworks. One of the chief tenets of effective data management, especially when intertwined with AI applications, is ensuring both transparency and traceability. This goes beyond mere access to data–it touches upon the ethics, processes, and implications of data collection, processing, and utilization.

5.3.1.   The Imperative of Data Transparency

The foundation of any trust-based relationship between organizations and their stakeholders (customers, partners, regulators) is transparency. Data transparency, in the context of AI, implies:

- **Open Algorithms:** While proprietary algorithms might be a company's secret sauce, an understanding of how these algorithms work is crucial. Even if the intricate details are not revealed, providing a broad overview of how algorithms make decisions can foster trust.

- **Clear Data Policies:** Organizations should have clear, comprehensible, and accessible policies detailing how data is collected, processed, stored, and utilized. These should be free from jargon and easily understandable by the average user.

- **Data Provenance:** It's not just about the data you have but where it came from. Provenance involves tracking the journey of data, ensuring its authenticity and reliability.

5.3.2.   Traceability: The Unsung Hero of Accountability

Where transparency is about clarity, traceability is about accountability. It involves:

- **Data Lineage:** This refers to visualizing data's journey throughout its lifecycle – from its source, through transformation processes, to its final destination. Data lineage tools can visually represent this journey, ensuring that data hasn't been tampered with and remains integral.

- **Audit Trails:** In the event of discrepancies, anomalies, or breaches, a robust audit trail can pinpoint where things went wrong. This isn't just about finding faults but is integral for rectifications and future preventions.

- **Machine Learning Model Versioning:** Just as software development uses version control to track changes, AI implementations should have a system in place to keep tabs on the various iterations of machine learning models. This helps in understanding how and why decisions were made at different times.

5.3.3.   *The Intersection of Transparency and Traceability*

When both these principles work in tandem, they form a robust framework that can:

- Facilitate regulatory compliance.

- Enhance consumer trust and brand reputation.

- Ensure ethical AI practices, preventing inherent biases or discriminatory practices.

- Offer a clear roadmap for data rectification, should the need arise.

Despite the obvious advantages, there are hurdles to achieving total transparency and traceability:

- **Proprietary Systems:** Many AI systems are black boxes, with their inner workings hidden. This can make transparency challenging.

- **Massive Data Volumes:** The sheer volume of data processed can make traceability a daunting task, necessitating advanced tools and methodologies.

In the grand tapestry of AI-driven operations, data transparency and traceability are not mere buzzwords—they are the pillars on which ethical, efficient, and effective AI systems stand. As AI continues to shape our world, understanding and advocating for these principles will be paramount for all stakeholders involved.

5.3.4.   AI Decision-Making: Explaining the "Black Box"

As AI becomes increasingly pervasive in various sectors and applications, from healthcare diagnoses to financial risk assessments, the decisions made by these systems wield significant influence. However, a key challenge that has persisted since the dawn of complex AI models is understanding the intricate web of calculations and processes within them. The opaque nature of such systems, often referred to as the "black box" of AI, has raised concerns among regulators, industry professionals, and the general public alike.

The term "black box" in AI refers to systems where inputs and outputs are visible, but the internal mechanisms that drive decisions remain obscured. The lack of transparency has implications:

- **Trust:** Without understanding how AI reaches conclusions, it becomes challenging for users to trust its decisions. This is particularly pertinent in sectors where stakes are high, like in medical diagnoses or criminal justice.

- **Accountability:** If an AI system makes a flawed decision, pinpointing the root of the error is vital for rectification. Without insight into the decision-making mechanics, accountability is elusive.

- **Regulatory Compliance:** Many modern regulatory frameworks demand explainability in automated decision-making processes, especially when they impact consumers directly.

Several methodologies and techniques are emerging to provide clarity:[65]

- **Interpretable Machine Learning Models:** While deep learning models like neural networks are notably complex, there are simpler models like decision trees or linear regression that are inherently more interpretable. Sometimes, a trade-off between accuracy and interpretability is worth considering.

---

[65] https://towardsdatascience.com/counterfactual-explanations-in-model-interpretations-a73caec5b74b, https://ml-retrospectives.github.io/neurips2020/camera_ready/5.pdf, and https://christophm.github.io/interpretable-ml-book/

- **Feature Visualization:** Techniques such as saliency maps highlight which parts of input data (like pixels in an image) were pivotal in an AI's decision. This can offer insights into what the model "sees" as significant.

- **Model Agnostic Methods:** Tools like LIME (Local Interpretable Model-agnostic Explanations) probe AI models by perturbing the input data and observing changes in output. This provides a localized understanding of the model's behavior.

- **Counterfactual Explanations:** These offer insights by answering hypotheticals. For instance, "If X hadn't occurred, Y would've been the outcome" can help in grasping why certain decisions were made.

5.3.5.   The Ethical and Practical Implications

Peering into the AI black box isn't just a technical challenge—it's an ethical imperative. If society is to increasingly rely on AI for critical decisions, there must be mechanisms to understand, question, and, if necessary, contest these decisions.

Furthermore, from a pragmatic viewpoint, businesses stand to benefit from explainable AI. When stakeholders, whether they are customers or internal teams, understand and trust AI-driven processes, it can lead to smoother implementations, fewer roadblocks, and more comprehensive integration into existing workflows.

In conclusion, explaining the "black box" is more than a mere academic endeavor. It's a journey towards establishing trust, ensuring accountability, and paving the way for a future where AI and humans coexist in a transparent symbiosis.

5.3.6.   Tracking Data Movement: From Collection to Processing

In an era defined by data ubiquity, understanding the journey of data—right from its collection to eventual processing—is of paramount importance. The circulation of data within and across organizations is analogous to a lifeblood flow within an intricate digital ecosystem. This flow sustains various functionalities, informs critical decisions, and empowers innovative solutions. Yet, this circulation also poses challenges, and managing these challenges requires diligent tracking of data movement.

5.3.7.   The Evolving Dynamics of Data Movement

Gone are the days when data was static, siloed, and confined within the boundaries of a singular database or repository. Today, data is dynamic. It flows seamlessly across systems, gets ingested into advanced analytics platforms, gets transferred across borders, and is continually transformed and enriched. This fluidity, while powerful, has brought to the fore the pressing need for transparency in data movement.

Tracking data movement is important because:[66]

- **Regulatory Compliance:** Many contemporary data protection regulations like the GDPR, CCPA, and others mandate businesses to maintain records of data processing activities. They require organizations to document where data comes from, where it's stored, who accesses it, and where it might be transferred.

- **Data Integrity and Quality:** As data moves and gets transformed, there's potential for corruption, degradation, or loss. Tracking its movement helps in maintaining data integrity and quality throughout its lifecycle.

- **Security:** By monitoring the flow of data, security teams can identify unauthorized data access or transfers, potentially thwarting breaches or leaks.

- **Operational Efficiency:** Understanding the flow of data helps in optimizing processing pipelines, ensuring that data is available when and where it's needed, and preventing bottlenecks.

Techniques and tools to track data movement include:[67]

- **Data Flow Diagrams (DFD):** A graphical representation that showcases the flow of data within a system. DFDs can be invaluable in visualizing the movement and transformation of data from one system component to another.

---

[66] https://lakefs.io/data-quality/data-integrity-vs-data-quality/, https://blog.quest.com/data-movement-why-its-necessary-why-it-should-start-with-data-modeling/, and https://atlan.com/data-integrity-vs-data-quality/

[67] https://guides.visual-paradigm.com/comprehensive-guide-to-data-flow-diagrams-in-software-engineering/, https://support.scitools.com/support/solutions/articles/70000641375-data-flow-diagrams, and https://sbscyber.com/blog/data-flow-diagrams-101

- **Data Lineage Tools:** These tools provide a visual representation of where data comes from, where it moves over time, and how it gets transformed. Tools like Talend, Collibra, and Alation are prime examples.

- **Audit Logs:** These are detailed records that track who accessed data, what changes were made, when, and why. Modern databases and data platforms come with robust auditing capabilities.

- **Data Catalogs:** These are centralized repositories that allow organizations to manage their data's metadata. They offer context about data sources, transformations, and usage, facilitating better governance and understanding of data movement.

Embracing the dynamism of modern data infrastructures doesn't mean relinquishing control. In fact, it's entirely possible—and necessary—to strike a balance where data can flow flexibly to fuel innovation while being meticulously tracked to ensure compliance, security, and operational efficiency.

In our journey towards AI-driven futures, understanding and monitoring the voyage of data becomes an imperative. Only when we know the paths our data treads can we ensure that it serves our needs while respecting the boundaries of privacy and security.

The digital landscape is vast and intricate. Each data point that enters this terrain undergoes numerous transformations, commutes across varied platforms, and might even transcend international boundaries before it is processed. Each movement and every transformation have potential implications, especially in the context of privacy and security. Consequently, understanding the precise journey of data, from the moment of its collection to its final processing, becomes a cornerstone of modern digital operations.

Before we delve into the nuances of tracking, it's essential to understand the nature of today's data ecosystem. In earlier times, data mostly resided in static environments, rarely moving beyond its original storage location. Fast forward to our current age, and data is now perpetually on the move. Be it through integrated systems, cloud migrations, or analytics engines, data today is ever-evolving, continually shifting, and always working. Movement is crucial because:

- **Upholding Regulatory Demands:** Many modern data protection regulations, including GDPR and CCPA, obligate businesses to not only protect data but also to be fully aware of its whereabouts and transformations. Companies must now maintain meticulous records detailing the data's origin, storage locations, access logs, and transfer points.

- **Ensuring Data Authenticity:** As data navigates through various systems, its authenticity and integrity can be at risk. Tracking its movement ensures the preservation of its originality and the prompt identification of any potential tampering.

- **Security Paradigms:** Continuous monitoring of data flows can swiftly highlight any anomalies, such as unauthorized data access or unscheduled transfers. This swift detection can be the difference between a secure system and a massive data breach.

- **Boosting Operational Efficiency:** A thorough understanding of data flow can illuminate operational bottlenecks, ensuring seamless processing and optimal utilization of resources.

Tools and strategies for effective data tracking include:

- **Data Flow Diagrams:** An illustrative tool that visually depicts the path data takes through systems. It's a simplified yet powerful way to understand how data moves and interacts with different system components.

- **Data Lineage Solutions:** Such tools present a comprehensive view of data's origin, its subsequent touchpoints, and the transformations it undergoes. Tools like Informatica, Apache Atlas, and Waterline Data stand out in this realm.

- **Audit Trails:** These are chronological records detailing every action performed on the data—be it access, modification, or deletion. Modern data management platforms have advanced audit capabilities, offering granular insights into data activity.

- **Centralized Data Catalogs:** Serving as repositories, these catalogs manage metadata associated with data, providing essential context about data sources, transformations, and usage patterns.

The rapid advancements in AI and digital technologies suggest that the complexity and volume of data movements are only set to increase. Ensuring that we can track every byte of this data is not just about compliance—it's about building trust. As data continues to shape our futures, understanding its journey becomes foundational to building transparent, secure, and efficient digital ecosystems.

5.3.8.   *User Access: Empowering Individuals to Understand Their Data*

In the age of data-driven decision-making, data has often been labeled the 'new oil.' But unlike oil, data is about individuals—it's personal, intimate, and often reveals more about a person than even close acquaintances might know. In this vast data-driven ecosystem, one of the vital tenets of privacy is the right of individuals to access and understand their data. Such empowerment is not just an ethical imperative but is also a regulatory necessity under various data protection regimes.

When we look at the crux of why individuals should have access to their data, several compelling arguments arise:

- **Personal Autonomy:** Data, at its heart, represents individual actions, preferences, beliefs, and histories. Ensuring that individuals can access and verify their data underscores the principle of personal autonomy in the digital age.

- **Transparency and Trust:** By allowing individuals to see what data an entity holds about them, companies can foster an environment of transparency, which in turn can bolster trust, a currency that's invaluable in our interconnected world.

- **Correction of Inaccuracies:** Humans, like the systems they create, are fallible. By allowing users to access their data, errors or inaccuracies can be identified and rectified, ensuring more accurate decision-making processes.

Achieving meaningful user access in AI-driven environments presents unique challenges.[68] Here's a brief exploration:

- **Complex Data Structures:** AI often works with intricate data structures, making it challenging to present data in an easily understandable format. Overcoming this requires thoughtful design and a user-centric approach.

---

[68] https://neptune.ai/blog/managing-dataset-versions-in-long-term-ml-projects and
https://neptune.ai/blog/data-versioning-control-for-various-data-sources

- **Derived Data and Predictions:** AI doesn't just store data—it derives new data, making predictions and inferences. Ensuring that users can understand not just the raw data but also its derived forms is essential.

- **Historical Data Snapshots:** AI models evolve over time. A user's data might have contributed to a model in a particular state but might not influence it in its current state. Providing users with snapshots of their data's influence over time is a step towards comprehensive access.

Several strategies and tools can help companies facilitate robust user access:

- **User Portals with Data Dashboards:** Many forward-thinking companies have developed user-centric portals where individuals can log in, view, and, in some cases, download all the data associated with them.

- **Plain-Language Summaries:** Especially relevant in AI scenarios, these summaries accompany raw data, providing users with a contextual understanding of what the data means.

- **Data Ambassadors:** Some organizations have begun employing 'data ambassadors' or 'data stewards.' These are individuals tasked with helping users navigate and understand their data, serving as a bridge between complex systems and the layperson.

- **Automated Data Access Tools:** With advancements in technology, there are tools that allow for automated extraction and presentation of user data upon request. Such tools not only streamline the access process but also ensure timely responses to user requests.

In the final analysis, user access to data is about reaffirming the centrality of the individual in a digital ecosystem. It's a gesture that says, "You matter, your data matters, and you have a right to it." As AI continues to play an increasingly pivotal role in our lives, we must ensure this right becomes not just a regulatory mandate but a moral one.

5.4.   Secure AI Deployment: Beyond Compliance

The integration of AI into businesses and society at large brings a promise of innovation and increased efficiency. However, as with all technological advancements, it's not without its risks. The nature of AI, its pervasive influence, and the vast amounts of data it handles necessitate security measures that go beyond standard compliance checkboxes.

5.4.1.   The Essence of Secure Deployment

The term 'secure deployment' in the context of AI isn't merely about protecting an AI system from external attacks. It's a holistic approach encompassing data integrity, system robustness, ethical considerations, and user trust. It's the assurance that when an AI system makes a decision, it does so based on untainted data, under ethical guidelines, and in a manner transparent enough for users to trust its judgment.

Several unique challenges arise when trying to secure AI systems:

- **Adversarial Attacks:** Unlike traditional systems, AI models can be misled by carefully crafted inputs, known as adversarial examples, that can trick the model into making incorrect predictions or classifications.

- **Model Stealing:** Competitors or malicious actors might attempt to recreate a proprietary AI model by continuously querying it.

- **Data Poisoning:** Introducing tainted data during the training phase can lead to skewed or malicious outputs when the model is later used in real-world scenarios.

5.4.2.   Strategies for Secure Deployment

To overcome these challenges, organizations can adopt several strategies:

- **Regular Model Updates:** Keeping AI models updated ensures they remain robust against evolving adversarial tactics. It's the digital equivalent of an immune system that learns from new threats.

- **Model Hardening:** Techniques such as adversarial training, where a model is exposed to and trained on adversarial examples, can make it more resilient to such attacks in the future.

- **Differential Privacy:** This ensures that the AI system's outputs don't compromise individual data points, even if the overall patterns or trends are revealed.

- **Federated Learning:** Instead of centralizing user data to train AI models, federated learning trains algorithms locally on devices (like smartphones). Only the learnings (and not the data) are sent back to a central server.

- **Ethical Review Boards:** Instituting boards or committees to oversee AI deployments ensures that the AI's decisions remain within ethical bounds, taking into consideration societal norms and values.

- **User Feedback Mechanisms:** By allowing users to provide feedback on AI-driven decisions, organizations can harness the collective intelligence of their user base to identify and rectify biases or inaccuracies.

- **Transparent Algorithm Practices:** Companies can adopt a practice of clarity by sharing (as far as proprietary considerations allow) the broad strokes of how their algorithms work. This doesn't mean revealing trade secrets but rather providing users with an understanding of the algorithm's decision-making criteria.

5.4.3.   The Journey Beyond Compliance

While regulatory compliance sets a baseline, true security in AI deployment is a journey. As AI systems evolve, so too will the threats against them. By understanding that security is not a destination but an ongoing process, organizations can better prepare themselves for the challenges of tomorrow. Secure AI deployment becomes a blend of technology, ethics, and human oversight.

5.4.4.   Encryption in the Age of AI: From Data at Rest to Data in Use

The encryption landscape has witnessed an upheaval in the era of AI. With AI systems continually processing and analyzing vast datasets, ensuring the confidentiality and integrity of this data becomes paramount. But the challenge is multi-fold. Not only must the data be secure when stored (data at rest) but also when transmitted (data in transit) and, crucially, even when it's being actively used or processed (data in use).

Historically, encryption practices primarily focused on data at rest and data in transit. Data at rest encryption ensures that databases, files, or disks are unreadable without the correct decryption keys. Similarly, data in transit encryption, like the SSL/TLS protocols, guarantees secure data transfers over networks. But decrypted data becomes vulnerable. Traditional encryption models struggled with securing data in use, as operations on encrypted data often required decryption first, creating potential security vulnerabilities.

Homomorphic encryption offers a groundbreaking solution to this age-old problem. It allows computations on ciphertexts, generating an encrypted result that, when decrypted, matches the result of the operations performed on the plain text. In simpler terms, it permits AI models to analyze and process encrypted data without ever needing to decrypt it, ensuring data remains confidential even during active use.

Examples of AI use cases:

- **Healthcare AI Models:** In fields like healthcare, where patient data privacy is a primary concern, homomorphic encryption can be a boon. AI models can analyze encrypted medical records to generate insights, make predictions, or even recommend treatments without exposing individual patient details.[69]

- **Financial Services:** For banks and financial institutions, protecting transaction data and financial records is crucial. AI systems can utilize homomorphic encryption to process and analyze encrypted transactions, offering insights without compromising security.[70]

---

[69] https://www.openaccessgovernment.org/fully-homomorphic-encryption-revolutionises-healthcare-data-privacy-and-innovation/167103/

[70] https://www.turing.ac.uk/blog/homomorphic-encryption-future-secure-data-sharing-finance

- **Smart Cities:** As urban centers become smarter with interconnected IoT devices, they collect vast amounts of data. AI can analyze this data for traffic management, energy optimization, etc., without endangering the privacy of individual citizens.

While homomorphic encryption is revolutionary, it's computationally intensive and might not be suitable for all applications due to latency issues. Companies must balance security requirements with operational efficiency.

AI itself is playing a role in advancing encryption methods. Machine learning models can predict potential threats and vulnerabilities in encryption algorithms, leading to the development of more secure cryptographic methods. Additionally, AI can automate and optimize key management processes, ensuring keys are rotated, stored, and distributed securely and efficiently.

In the sprawling landscape of AI, where data is the lifeblood, encryption methods have had to evolve to ensure that this data remains sacrosanct at every stage. From data at rest to the revolutionary realm of data in use, modern encryption practices, enhanced by AI, are making it possible for organizations to harness the power of AI without compromising on security.

5.4.5.   AI-Powered Data Anonymization Techniques

The increasing demand for data in AI applications has brought forth a critical challenge: how can we harness vast datasets without violating individual privacy? As regulations become stricter and public awareness of data privacy grows, there's a pressing need for advanced data anonymization techniques that can protect individual identities. AI is at the forefront of shaping these techniques, making data both useful for analysis and safe from breaches.

Traditional data anonymization methods include tactics like data masking, pseudonymization, and basic aggregation. These methods replace, obscure, or generalize personal data to make re-identification difficult. However, as datasets grow larger and analytical tools become more sophisticated, the chance of 're-identifying' individuals from such anonymized data increases.

AI-driven techniques are revolutionizing the data anonymization landscape. By learning from vast amounts of data, AI models can develop more effective strategies for anonymization, ensuring both data utility and privacy. Some cutting-edge AI-powered anonymization techniques include:

- **Differential Privacy:** Rooted in advanced mathematics, differential privacy ensures that the inclusion (or exclusion) of an individual's data in a dataset does not significantly affect the outcomes of any analysis, thereby maintaining the person's privacy. Apple, for instance, has used differential privacy to gather user insights without compromising individual user data.[71]

- **Generative Adversarial Networks (GANs):** GANs are neural network architectures where two networks, a generator and a discriminator, work against each other. For data anonymization, GANs can generate synthetic datasets that maintain the statistical properties of the original dataset without containing any actual individual data points. We can then use this synthetic data for AI training and analysis without privacy concerns.[72]

- **Automated Feature Engineering:** AI automatically identifies and selects features that maintain data utility but don't compromise privacy. These models apply complex transformations to data features, enhancing data privacy while preserving the dataset's analytical value.[73]

- **Federated Learning:** While not an anonymization technique in itself, federated learning changes the approach to data access, which has significant privacy implications. Rather than centralizing data, federated learning leaves personal data on the user's device and only sends model updates to the cloud. This

---

[71] https://arxiv.org/pdf/2008.01916.pdf, https://neptune.ai/blog/using-differential-privacy-to-build-secure-models-tools-methods-best-practices, and https://www.nist.gov/news-events/news/2023/12/nist-offers-draft-guidance-evaluating-privacy-protection-technique-ai-era

[72] https://ieeexplore.ieee.org/ielaam/6221020/9159696/9034117-aam.pdf, https://www.statworx.com/en/content-hub/blog/generative-adversarial-networks-how-data-can-be-generated-with-neural-networks/, and https://link.springer.com/article/10.1007/s11042-022-13917-6

[73] https://www.k2view.com/what-is-data-anonymization/ and https://www2.deloitte.com/content/dam/Deloitte/de/Documents/Innovation/Deloitte_Trustworthy%20AI%20_Data%20Anonymization_Feb2022.pdf

technique decreases the risk of data breaches, minimizing the exposure of sensitive data.[74]

Incorporating AI-powered data anonymization techniques into your privacy framework offers several benefits. First, you'll significantly reduce the risk of data breaches and resultant regulatory penalties. Second, it gives your business a competitive edge. As privacy becomes a major concern for customers, companies that can prove they respect and protect user data stand to gain.[75]

However, integrating AI-powered data anonymization into your privacy framework requires careful consideration. Like any AI solution, these techniques should be transparent, controllable, and subject to human oversight. They should also be monitored and regularly updated to respond to evolving privacy risks and regulatory requirements.

Additionally, as these techniques often involve complex mathematical algorithms and AI models, having a team with the requisite skills is critical. Some organizations may find it beneficial to engage with external AI and data privacy experts to implement these techniques effectively.

In conclusion, as AI continues to drive data-driven strategies, finding ways to harness data without compromising privacy becomes paramount. AI-powered data anonymization techniques offer a promising solution, bridging the gap between data utility and privacy. However, as with any advanced technology, careful implementation and continuous monitoring are vital to ensuring these techniques serve their purpose without introducing new risks.

In an age where data is continuously being generated, processed, and analyzed, preserving the privacy of individuals is a mounting challenge. AI has not only become an enabler for businesses to gain insights from this data but also a facilitator in enhancing data protection techniques. AI-driven anonymization techniques play a pivotal role in

---

[74] https://queue.acm.org/detail.cfm?id=3501293,
https://www.ncbi.nlm.nih.gov/pmc/articles/PMC10418741/, and
https://pair.withgoogle.com/explorables/federated-learning/

[75] https://amlegals.com/ai-powered-data-anonymization-techniques-for-preserving-privacy/,
https://mostly.ai/what-is-data-anonymization, and https://www.iterates.be/2024/02/23/data-privacy-anonymization-with-ai-tools-a-complete-guide/

this realm, offering more sophisticated ways to anonymize data compared to traditional methods.

Traditional data anonymization methods, such as masking or redaction, simply hide or alter specific data elements. However, they can sometimes still allow data miners to reconstruct the original data or infer personal details. With the exponential growth in data volumes and the sophistication of cyber threats, the need for enhanced data anonymization has never been more urgent.

Enter AI-powered data anonymization techniques. By employing advanced algorithms and learning mechanisms, AI can create multi-layered and complex anonymization methods that are harder to reverse-engineer.

Popular AI-powered anonymization methods include:[76]

- **Differential Privacy:** Originating from the realm of cryptography, differential privacy ensures that the risk to one's privacy is not substantially increased by one's participation in a statistical database. AI models, particularly deep learning ones, can be trained to satisfy differential privacy requirements, ensuring individual data points are indistinguishable from the rest.

- **Generative Adversarial Networks (GANs):** GANs are neural network architectures where two networks (the generator and the discriminator) are trained together. When applied to data anonymization, the generator tries to produce fake data while the discriminator attempts to distinguish between real and fake data. Over time, the generator gets better, producing anonymized data that is almost indistinguishable from real data.

- **Feature Selection and Transformation:** Advanced machine learning models can be designed to select and transform features of a dataset automatically. This ensures data remains useful for analysis, but the personal identifiers are transformed so that they can't be traced back to the original.

- **Federated Learning:** While not a direct anonymization method, federated learning offers a new paradigm in how data is accessed and processed. It trains algorithms across decentralized devices or servers holding local data samples

---

[76] https://www.respeecher.com/blog/impact-deepfake-technology-digital-marketing-advertising and https://www.techmagic.co/blog/ai-in-cybersecurity/

without exchanging them. This ensures personal data remains local, minimizing exposure.

Incorporating AI-driven anonymization has its set of challenges. The complexity of AI models, coupled with the intricacies of data privacy, demands a robust framework. It's essential for businesses to understand the underpinnings of the AI models they employ, ensuring that they don't unintentionally introduce biases or vulnerabilities.

Moreover, the evolving landscape of data privacy regulations necessitates continuous monitoring and updating of these AI-driven techniques. Organizations must strike a balance: use advanced techniques to protect data and simultaneously ensure they remain compliant with privacy laws.

> *AI-powered data anonymization techniques present a promising avenue for businesses to harness the potential of their data without compromising individual privacy. But like all powerful tools, they come with the responsibility of careful and knowledgeable application.*

5.4.6.   Robust Access Controls and Data Integrity Checks

In a digital world increasingly dominated by vast amounts of data, ensuring the right access and maintaining the integrity of this data becomes paramount, especially when AI systems are integrated into the infrastructure. AI, by its very nature, is hungry for data, processing vast amounts of it to provide accurate outputs. However, this appetite for data also raises concerns: Who should have access to the data? How can one ensure the data hasn't been tampered with? Addressing these concerns are the realms of robust access controls and data integrity checks.

There is an imperative of robust access controls because:[77]

- **The Risk Landscape:** With the adoption of AI systems, data isn't just stored—it's actively processed, analyzed, and acted upon. Each interaction point becomes a potential vulnerability. Unauthorized access could lead not just to data breaches but also to manipulated AI outcomes.

---

[77] https://frontegg.com/guides/rbac-vs-abac, https://www.linkedin.com/advice/1/what-pros-cons-role-based-access-control-rbac-versus, and https://support.pega.com/question/rbac-vs-abac-performance-consideration-and-use-cases

- **Role-Based Access Control (RBAC):** A widely adopted method, RBAC, assigns roles to users and grants permissions based on these roles. In an AI-integrated infrastructure, this might mean that data scientists have access to raw data for model training, but marketing personnel might only see aggregated insights.

- **Attribute-Based Access Control (ABAC):** Going beyond roles, ABAC uses policies to determine access, taking into account attributes like the user's department, time of request, type of data requested, and more. This granularity becomes crucial when dealing with sensitive data processed by AI, allowing fine-tuned control over who can access what, when, and under what circumstances.

Checks and balances to preserve data integrity include:

- **Cryptographic Hash Functions:** These are algorithms that take input data and return a fixed-size string, which is typically a hash value. Any minor change in input will result in a dramatically different hash. One can verify that the data hasn't been tampered with by comparing hash values before and after data transfers or at various checkpoints.

- **Blockchain and Distributed Ledgers:** A growing field of interest, especially for maintaining the integrity of vast datasets. Every change or addition to the data creates a new 'block' in the 'chain.' This block contains a cryptographic hash of the previous one, forming a linked chain. As AI systems process data, these chains can provide immutable, transparent logs of all interactions, making unauthorized alterations almost impossible.

- **Digital Signatures:** These are cryptographic equivalents of handwritten signatures or stamped seals but are much more secure. They provide proof of the origin, identity, and status of an electronic document, transaction, or message and can acknowledge informed consent by the signer.

- **The AI Angle:** Advanced AI and machine learning models are now being developed to monitor and manage access controls and integrity checks. These systems can learn typical user behavior and raise flags on anomalous access requests or data interactions, providing an extra layer of security.

In conclusion, as businesses become deeply intertwined with AI systems, the principles of access control and data integrity aren't just best practices—they are necessities. Ensuring that only authorized individuals have access to specific data and maintaining a vigilant eye on the sanctity of data are essential steps in building trust in AI-driven digital infrastructures.

5.5.   AI and The Right to Erasure ("Right to be Forgotten")

The 'Right to Erasure,' also known as the 'Right to be Forgotten,' is a foundational pillar of modern data protection regulations. Rooted in the European Union's General Data Protection Regulation (GDPR), this principle gives individuals the right to request the deletion or removal of personal data when there's no compelling reason for its continued processing. However, integrating artificial intelligence into digital infrastructures presents new challenges and considerations in upholding this right.[78]

5.5.1.   The Complexities Introduced by AI

AI systems, by design, are vast repositories of data, continuously learning and evolving based on the information they ingest. This continuous learning process, known as *training*, can make the erasure of specific data points challenging:

- **Entwined Data:** When personal data becomes part of an AI model's training set, it becomes deeply woven into the fabric of the model. Erasing a specific individual's data doesn't just involve removing it from a database, but potentially retraining the model to ensure the data is genuinely forgotten.

- **Data in Neural Networks:** Advanced AI systems, especially deep neural networks, don't store data in recognizable forms. Instead, they maintain weights and adjust their biases through training. This means that even if the original data is deleted, its 'essence' might still impact the model's behavior.

---

[78] https://gdpr.eu/right-to-be-forgotten/ and https://dig.watch/updates/challenges-in-removing-data-from-ai-models

5.5.2.   *Practical Steps Towards Upholding the Right*

While the right to erasure poses challenges in an AI-driven world, there are methods and best practices to ensure compliance:

- **Regular Model Retraining:** Instead of trying to 'remove' data from an already trained model, organizations can store training data separately and, upon a request for erasure, retrain the model from scratch without the data in question. This method, although resource-intensive, is one of the most effective ways to ensure compliance.

- **Differential Privacy:** This technique adds statistical noise to data queries, allowing data analysts to extract useful insights without accessing specific personal data. By ensuring that AI models don't have access to precise personal data, the right to erasure becomes more straightforward to uphold.

- **Use of Synthetic Data:** Synthetic data, which is artificially generated, mimics the characteristics of real-world data without containing actual personal information. Training AI models on synthetic data can significantly reduce the complexities associated with the right to erasure.

5.5.3.   *Balancing Innovation and Privacy*

As the 'Right to be Forgotten' becomes more globally recognized, its intersection with AI will continue to be a topic of debate. On the one hand, AI needs vast amounts of data to function optimally, and on the other hand, individuals have a fundamental right to data privacy.

The ultimate challenge lies in striking the right balance. Organizations must prioritize innovative methods that respect individual privacy rights while still harnessing the transformative power of AI. Proactively building systems with the 'Right to Erasure' in mind will not only ensure regulatory compliance but also foster trust among users and stakeholders in an increasingly data-driven world.

5.5.4.   Implementing and Respecting Data Deletion Requests

In an era where personal data has become a valuable commodity, the ability for individuals to reclaim their digital autonomy by exercising their right to erasure is profound. As the intricate webs of data entanglement become more complex with AI's intervention, companies must have robust systems in place to not only implement data deletion requests but also to respect and uphold them consistently.

Individuals may have a myriad of reasons for wanting their data erased, ranging from concerns about privacy and potential misuse to simply wanting to reduce their digital footprint. Irrespective of the reason, it's vital for organizations to recognize that these requests are rooted in fundamental rights.

Key steps to implementing data deletion requests include:[79]

1. **Unified Data Inventory:** Before any deletion can occur, companies must know where the data resides. The first step is implementing a unified data inventory that provides a holistic view of where an individual's data is stored across various databases and systems.

2. **Automated Processes:** Given the scale of data that large organizations handle, automation is key. Tools and solutions that can automatically detect and delete specific data sets in response to user requests are invaluable.

3. **Validation of Request:** While it's essential to respect users' wishes, validating the legitimacy of a deletion request is crucial. This helps prevent malicious requests that aim to disrupt service or compromise data integrity.

4. **Timely Response:** Regulations like the GDPR mandate a one-month window for companies to respond to data subject requests. Adhering to these timelines is not just about compliance—it's about building trust.

5. **Feedback Loop:** Once the data has been deleted, inform the user about the completion of the process. This confirmation serves as a closure to their request and reinforces the company's commitment to data privacy.

---

[79] https://www.mineos.ai/articles/right-to-erasure-time-frame and
https://www.privacyworld.blog/2021/03/consumers-right-to-delete-under-us-state-privacy-laws/

Traditional databases offer a straightforward process when it comes to data deletion. However, AI systems, particularly machine learning models, pose unique challenges:

- **Backup Systems:** AI systems often have backup datasets used for recovery and retraining. Ensuring data is deleted from these backups is just as crucial as the primary datasets.

- **Repercussions on Model Integrity:** Deleting data might require retraining AI models, especially if the removed data played a significant role in predictions or outcomes. This retraining ensures the model remains accurate without the now-erased data.

- **Propagation of Data:** In federated learning systems, data might be distributed across multiple nodes or devices. Ensuring complete erasure in such systems can be challenging.

The implementation of data deletion requests in an AI-centric ecosystem is undoubtedly complex, but it's far from insurmountable. With a combination of technological solutions, proactive data management strategies, and a genuine commitment to respecting user rights, organizations can navigate this challenge efficiently. This not only satisfies regulatory requirements but also solidifies the company's reputation as a trustworthy custodian of user data.

5.5.5.   Challenges and Considerations: Data Retention in AI Systems

The complex architectures and data-driven nature of AI systems have introduced a new set of challenges when it comes to data retention and management. While organizations have been managing data retention for traditional IT systems for years, AI introduces unique concerns and nuances that demand a rethink of established protocols. Let's delve into the primary challenges and considerations associated with data retention in AI environments.

One of AI's strengths is its ability to learn from historical data, enabling it to make predictions or decisions based on vast data sets that humans could not process in real-time. This dependency on past data creates tension between the need to retain data for AI's effectiveness and the demand to respect data retention policies and regulations.

Once an AI model is trained on specific data, removing or altering that data can change the model's behavior or accuracy. It's a challenge to determine how much historical data an AI system should retain to ensure its effectiveness while complying with retention policies and deletion requests.

Organizations have begun to utilize differential privacy techniques and synthetic data generation to counteract the potential pitfalls of data deletion. These methods allow AI systems to be trained on data without directly accessing the original, potentially sensitive information. However, the balance between utility and privacy in these solutions remains a point of contention.

For AI systems, especially in regulated industries, it's paramount to have traceable audit trails showcasing when data was used, for what purpose, and when it was deleted or altered. This not only ensures regulatory compliance but also provides a means to verify and validate AI decisions retrospectively.

The rise of decentralized data storage solutions and federated learning, where AI models are trained on multiple devices or nodes, further complicates data retention. Ensuring consistent data retention policies across a distributed network is challenging, especially when varying regional regulations might govern different nodes.

Some AI systems operate in real-time, ingesting and processing data streams continuously. Establishing retention policies for such systems can be challenging. Should the data be retained momentarily, just long enough for the AI to process, or should it be stored for potential future retraining or auditing?

Managing data retention in AI systems isn't just a technical challenge—it's an organizational and cultural one. It requires cross-functional collaboration between legal teams, data scientists, IT professionals, and organizational leadership. Proactive strategies, underpinned by a clear understanding of both regulatory demands and AI's unique requirements, are crucial. By addressing these challenges head-on, organizations can harness the power of AI while safeguarding user rights and ensuring compliance.

5.5.6.   *Best Practices: Ensuring User Data is Truly Erased*

The evolution of digital information and the sprawling nature of data storage have made the task of completely erasing user data more intricate than ever before. Especially in AI, where data often serves as the backbone of algorithms, ensuring a comprehensive erasure is challenging yet crucial. Adopting robust practices for data deletion safeguards user rights and bolsters trust. Let's delve into the best practices organizations should consider when ensuring user data is truly removed:

- **Comprehensive Data Mapping:** Before any data can be deleted, it must first be located. Organizations should maintain a detailed map of where user data resides. This encompasses not just primary databases but also backups, logs, caches, and external storage facilities. Data mapping tools, many equipped with AI capabilities, can aid in continuously updating these maps, reflecting the dynamic nature of data storage.

- **Multiple Layer Deletion Protocols:** Simply deleting data from a frontend application doesn't guarantee its removal from backend databases or backup systems. A multi-layered deletion protocol ensures that data is erased from primary storage, secondary storage, caches, and any other residual repositories.

- **Secure Data Shredding:** Data shredding refers to overwriting deleted data multiple times with random information, ensuring the original data is irretrievable. This practice is especially essential when dealing with sensitive information. Many modern storage systems come equipped with secure deletion features that perform this function.

- **Regular Data Audits:** Scheduled audits of data repositories can identify lingering personal data that should have been deleted. This step is essential in verifying that data deletion processes are effective and compliant. Automated tools can be employed to facilitate this continuous monitoring process.

- **Monitor Third-party Handlers:** Often, user data is shared with third-party vendors or service providers. Contracts and agreements should clearly specify the data deletion procedures these parties must adhere to, and regular checks should ensure their compliance.

- **Immutable Logs for Accountability:** While user data should be deleted, the action of deletion itself should be logged in an immutable manner. This provides an audit trail, proving that data was erased in compliance with requests and regulations.

- **Update AI Models:** When data is deleted, especially in large amounts, AI models that were trained on this data might require updates or retraining to ensure they don't inadvertently recall or act on erased data patterns.

- **Education and Training:** Human error remains a significant challenge in data management. Continuously educating IT teams about the importance of thorough data deletion and training them on the latest tools and best practices reduces the risk of oversight.

- **Establishing a Data Retention Policy:** An explicit data retention policy that clearly outlines the duration for which different data types are retained and the criteria for their deletion ensures a structured approach to data management. Periodically revisiting and revising this policy ensures it remains relevant in the ever-evolving digital landscape.

- **Seek Feedback and Continuously Improve:** Given the rapid advancements in technology and the changing regulatory environment, organizations should maintain a feedback loop with both internal stakeholders and users. Feedback can spotlight areas of improvement in the data deletion process, ensuring that practices are continuously refined.

Truly erasing user data in today's digital landscape requires a mix of robust technological practices and a commitment to transparency and ethics. As AI systems continue to play an integral role in data management, adapting and refining these practices becomes paramount in upholding user rights and maintaining trust.

5.6.   The Role of Human Oversight in AI Privacy

In the evolving digital realm where AI systems take on increasingly autonomous roles, the significance of human oversight in preserving privacy cannot be understated. Human judgment provides the nuance, context, and ethical considerations that algorithms, no matter how sophisticated, might not always fully grasp. The blend of human expertise with AI efficiency strikes the right balance in navigating the challenges of privacy in the age of AI.

5.6.1.   The Limits of Algorithms: Context and Nuance

Algorithms, at their core, are rule-based and operate within the parameters they are set. However, privacy concerns often tread in the gray areas where strict rules may fall short. A particular data-sharing action might be technically permissible but ethically questionable. Human oversight fills these gaps, bringing a deeper understanding of context, culture, and ethics into decision-making.

5.6.2.   The Ethical Compass: AI is Amoral

While we can design AI to recognize patterns, make decisions, and even learn from new data, it doesn't possess a moral or ethical compass. Humans, with their collective societal, cultural, and individual values, play a pivotal role in ensuring that AI systems respect privacy norms and uphold ethical standards.

5.6.3.   Continuous Monitoring and Auditing

Even the most well-designed AI systems can go awry. Continuous human monitoring and periodic auditing ensure that AI behaviors align with intended outcomes and ethical standards. Any anomalies or drifts in AI behavior that might compromise user privacy can be promptly addressed with timely human intervention.

5.6.4.   Training and Calibration of AI Systems

AI systems often require training data to improve their performance. Humans play a critical role in curating this data, ensuring its quality, and eliminating biases. Furthermore, they decide when an AI system has been adequately trained and is ready for deployment or when it needs recalibration to better serve its purpose.

5.6.5.   Handling Ambiguities and Edge Cases

Despite vast datasets and advanced algorithms, AI might occasionally encounter situations that are ambiguous or don't fit within its trained parameters. Human expertise becomes invaluable in such scenarios, guiding the system through complex decisions and handling edge cases that might have privacy implications.

5.6.6. Ensuring Accountability and Transparency

Accountability in AI-driven decisions, especially those impacting privacy, is crucial. Human oversight ensures that there's a clear chain of responsibility. When things go wrong, it's essential to have a human point of contact who can explain the situation, take corrective actions, and ensure transparency in the process.

5.6.7. Feedback Loop for System Improvement

Humans, as end-users and overseers, provide feedback that's invaluable for refining AI systems. Their experiences, observations, and insights feed into system updates, ensuring that AI evolves in a manner that remains sensitive to privacy concerns.

5.6.8. Balancing Efficiency with Ethics

While AI systems offer unparalleled efficiency and speed, there's a risk of sidelining ethical considerations in the quest for optimization. Human oversight ensures that the drive for efficiency doesn't overshadow the fundamental rights of individuals, particularly their privacy.

The integration of AI into our digital lives offers immense possibilities but also presents privacy challenges. Human oversight acts as a guardian, ensuring that as we leverage AI's capabilities, we do so in a manner that respects individual rights, understands nuanced contexts, and upholds the highest ethical standards. In the age of AI, the human touch remains as vital as ever.

6. Human Element: Training and Awareness in AI Security

6.1. Recognizing the Risk of Human Error

In the rapidly evolving world of AI, where machines exhibit learning capabilities and can operate autonomously, it's tempting to trust them blindly. We often hear of their efficiencies, reduced operational costs, and improved accuracy. But behind every sophisticated algorithm and every neural network lies the fundamental element: the human. And humans, by their very nature, are susceptible to errors.

Humans design, code, train, and oversee AI systems. They decide on the data that trains AI, the algorithms that get used, and the context in which AI decisions are applied. Therefore, even in a landscape dominated by machines, human error remains a significant risk factor.

This is especially true when considering the chain of events leading to an AI's decision. For instance, if an AI system is to identify potential loan defaulters, its predictions are based on the data it has been trained on. If a human mistakenly includes incorrect data or excludes crucial data sets, the AI's predictions could result in serious financial and reputational consequences for a banking institution.[80]

Moreover, as AI systems become more intricate and their applications more widespread, the room for human error expands. The complexity of these systems means that mistakes might not be immediately evident, and by the time they are identified, the consequences could be magnified.

6.1.1.   The Weakest Link in Security

Human error has always been a weak link in security. Whether it's weak passwords, susceptibility to phishing attacks, or configuration errors, these oversights often lead to significant breaches. Within the context of AI, a minor human error can have magnified repercussions. AI operates at a scale and speed that humans cannot match, so a misstep can lead to rapid and widespread consequences. For instance, Microsoft's chatbot Tay was corrupted into making inappropriate remarks due to oversight in training data and inadequate filtering, resulting in a PR nightmare.[81]

AI systems are often trained on biased and inaccurate data, which can reinforce and amplify societal inequalities. For example, AI technologies used by U.S. police forces for predictive analytics relied on "dirty data" plagued by corrupt practices and underlying racist ideologies, leading to biased outcomes.[82] Additionally, human judgment can be adversely affected when participants receive incorrect algorithmic support, leading to excessive compliance when the system errs.[83] Therefore, while AI can help mitigate some human errors, it also introduces new risks that need to be carefully managed to prevent significant security breaches.

---

[80] https://kodexolabs.com/how-does-ai-reduce-human-error/

[81] https://www.bloomberg.com/news/articles/2016-03-24/microsoft-removes-racist-comments-from-millennial-focused-ai-bot

[82] https://www.theverge.com/2016/3/24/11297050/tay-microsoft-chatbot-racist

[83] https://www.bloomberg.com/news/articles/2016-03-24/microsoft-removes-racist-comments-from-millennial-focused-ai-bot

6.1.2. Real-world Consequences of Oversights

Historical records show that even without AI, human errors in IT can lead to disastrous outcomes. For example, the 2017 Amazon S3 misconfiguration resulted in the exposure of nearly 200 million US voter records. When we extrapolate such mistakes to AI-driven scenarios,[84] the potential harm is even greater. An error in an AI system controlling a city's traffic lights, for example, could result in chaos, accidents, and even fatalities.

6.1.3. Avoiding Common Pitfalls

Proactively addressing the risk of human error in AI requires a multi-faceted approach. Organizations must develop specific training modules, checklists, and best practices targeting AI deployments. These measures, combined with frequent audits and a culture of continuous learning, can significantly reduce the potential for human error. Embracing a mindset where mistakes are viewed as learning opportunities rather than causes for punitive action can also encourage individuals to report and rectify their errors more promptly.

6.2. Cultivating an AI-proof Organizational Culture

As AI systems become ubiquitous in the business world, organizations must ensure that their internal cultures are attuned to the challenges and opportunities that these technologies bring. An AI-proof organizational culture prioritizes knowledge, adaptability, collaboration, ethics, and constant vigilance in its AI endeavors.

The blend of human intellect with machine capabilities offers unparalleled benefits, but this confluence can be a double-edged sword. On the one hand, AI can augment human capabilities, while on the other hand, it poses novel risks and challenges. By nurturing an organizational culture that's sensitive to both these aspects, businesses can harness AI's potential safely and ethically.

---

[84] https://www.zdnet.com/article/security-lapse-exposes-198-million-united-states-voter-records/

6.2.1.   Emphasizing Continuous Learning

In a realm where change is the only constant, continuous learning becomes a crucial asset. Organizations must prioritize upskilling and reskilling their staff, particularly in AI and related areas. Workshops, courses, and hands-on training sessions can be instrumental. Not only does this bolster the employees' expertise, but it also instills a sense of value and growth, fostering loyalty and dedication.[85]

6.2.2.   Promoting Ethical AI Use

With the myriad capabilities of AI comes the responsibility to use it ethically. This responsibility isn't just limited to the developers and coders but extends to everyone in the organization. From marketing teams using AI to target potential clients to HR departments leveraging AI for recruitment, every team should be trained on the ethical ramifications of their AI tools. Regular ethics workshops and discussions can promote responsible AI usage.[86]

6.2.3.   Fostering Collaboration

As AI systems touch various parts of a business, silos can be detrimental. Cross-departmental collaboration is essential to ensure that the potential pitfalls and benefits of AI are clearly understood and addressed. Monthly meetings, workshops, and brainstorming sessions where different teams share their experiences with AI can pave the way for more integrated and holistic AI strategies.

6.2.4.   Encouraging Vigilance and Accountability

It's crucial that everyone in the organization, from top-tier leadership to the newest intern, understand their role in AI security. This involves recognizing potential threats, reporting anomalies, and proactively suggesting improvements. A culture that rewards

---

[85] https://www.techtarget.com/searchenterpriseai/tip/Why-continuous-training-is-essential-in-MLOps

[86] https://techxplore.com/news/2023-03-humans-artificial-intelligence.html

vigilance and holds individuals accountable for their actions can be a formidable defense against AI-driven threats.

6.2.5.   Championing Transparency

As AI systems often operate as black boxes, there's a pressing need for transparency in how they're implemented and utilized. Encouraging teams to document their processes, share their methodologies, and openly discuss their AI tools' outcomes can demystify AI for everyone in the organization. This not only boosts trust but also facilitates more informed decision-making.[87]

Embedding these principles into the core of an organization's culture will not only make it more resilient to AI-associated risks but also position it to capitalize on the myriad opportunities AI offers. By placing humans at the heart of their AI strategies, businesses can navigate the AI revolution in a balanced, ethical, and prosperous manner.

6.3.   Continuous Training and Simulation Drills

Incorporating AI into business processes isn't just about integrating the technology—it's about ensuring that the humans who interact with these systems are prepared and well-versed in their operation and potential pitfalls. This human-AI interactivity dynamic is unlike any challenge businesses have faced before, demanding a new approach to training and readiness. Continuous training and simulation drills are among the most effective methods to prepare organizations for these challenges.

6.3.1.   The Importance of Regular Updates

As AI systems and the threats associated with them evolve, so too must the training materials and modules. Organizations can't rely on one-off training sessions or outdated materials. Instead, there should be a commitment to regular updates, ensuring that all

---

[87] https://www.worldprivacyforum.org/2023/12/new-report-risky-analysis-assessing-and-improving-ai-governance-tools/

team members are familiar with the latest developments in AI technology, potential threats, and best practices.

6.3.2.   Real-world Simulation Drills

Theoretical knowledge is essential, but practical application solidifies understanding. By simulating real-world scenarios where AI systems might be vulnerable or misused, staff can gain hands-on experience in dealing with these situations. These drills can range from simple problem-solving exercises with AI tools to full-blown cyberattack simulations targeting AI systems.

6.3.3.   Feedback and Iteration

After each training session or simulation, it's vital to gather feedback from participants. This can provide insights into areas that might need more focus or clarification in future training iterations. Continuous feedback loops ensure that training remains relevant and effective.

6.3.4.   Role-specific Training Modules

Not every employee interacts with AI in the same manner. A developer working on an AI algorithm might face different challenges than a marketing executive using AI-driven analytics tools. Tailoring training modules to specific roles ensures that each individual is equipped with the knowledge pertinent to their interaction with AI.

6.3.5.   Encouraging a Culture of Curiosity

There must be a supportive culture for continuous training to be effective. Organizations should encourage a mindset of constant learning and curiosity. Providing resources, platforms, or even time for employees to explore and experiment with AI tools can foster this culture. Regular AI-focused seminars, talks, or even AI hackathons can keep the enthusiasm and curiosity alive.

Continuous training and simulation drills ensure that the organization remains not just compliant but competent in the face of ever-evolving AI challenges. By proactively preparing its human assets, businesses can ensure they harness AI's potential while mitigating associated risks.

6.4. Adapting to the Evolving Threat Landscape

With the rapid progression of technology and the increasing sophistication of cyber threats, it's clear that the AI-driven threat landscape is not static. As AI finds its way into more business processes and consumer products, the nature and number of vulnerabilities will inevitably change. An organization's defensive posture must, therefore, be fluid, adaptive, and ever-aware of the shifting sands of the digital frontier.

Staying one step ahead is a dance, and adaptation is the rhythm.

6.4.1. Continuous Threat Assessment

As new threats emerge, organizations must develop the habit of continuously assessing their AI systems for vulnerabilities. This includes keeping abreast of the latest research on AI vulnerabilities, tapping into threat intelligence networks, and having a dedicated team or individual tasked with understanding the evolving threat landscape.

6.4.2. Collaborative Defense Strategies

Given the complex nature of AI threats, many organizations are finding value in collaborative defense. This involves partnering with other businesses, industry groups, and even competitors to share information about threats and best practices. Collective wisdom and shared resources can offer more robust protection than going it alone.

6.4.3.   Dynamic Security Protocols

Traditional security protocols often operate on a set-and-forget principle. In the realm of AI, such an approach can be fatal. Security protocols need to be dynamic, with automated systems in place to adjust defenses based on the nature of the detected threat.

6.4.4.   Investing in Threat Research

Some of the most significant breakthroughs in understanding AI threats come from dedicated research. Organizations should consider investing in AI security research or partnering with academic institutions that specialize in this field. This proactive approach not only helps the organization but also contributes to the broader community's understanding of AI threats.

6.4.5.   Engaging with the Ethical Hacking Community

Ethical hackers, also known as "white hat" hackers, can be invaluable allies. They can probe systems for weaknesses before malicious actors do, providing feedback to bolster defenses. Organizations can engage with this community through bug bounty programs or by attending and sponsoring hackathons.[88]

Adapting to the evolving threat landscape is not just about defense—it's about maintaining trust. Trust in the systems, trust between the organization and its customers, and trust in the idea that technology, despite its challenges, can be harnessed for the greater good. By understanding and adapting to these evolving threats, organizations can ensure that their AI-driven innovations continue to deliver value while safeguarding their stakeholders.

---

[88] https://www.linkedin.com/pulse/benefits-bug-bounties-saving-time-money-penetration and
https://www.hackerone.com/bounty/bug-bounty-benefits-why-you-need-bug-bounty-program

6.5.   Building a Resilient Mindset

In the digital age, especially in the sphere of AI, the term 'resilience' gains profound significance. Resilience isn't just about recovering from setbacks—it's about anticipating them, planning for them, and emerging stronger after encountering them. AI introduces a complex landscape where the unforeseen can swiftly lead to a disaster, but a resilient mindset among stakeholders can be the difference between a brief interruption and a sustained debacle.

6.5.1.   Embracing Failure as a Learning Opportunity

No system, no matter how advanced, is impervious to failures or vulnerabilities. Instead of seeing these setbacks as final defeats, organizations should embrace them as learning opportunities. Each failed simulation or security breach is a lesson, pointing precisely to where enhancements are needed.

6.5.2.   Stress-Testing AI Systems

Just as infrastructure is stress-tested to anticipate how it would respond to natural calamities, AI systems should be rigorously challenged. These tests shouldn't just simulate expected challenges but also improbable ones. It ensures that when the unforeseen strikes, the AI system and the human team behind it aren't caught off guard.

6.5.3.   Fostering a Culture of Open Communication

A resilient mindset can only thrive in an environment where there's open communication. Employees should feel empowered to voice concerns, share insights, or report potential vulnerabilities without fear of retribution. A transparent dialogue can often be the first line of defense against emerging threats.

6.5.4.   *Encouraging Cross-Functional Collaboration*

AI security is not just the domain of the IT department. Every function, from marketing to human resources, can play a role. By fostering a culture where different departments actively collaborate and share insights, organizations can create a multi-dimensional defense strategy against AI threats.

6.5.5.   *Continuous Learning and Upskilling*

AI is advancing at a rapid pace. What's cutting-edge today might become obsolete tomorrow. Building resilience means continuously learning and upskilling, ensuring that the organization remains at the forefront of AI security practices. Investing in employee training and seeking external experts' insights can help maintain this momentum.

In essence, resilience in the context of AI is a composite of mindset, culture, processes, and continuous learning. When these elements come together, they form a formidable barrier against threats, ensuring that the organization can navigate the AI landscape with confidence and agility.

7. AI Risk Management

7.1. Understanding AI Risk: Types and Consequences

The infusion of AI into contemporary operations, while being transformative, has also opened up an array of risks. These risks, unique to AI or augmented by it, necessitate a deeper understanding. They cannot be viewed through the same lens as traditional technological risks, as AI has distinctive characteristics like adaptability, self-learning, and vast data handling.

7.1.1. Technological Risks

AI's strength lies in its algorithms, its ability to process vast amounts of data, and its capability to learn and adapt. However, these strengths can turn into vulnerabilities if not properly managed.[89]

- **Adversarial Attacks:** As mentioned previously, adversarial attacks can deceive AI systems. What makes them particularly concerning is that they can be designed to exploit the way AI models are built. For example, in image recognition, a subtle, almost imperceptible alteration to an image can make an

---

[89] https://www.forbes.com/sites/forbestechcouncil/2023/07/27/adversarial-attacks-on-ai-systems/?sh=58d1609832be and https://leoforce.com/blog/amazon-ai-hiring-bias-case-study/

AI system wrongly identify it. Imagine the potential chaos if traffic sign recognition systems in autonomous cars were tricked in real-world scenarios.

- **Algorithmic Biases:** AI systems are only as good as the data they're trained on. If this data carries biases, the AI system will reflect them. A case in point is the AI recruiting tool used by a global tech giant that was found to be biased against female candidates. The tool was trained on resumes submitted over a decade, which predominantly came from males, resulting in a skewed AI system.

- **Complexity of Neural Networks:** Deep learning models, especially neural networks, are incredibly complex. Their complexity makes it hard to pinpoint why a particular decision or prediction was made, often referred to as the 'black box' dilemma.

7.1.2.   Operational Risks

Operational risks in the context of AI arise from the practical application and day-to-day functioning of these systems within an organizational setting.

- **Integration Challenges:** As AI systems become more embedded in operations, their seamless integration with existing technologies becomes paramount. An oversight or glitch here can result in operational disruptions. For instance, if an AI-powered customer service chatbot isn't fully integrated with the inventory system, it might provide incorrect product availability information to customers.

- **Human-AI Interaction:** Operational risks are not limited to system operations. The human element, which includes how employees interact with and interpret AI outputs, is critical. Misunderstandings or misinterpretations can lead to operational mishaps.

- **Maintenance and Upkeep:** Like any system, AI models can degrade over time, especially if the environment in which they operate changes. Continuous maintenance, recalibration, and training are required, and neglect can lead to operational inefficiencies.

7.1.3.   Strategic Risks

Adopting AI can be a strategic move for companies looking to optimize operations, gain competitive advantage, or innovate. But this strategic adoption carries inherent risks.

- **Over-reliance on AI:** In the rush to adopt AI, companies might sideline or completely do away with traditional systems that serve as valuable backups. This over-dependence can be risky if the AI system malfunctions or is compromised.

- **Misaligned Objectives:** AI is a tool, and like all tools, it needs to align with the broader strategic objectives of the organization. If the AI's goals don't align with the company's, it can lead to misdirected efforts and resources.

- **Ethical and Brand Implications:** How a company uses AI can have profound implications for its brand. If an AI system is found to be biased, discriminatory, or invasive in terms of privacy, it can tarnish the company's image and erode trust.[90]

7.2.   Risk Assessment in AI Systems

Risk assessment, a staple in the conventional technology and business fields, confronts new intricacies when approached through the lens of artificial intelligence. As AI continues its march into numerous sectors, the significance of performing comprehensive risk assessments for such systems surges. These evaluations offer pivotal insights into potential threats, establishing a foundation upon which an organization's risk tolerance can be gauged and relevant protective measures can be deployed.

---

[90] https://online.maryville.edu/blog/ai-ethical-issues/

7.2.1.   Understanding the Landscape

Every risk assessment begins by immersing oneself into the world of the subject at hand. In AI, this implies discerning the vast applications, from customer service chatbots to intricate data analytics tools. Here are the essential steps to undertake:

- **System Boundaries:** Before anything else, it's imperative to demarcate the AI system's boundaries. One must pose questions like: What external systems does it interact with? How do these interactions manifest? For instance, consider a recommendation algorithm on an e-commerce site. Its interactions could span user profiles, their past purchase records, and the site's current inventory data.

- **Data Flow Mapping:** A profound comprehension of how data transits within the system is pivotal. Pictorially charting this journey can unveil vulnerable junctures where data may be susceptible to misuse or unwarranted exposure.

- **Stakeholder Identification:** Beyond the core developers and users, an AI system invariably impacts a wider circle. It becomes indispensable to recognize all parties, direct and indirect, who find themselves in the system's ripple effect.

7.2.2.   Probing the Shadows for Threats

AI's novelty doesn't shield it from threats—it simply presents a fresh set. Rooted in the system's function, the nature of the data it manages, and its inter-system interactions, these threats necessitate identification.

- **Historical Data Analysis:** Past incidents, especially those entwined with similar AI systems, can offer enlightening glimpses into plausible threats. Reflect upon past scenarios—was a chatbot manipulated to spew inappropriate responses? Did an AI model falter in its classification task?

- **Threat Modelling:** Systematic threat identification methods, such as the STRIDE technique, can be invaluable. This approach encompasses various threat vectors: Spoofing, Tampering, Repudiation, Information Disclosure, Denial of Service, and Elevation of Privilege.

- **External Threat Intelligence:** The world of AI is vast and evolving. To stay abreast of the emerging threats, organizations could consider allying with external entities or subscribing to specialized threat intelligence services.[91]

7.2.3.   *Vulnerability: AI's Achilles' Heel*

Threats, while crucial, represent only half the narrative. The other half lies in recognizing one's vulnerabilities against these threats.

- **Penetration Testing:** Analogous to its role in traditional IT setups, penetration tests in the AI domain involve ethical hackers attempting to exploit system vulnerabilities within a controlled milieu.

- **AI-specific Vulnerability Assessment Tools:** The market today brims with tools tailor-made for AI vulnerability assessments. Leveraging these specialized tools can unearth weak points that more generic counterparts might fail to spot.

- **Feedback Loops:** The beauty of AI lies in its adaptability. However, this evolution requires monitoring. Establishing feedback mechanisms where irregularities or concerns are flagged can be instrumental in continually spotlighting and addressing vulnerabilities.

7.2.4.   *Quantifying the Consequences*

Once threats and vulnerabilities are laid out on the table, the subsequent step revolves around gauging the fallout of a potential risk manifestation.

- **Quantitative Analysis:** Here, the focus narrows down to numbers. Assigning tangible monetary figures to potential damages is essential. Consider an AI-driven sales prediction model: if it derails, what could be the ensuing revenue loss?

---

[91] https://www.practical-devsecops.com/what-is-stride-threat-model/

- **Qualitative Analysis:** Beyond numbers, there exists a realm of subjective repercussions—brand erosion, diminished trust, and looming legal entanglements.

- **Scenario Planning:** With the assembled data, construct hypothetical risk scenarios. These scenarios should draw from identified threats and vulnerabilities, offering a panoramic view of potential outcomes.

With the AI terrain in perpetual flux, risk assessment is not a one-off task. It's an iterative process demanding frequent revisits and recalibrations.

7.3.   AI Risk Mitigation Strategies

In the rapidly evolving domain of AI, risks emerge as quickly as new applications and advancements. The inherent complexities tied to AI systems, including their data dependence, algorithmic intricacies, and integration into critical processes, make risk mitigation a paramount concern. Crafting a resilient and effective risk mitigation strategy requires an understanding of both generic cybersecurity best practices and those unique to the AI ecosystem.

7.3.1.   Contextual Security Measures

When it comes to AI, one size does not fit all. Depending on the specific application of an AI system, different threats and vulnerabilities may be present. Contextual security measures are designed to address these unique risks.

- **Domain-specific AI Shields:** Implementing protective measures tailored to the specific industry or use-case, such as finance, healthcare, or autonomous driving.

- **AI Function-Based Protocols:** Different AI functions, like image recognition or natural language processing, have unique threats. Implementing protocols that focus on function-specific vulnerabilities is crucial.

- **Adaptive Trust Levels:** Dynamically changing trust levels based on AI behavior, data sources, and interaction contexts.

- **Operational Environment Scanning:** Tools that continuously monitor the environment in which the AI operates, adjusting security postures based on detected context changes.

- **Contextual Behavior Baselines:** Establishing normative behaviors for AI models based on their operational context, ensuring that deviations can be quickly detected and addressed.

7.3.2.   Robust Data Management

An AI system's potency is directly proportional to the quality and integrity of its data. As such, data forms the lifeblood of AI, necessitating rigorous protective measures. These measures shouldn't merely focus on preventing breaches but should also ensure data quality, as tainted data can lead to skewed AI decisions.[92]

- **Data Quality Checks:** Routine verifications are crucial. Regular audits can prevent malevolent, misleading, or incorrect data from influencing AI operations. By maintaining high data quality, organizations can ensure the reliability of AI outputs.

- **Differential Privacy:** As organizations strive to extract insights from data, there's a pressing need to protect individual data points. Differential privacy, a novel approach to data privacy, helps in this regard. It allows for data analysis without revealing personally identifiable information, adding a layer of obfuscation that ensures privacy.

- **Data Encryption:** A fundamental tenet of data security, encryption transforms data into a code, thwarting unauthorized access. It's vital not just for data at rest but also for data in transit, ensuring comprehensive protection.

- **Version Control for Datasets:** To track changes and modifications made to datasets over time, employing version control is beneficial. This can help trace

---

[92] https://dualitytech.com/blog/what-is-differential-privacy/, https://www.statice.ai/post/what-is-differential-privacy-definition-mechanisms-examples, and https://www.immuta.com/blog/understanding-differential-data-privacy/

anomalies or biases introduced to AI models and restore data to its previous state if needed.

- **Automated Data Cleansing Tools:** Utilize tools that automatically identify and rectify errors, inconsistencies, or outliers in datasets. This not only enhances the quality of data but also optimizes AI model training.

- **Data Redundancy Protocols:** Implement strategies to maintain copies of critical data across various storage mediums, ensuring data availability even when a primary source fails.

- **Continuous Monitoring for Data Integrity**: Adopting systems that consistently monitor data storage and access patterns can detect and alert anomalies, suggesting possible breaches or tampering.

- **Data Masking:** A technique that disguises original data with modified yet structurally similar content to protect sensitive data, especially in non-productive environments.

7.3.3.   System Transparency and Interpretability

A significant challenge with many advanced AI models, particularly deep learning, is their opaqueness. Such "black box" systems, while powerful, can be a hotbed for vulnerabilities, as it's challenging to diagnose and rectify underlying issues. Therefore, driving transparency and ensuring system interpretability is not just a matter of trust but also of security.

- **White-box Testing:** Diverging from the obscurity of black-box systems, white-box testing provides a thorough evaluation. Equipped with a complete understanding of the system's architecture, testers can probe deeply, identifying vulnerabilities that might otherwise remain hidden.

- **Adopting Explainable AI (XAI):** The realm of XAI is gaining traction. Here, AI models are designed to provide insights into their decision-making logic. It's a paradigm shift that balances between AI's potency and the user's need for transparency.

A significant challenge with many advanced AI models, particularly deep learning, is their opaqueness. Such "black box" systems, while powerful, can be a hotbed for vulnerabilities, as it's challenging to diagnose and rectify underlying issues. Therefore, driving transparency and ensuring system interpretability is not just a matter of trust but also security:[93]

- **White-box Testing:** Diverging from the obscurity of black-box systems, white-box testing provides a thorough evaluation. Equipped with a complete understanding of the system's architecture, testers can probe deeply, identifying vulnerabilities that might otherwise remain hidden.

- **Adopting Explainable AI (XAI):** The realm of XAI is gaining traction. Here, AI models are designed to provide insights into their decision-making logic. It's a paradigm shift that balances between AI's potency and the user's need for transparency.

- **Feature Visualization Techniques:** Leveraging tools and methodologies to visually represent how an AI model perceives input data and which features it deems important for decision-making can offer insights into its internal workings.

- **Sensitivity and Perturbation Analysis:** This analyzes how slight changes in input can impact an AI model's output. By understanding these sensitivities, organizations can gauge the robustness and reliability of their AI systems.

- **Auditing and Logging AI Decisions:** Establishing rigorous audit trails for decisions made by AI systems. This helps in retrospective analysis, ensuring decisions can be traced back, understood, and validated.

- **Collaborative AI Development:** Promote an open-source ethos, enabling multiple eyes on the model development process. This communal scrutiny can lead to the identification and rectification of potential vulnerabilities or biases.

- **Human-in-the-loop Systems:** Introducing human oversight in AI decision-making processes. This ensures there's a check and balance system where AI outputs are verified by human experts before final implementation, adding an extra layer of scrutiny.

---

[93] https://www.frontiersin.org/articles/10.3389/frai.2022.879603/full, https://www.techtarget.com/whatis/definition/explainable-AI-XAI, and https://papers.ssrn.com/sol3/papers.cfm?abstract_id=4317938

7.3.4. Tailored AI Monitoring Systems

AI systems require monitoring that extends beyond standard IT surveillance. As AI evolves and learns, the system's behavior can change. Standard monitoring solutions might not always detect anomalies in such an environment. Tailored AI monitoring focuses on nuances peculiar to artificial intelligence:

- **Behavioral Analytics:** Using machine learning, behavioral analytics track the typical behavior of AI models. When deviations occur, possibly because of tainted data or external interference, alerts are triggered.

- **AI Health Dashboards:** These tools provide real-time insights into an AI model's performance, giving an immediate overview of potential discrepancies or inefficiencies.

- **Model Debugging Tools:** Unlike conventional software, AI models can make decisions that are hard to predict. Debugging tools tailored for AI can trace decision paths, helping to pinpoint issues.

- **Automated Threat Hunting:** AI can be employed to actively seek out threats in an AI environment, learning from each detection and improving its efficacy over time.

7.3.5. Adaptive Security Protocols

As AI systems continuously evolve, so too must the security protocols guarding them. Adaptive security isn't about merely reacting to threats but anticipating them based on trends, system evolution, and changing contexts:[94]

- **Predictive Threat Analysis:** Using AI to forecast potential future threats by analyzing current data and historical threat patterns.

---

[94] https://www.advsyscon.com/blog/self-healing-it-operations/ and https://bigid.com/blog/ai-threat-intelligence/

- **Self-healing Systems:** Infrastructure designed to automatically detect vulnerabilities and deploy fixes without human intervention, ensuring swift response times.

- **AI-assisted Security Playbooks:** Dynamic guidelines and procedures that evolve with threat intelligence, ensuring that responses are always aligned with the latest threat landscape.

- **Real-time Policy Enforcement:** Using AI to enforce security policies in real-time, adapting to changing contexts and scenarios on the fly.

7.3.6.   Collaborative Threat Intelligence

The vast and interconnected landscape of AI presents challenges that are often beyond the scope of individual organizations. Collaborative threat intelligence involves pooling resources, data, and insights to collectively combat threats in the AI ecosystem:

- **Shared Threat Databases:** Central repositories where organizations can share details of identified threats, ensuring collective awareness.

- **Decentralized AI Security Platforms:** Platforms where threat data, tools, and insights are distributed across nodes, reducing single points of failure.

- **Open-source AI Security Tools:** Tools that are continuously improved by a community, ensuring they remain at the cutting edge of threat detection and mitigation.

- **Collective Simulation Drills:** Multi-organization drills that mimic large-scale AI threats, testing and refining collaborative response strategies.

7.4.   AI Risk Communication and Reporting

With AI systems becoming pervasive in modern business operations, communication about risks associated with them requires a structured, in-depth approach. Whether it's internal stakeholders or the external world, clear channels of communication about potential AI risks and actual incidents are essential to ensure trust, facilitate swift responses, and aid in strategic decision-making.

7.4.1. Incident Notification Protocols

Every organization hopes to avoid security breaches or operational failures in its AI systems, but the reality is that risks exist. When these incidents do occur, an established, comprehensive notification protocol is vital:

- **Timely Alerts:** Implementing sophisticated real-time monitoring mechanisms can help identify any unusual patterns or potential breaches. Systems that not only detect these anomalies but also initiate automatic alerts can drastically reduce the damage scope by ensuring immediate action.

- **Predefined Communication Channels:** Whether it's emails, phone trees, or specialized internal messaging systems, having predefined channels ensures that the reaction time post-incident is minimized. These channels should be tested periodically to ensure their effectiveness.

- **Stakeholder Categorization:** Different stakeholders have varied interests and stakes in AI operations. By classifying them in advance based on the potential risk impact, you can streamline the communication process, ensuring that relevant parties receive pertinent information without unnecessary panic.

- **Escalation Matrix:** This predefined hierarchy determines who gets informed based on the incident severity. By establishing this in advance, you eliminate any guesswork during critical moments and ensure the right leadership levels are involved when needed.

- **Drafted Templates:** Preparing communication templates for various potential incidents can facilitate faster and clearer communication during real incidents. These templates can then be customized as per the specific event details.

7.4.2.   Maintaining Transparency with Stakeholders

Transparent communication about AI systems and associated risks is a cornerstone of stakeholder trust. This trust is not just about sharing good news but also involves candidly discussing challenges, failures, and remediation strategies:

- **Regular Reporting:** Transparency is an ongoing effort. Regular reports on AI system performance, challenges faced, risks identified, and remediation actions can ensure stakeholders are continuously informed.

- **Open Forums:** Designing platforms where stakeholders can express concerns, ask questions, or even provide feedback fosters a sense of involvement and ownership. These forums can be periodic webinars, Q&A sessions, or feedback portals.

- **Transparent Metrics:** Using jargon-filled, complex metrics can obscure understanding. Instead, choose metrics and performance indicators that a layperson can comprehend, ensuring inclusivity and transparency.

- **Feedback Loop:** A transparent system is a two-way street. While the organization provides information, it's equally crucial to listen. By incorporating stakeholder feedback into AI systems and risk strategies, you emphasize the collaborative nature of the journey.

7.4.3.   Post-Incident Analysis and Learning

An incident, while regrettable, can be a treasure trove of insights if analyzed correctly. By dissecting the event, its causes, its handling, and its aftermath, organizations can prevent future occurrences and improve their AI risk posture:

- **Root Cause Analysis:** A superficial understanding of incidents might offer immediate remedies, but diving deep to unearth systemic issues or procedural lapses provides longer-term solutions.

- **Lessons Learned Log:** This isn't just a record—it's an evolving document reflecting the organization's growth in understanding AI risks. Each incident, its analysis, findings, and resultant actions enrich this log, making it a reference point for future risk strategies.

- **Feedback Incorporation:** Analysis without action is futile. Every insight gleaned from post-incident analysis should find its way into action items—be it system upgrades, process changes, or training enhancements.

- **Stakeholder Communication:** Once the dust settles, revisiting the incident with stakeholders communicates two things: the organization's commitment to transparency and its determination to learn and improve.

7.4.4. *Real-World Examples of Risk Communication*

Drawing lessons from real-world situations helps crystallize the importance and approach of risk communication. Let's explore a few examples where companies faced significant challenges and how their communication strategies affected outcomes:[95]

- **Equifax Data Breach (2017):** One of the most significant data breaches in history, where the personal data of 143 million individuals was compromised. The company faced criticism not only for the breach itself but also for the delay in disclosing it. A transparent and immediate communication plan could have better managed stakeholder trust and regulatory response.

- **Cambridge Analytica and Facebook (2018):** The scandal unveiled how the personal data of millions of Facebook users was harvested without consent for political advertising. Facebook's initial response was seen by many as insufficient, leading to significant trust erosion. The event underscores the importance of timely, transparent, and comprehensive risk communication to stakeholders.

- **Uber Data Breach (2016):** Uber paid hackers $100,000 to conceal a data breach affecting 57 million users. When the cover-up surfaced in 2017, it exemplified the potential repercussions of not following clear risk communication

---

[95] https://store.samhsa.gov/sites/default/files/pep19-01-01-005.pdf and https://simplicable.com/risk/risk-communication

protocols. The incident resulted in significant legal, financial, and reputational ramifications for the company.

- **OpenAI's GPT-2 Release Decision (2019):** OpenAI initially chose not to release the trained model of its GPT-2 language model, citing concerns about potential misuse. They communicated these risks transparently to the public, describing potential malicious uses. Over time, as they released increasingly larger models, their communication about the risks and their mitigation strategies showcased a balanced approach to innovation and responsibility.

- **Google Cloud Outage (2019):** Google Cloud experienced a significant outage affecting multiple services like YouTube, Gmail, and Google Cloud Platform. Google's timely and detailed communication about the cause of the disruption, its impact, and recovery measures helped manage customer concerns and showcased its commitment to transparency.

Through these instances, it becomes evident that the magnitude of an incident alone doesn't determine its overall impact. The manner in which organizations communicate during these crises plays a crucial role in shaping stakeholder trust, regulatory outcomes, and long-term reputational effects.

7.5. Ongoing Review and Updates to AI Risk Management

Artificial intelligence, with its transformative capabilities, is redefining industries and societal interactions. As it permeates deeper into our systems, the dynamics of risk and security evolve as well. For organizations, this means that AI risk management is not a one-time endeavor but a perpetual commitment. The vitality of this commitment stems not only from the evolving nature of AI but also from the complexities and intricacies that accompany its broader integration.

7.5.1.   Scheduled Risk Assessment Revisions

The dynamism of AI requires an equally dynamic approach to risk assessment. As models get refined, data sources expand, and integration points diversify, the potential threats and vulnerabilities shift:

- **Annual Audits:** Instituting an annual AI risk assessment is fundamental. Such audits delve deep into the existing systems, evaluating the protective measures in place, their efficacy, and their relevance in the current context. These audits also help forecast potential future vulnerabilities, giving organizations a proactive approach to risk management.

- **Quarterly Check-ins:** While annual audits provide a comprehensive overview, quarterly check-ins address the rapid changes that AI systems might undergo within shorter time frames. These periodic assessments monitor the pulse of AI integrations, ensuring that any discrepancies or vulnerabilities are promptly identified and rectified.

- **Trigger-based Reviews:** Significant milestones, such as integrating a new AI module or adopting a fresh data source, can pose unforeseen challenges. Thus, events like these should prompt a thorough risk review. This ensures that any new integration or change aligns with the organization's risk management strategy without introducing weak links.

- **Stakeholder Involvement:** A well-rounded risk assessment transcends technical evaluations. Incorporating views and insights from various stakeholders, be it operational leaders, regulatory experts, or even end-users, can shed light on vulnerabilities from multiple angles, leading to a holistic risk management strategy.

7.5.2.   Incorporating New Threat Intelligence

The cyber landscape isn't static. As cyber attackers evolve their methodologies, the defense mechanisms need to be steps ahead, anticipating and countering these threats proactively:

- **Real-time Cybersecurity Feed Integration:** Integrating live feeds detailing global cybersecurity threats offers AI systems the ability to prepare and counteract emerging threats. These insights enable dynamic adjustments, enhancing system robustness against fresh attack vectors.

- **Threat Intelligence Platforms:** Renowned platforms such as MITRE ATT&CK not only chronicle existing threats but also predict potential future vulnerabilities. Engaging with such platforms empowers organizations to refine their AI defenses continuously.[96]

- **Incident Response Team Feedback:** There's a wealth of knowledge in every security event. By dissecting each incident and understanding its genesis, progression, and impact, organizations can refine their risk protocols. This iterative feedback loop ensures a continuously evolving defense framework.

- **Adaptive AI Models:** Leveraging AI to safeguard AI might sound like a futuristic proposition, but it's increasingly becoming the norm. Adaptive AI models self-learn from the existing threat environment, autonomously enhancing defense protocols to counter emerging threats.

7.5.3. *Engaging with AI Security Communities*

AI's global nature means that challenges faced in one corner of the world can offer lessons to entities elsewhere. Collaborative engagement with global AI communities can be the key to unlocking collective wisdom:

- **AI Security Conferences Participation:** Renowned conferences, seminars, and workshops are treasure troves of insights. Active participation not only offers knowledge intake but also opens doors to collaborative projects and research ventures.

- **Collaboration on Open-Source Platforms:** Open-source communities like GitHub host lively discussions, innovative solutions, and a spirit of

---

[96] https://cyware.com/security-guides/cyber-threat-intelligence/everything-you-need-to-know-about-mitre-attck-framework-662a and https://www.attackiq.com/mitre-attack/

collaboration. Engaging here provides firsthand access to the latest in AI security, from tools to strategies.

- **Joining AI Security Consortiums:** Collective endeavors often lead to amplified results. Consortiums foster a spirit of shared learning, pooling resources, insights, and expertise to tackle common challenges.

- **Engaging with Academia:** Many groundbreaking AI solutions trace their origins to academic research. Collaborative engagements with academic institutions can give organizations an early-bird advantage, preparing them for future threats and challenges.

Embracing AI's potential also necessitates embracing the complexities of its risk environment. With an iterative, inclusive, and forward-looking approach to risk management, organizations can ensure that they're not just surviving but thriving in the AI era.

---

8. Advanced AI-Proof Data Storage Solutions

In the digital era, where data serves as the lifeblood of most technological innovations, especially AI, its protection has paramount importance. AI systems not only process vast amounts of data but also generate new patterns and insights. As these AI models become deeply integrated into societal frameworks, traditional data storage and protection mechanisms are being challenged. Advanced AI-proof data storage solutions ensure that while data is available for beneficial AI algorithms, it remains out of the reach of malicious entities.

8.1. Quantum-resistant Cryptography

The name "quantum-resistant" already hints at a futuristic landscape where our standard cryptographic systems, built on the presumed difficulty of certain mathematical problems, crumble under the power of quantum computers. These supercomputers, leveraging the principles of quantum mechanics, have the potential to break the encryption methods that secure our present-day internet.

8.1.1. The Advent of Quantum Computing

Quantum computing has been a theoretical concept for decades, but recent advancements in technology have made it a looming reality. Unlike classical computers, which use bits as their smallest unit of data (either a 0 or a 1), quantum computers use quantum bits or qubits. Due to the principles of superposition and entanglement, a qubit can represent both 0 and 1 simultaneously, enabling quantum computers to process a vast amount of information at once.[97]

For AI, quantum computing promises unparalleled processing power, allowing for complex computations in mere seconds. But for cryptography, it poses a genuine threat. Many of the cryptographic systems today, like RSA and ECC, rely on the difficulty of factoring large numbers or computing discrete logarithms—tasks that quantum computers could achieve much faster than today's classical machines.

8.1.2.   *Post-quantum Cryptographic Algorithms*

As the advent of quantum computing poses an undeniable threat to contemporary cryptographic mechanisms, the research community has been fervently working on formulating post-quantum cryptographic algorithms. These cutting-edge cryptographic measures are not merely iterative improvements–they represent a paradigm shift designed to stand firm even when confronted by the immense processing prowess of quantum computers.[98]

The cornerstone of these algorithms lies in their foundational strategies. Unlike current cryptographic systems that base their security on problems deemed difficult for classical computers—like factorizing large numbers—post-quantum algorithms delve into entirely new territories. From lattice-based cryptography, which rests its security on the intricate complexity of specific lattice problems, to hash-based and code-based cryptography. Each approach explores new realms of mathematical complexity.

The significance of these post-quantum algorithms transcends their innovative nature. They are emblematic of a broader global initiative to pre-emptively address and neutralize the vulnerabilities that quantum computers might exploit. By doing so, they

---

[97] https://threatresearch.ext.hp.com/anticipating-the-quantum-threat-to-cryptography/, https://arramton.com/blogs/quantum-computing-affect-artificial-intelligence-applications, and https://www.forbes.com/sites/jonathanreichental/2023/11/20/quantum-artificial-intelligence-is-closer-than-you-think/?sh=4057545f4818

[98] https://link.springer.com/article/10.1007/s11401-023-0053-6 and https://csrc.nist.gov/csrc/media/projects/post-quantum-cryptography/documents/call-for-proposals-final-dec-2016.pdf

aim to ensure that our digital world remains fortified against future technological advancements. Cryptography strategies include:

- **Lattice-based Cryptography:** Lattice-based cryptographic methods are rooted in the complexity of certain mathematical structures known as lattices. In simple terms, a lattice is a regular grid of points in multidimensional space. Some problems related to lattices, like the Shortest Vector Problem (SVP), have been shown to be incredibly difficult to solve, even with quantum computers. This innate difficulty is what makes lattice-based cryptography a promising avenue for post-quantum security. For example, one popular protocol in this realm is the Learning With Errors (LWE) problem. In LWE, one is given a nearly uniform random sample and must distinguish it from a truly uniform sample. Quantum computers, as of our current understanding, can't solve this efficiently, making it a cornerstone for future cryptographic systems.[99]

- **Hash-based Cryptography:** Hash functions are algorithms that take an input and produce a fixed-size string of bytes, typically a digest that is unique to the given input. Hash-based cryptographic methods don't directly encrypt data—instead, they produce a unique "signature" for data. Because of their simplicity and speed, they are highly regarded for post-quantum security, particularly for digital signatures. For example, the Merkle Signature Scheme (MSS) is a tree-based structure where individual signatures are formed from leaves, and each leaf corresponds to a one-time signature. A quantum adversary would face significant challenges trying to forge such signatures due to the cryptographic strength of the hash functions involved.[100]

- **Code-based Cryptography:** Originating in the late 1970s, code-based cryptography utilizes the challenges associated with decoding randomly generated linear codes. If you think of data as being sent over a noisy channel, then the problem is akin to accurately decoding the message despite the noise. For example, the McEliece cryptosystem, one of the earliest instances of code-based cryptography, remains unbroken. It employs Goppa codes, ensuring

---

[99] https://english.ncsc.nl/publications/factsheets/2019/juni/01/factsheet-post-quantum-cryptography, https://www.cybersecurity.blog.aisec.fraunhofer.de/en/a-somewhat-gentle-introduction-to-lattice-based-post-quantum-cryptography/, and https://utimaco.com/service/knowledge-base/post-quantum-cryptography/what-lattice-based-cryptography

[100] https://eprint.iacr.org/2023/411.pdf and https://crypto.stanford.edu/cs355/18sp/lec12.pdf

security by making it computationally tough for an attacker to decode without specific knowledge of the structure.[101]

- **Multivariate Polynomial Cryptography:** This type of cryptography is a branch of public-key cryptography that leverages the complexity of solving systems of multivariate polynomial equations over finite fields. This approach is particularly promising for post-quantum cryptography, as it is believed to be resistant to attacks from quantum computers. Multivariate polynomial cryptography is a promising field for developing secure cryptographic systems, especially in post-quantum cryptography. Its security relies on the inherent difficulty of solving systems of multivariate polynomial equations, making it a robust alternative to traditional cryptographic methods in the face of advancing computational capabilities. Key concepts include:

- **Multivariate Polynomials:** A multivariate polynomial is a polynomial that involves more than one variable. For example, $P(x,y) = 3x2 + 2xy + y2P(x,y) = 3x2 + 2xy + y2$ is a multivariate polynomial in variables x and y.[102] [103] The degree of a multivariate polynomial is the highest sum of the exponents of the variables in any single term. For instance, in $P(x,y) = 3x2 + 2xy + y2P(x,y) = 3x2 + 2xy + y2$, the degree is 2.[104]

  - **Public Key and Private Key:** In multivariate polynomial cryptography, the public key is typically a set of multivariate polynomial equations. These equations are designed to be difficult to solve without specific knowledge.[105] The private key is a trapdoor, a piece of information that allows the owner to solve these polynomial equations efficiently. This trapdoor is analogous to the factorization of a large number in RSA cryptography.

---

[101] https://arxiv.org/pdf/1907.12754.pdf and https://en.wikipedia.org/wiki/Binary_Goppa_code

[102] https://mathworld.wolfram.com/MultivariatePolynomial.html

[103] https://homepages.math.uic.edu/~jan/mcs320/polynomialsfactor.pdf

[104] https://study.com/skill/learn/identifying-degree-of-multivariate-polynomials-explanation.html

[105] https://en.wikipedia.org/wiki/Multivariate_cryptography

- o **Security Basis**: The security of multivariate polynomial cryptography is based on the NP-hardness of solving systems of nonlinear equations over finite fields. This means that, in general, there is no efficient algorithm to solve these equations, making it computationally infeasible for an attacker to break the encryption without the private key.[106]

Examples include:

- o **Multivariate Public Key Cryptosystems (MPKCs)**: MPKCs use multivariate polynomials to create public and private keys. Famous examples include the Hidden Field Equations (HFE) and the Unbalanced Oil and Vinegar (UOV) schemes. These systems are designed to be secure against both classical and quantum attacks, making them suitable candidates for post-quantum cryptography.

- o **Digital Signatures**: Multivariate polynomial cryptography is also used in digital signature schemes. For instance, the Unbalanced Oil and Vinegar (UOV) scheme and its variants like Rainbow are used to create secure digital signatures. These signatures are verified by checking the validity of the polynomial equations, ensuring that the message has not been tampered with.

- o **Cryptanalysis and Attacks**: Despite their theoretical security, many multivariate schemes have been broken through various attacks, such as Gröbner basis attacks and differential attacks. Continuous research is necessary to develop more robust schemes and to understand the vulnerabilities of existing ones.

- o **Hidden Field Equations (HFE)**: Public key is a set of multivariate quadratic polynomials over a finite field. Private key includes two affine transformations and a quadratic map that allow efficient inversion of the public key polynomials. Security is based on the difficulty of solving the system of quadratic equations without the private key. Variants like HFEv- (HFE with vinegar variables) have been proposed to enhance security.

---

[106] https://research.nccgroup.com/2023/03/18/demystifying-multivariate-cryptography/

8.1.3. Transitioning from Classical to Quantum-Resistant Security

The transition from classical cryptographic systems, which currently secure the digital world, to quantum-resistant alternatives is not just an upgrade–it's a paradigm shift. The era of quantum computing, while ushering in vast computational advantages, also threatens to dismantle many of the cryptographic methods we've relied upon for decades. Ensuring a smooth transition is imperative, and it's about more than just adopting new algorithms—it's about reimagining the whole security infrastructure.

- **Hybrid Cryptographic Systems:** One strategy for transitioning is the adoption of hybrid cryptographic systems. These systems combine the best of both worlds, using classical cryptographic methods alongside newer, quantum-resistant algorithms. This dual approach ensures immediate robustness against traditional and quantum attacks. For example, in a hybrid system, a communication channel might employ both RSA (a popular classical encryption scheme) and a lattice-based encryption method. Even if a quantum computer could break RSA, the lattice-based encryption would still hold firm, ensuring data remains confidential.[107]

- **Gradual Phased Integration:** Transitioning to a new security standard globally is daunting. A phased approach can be more practical, wherein organizations and critical infrastructure begin by integrating quantum-resistant algorithms in parallel with existing systems. This way, any potential issues with the new algorithms can be identified and addressed without compromising the entire security infrastructure. For example, financial institutions, which are at the forefront of cybersecurity risks, might initially introduce quantum-resistant cryptographic methods only for high-value transactions. As these systems prove their reliability, the institutions can gradually expand their usage.

- **Backward Compatibility and Interoperability:** As the world shifts towards quantum-resistant security, there will be a considerable period where both classical and quantum-resistant systems coexist. Ensuring that new systems can effectively communicate with legacy systems is crucial. This requires developing protocols and standards that prioritize backward compatibility and

---

[107] https://decentcybersecurity.eu/strategies-for-upgrading-existing-cryptographic-systems-to-quantum-resistant-models-in-2024/, https://www.linkedin.com/pulse/implementing-quantum-resistant-cryptography-hybrid-micai-garcia-ccsp, and https://semiengineering.com/getting-ready-for-the-quantum-computing-era-thoughts-on-hybrid-cryptography/

interoperability. For example, a cloud storage provider might use post-quantum algorithms to secure new data. Still, they'll need mechanisms in place to access and protect older data encrypted under classical methods, ensuring service continuity for all users, regardless of when their data was stored.[108]

- **Educating and Upskilling the Workforce:** Beyond the technical challenges, there's a human element to this transition. Cybersecurity professionals, software developers, and IT staff need to be educated about the nuances of quantum-resistant methods. Investing in training and development ensures that as the technology evolves, the people responsible for its implementation aren't left behind. For example, a multinational corporation could host annual cybersecurity seminars, bringing in experts in quantum computing and post-quantum cryptography. These sessions would keep their internal teams updated on the latest threats and defense strategies.

- **Public-Private Collaborations:** The magnitude of the challenge that quantum computing presents to cybersecurity necessitates collaborations beyond the confines of individual organizations. Governments, academic institutions, and private entities need to pool resources, share knowledge, and collaboratively draft the roadmap for a quantum-secure future. For example, the Post-Quantum Cryptography Alliance (PQCA) is an initiative focused on advancing the development and implementation of cryptography that is resistant to the potential threats of quantum computing. The alliance's efforts are particularly significant in the context of public-private collaborations, as it involves a concerted effort between various stakeholders to ensure the security of digital infrastructure in a post-quantum world. The Open Quantum Safe (OQS) project, part of PQCA's endeavors, exemplifies this collaborative approach. It is dedicated to supporting the creation and maintenance of high-assurance implementations of post-quantum cryptography algorithms that are on track to become industry standards.[109]

The PQCA's work is crucial in preparing for a future where traditional cryptographic methods may no longer be secure against the advanced computational capabilities of quantum computers. By bringing together expertise from both the public and private

---

[108] https://www.linkedin.com/pulse/transitioning-quantum-resistant-cryptography-cost-micai-garcia-ccsp and https://www.cyberdefensemagazine.com/post-quantum-cryptography-safeguarding-the-digital-future-and-bolstering-security-in-critical-sectors/

[109] https://pqca.org/

sectors, the alliance is working to prototype quantum-resistant cryptographic solutions. These efforts are aimed at safeguarding sensitive information and communications across various platforms and industries, thereby contributing to the overall resilience of cybersecurity infrastructure against emerging quantum threats.

The journey from classical to quantum-resistant security is intricate, requiring not just technological adaptations but also shifts in organizational strategies and mindsets. The future might be quantum, but with careful planning and collaborative efforts, it can also be secure.

8.2. The Future of Quantum-resistant Cryptography[110]

The future of quantum-resistant cryptography is a critical area of focus as the world prepares for the advent of quantum computing, which poses significant threats to current cryptographic standards. Quantum computers, with their ability to process information at unprecedented speeds, have the potential to break many of the cryptographic algorithms that currently protect our digital communications, financial transactions, and national security secrets. This looming threat has spurred intense research and development efforts aimed at creating quantum-resistant or post-quantum cryptographic methods that can withstand attacks from quantum computers.

One of the primary strategies in developing quantum-resistant cryptography involves designing algorithms based on mathematical problems that are believed to be secure against both classical and quantum computing attacks. Current research is largely focused on several promising approaches, including lattice-based cryptography, hash-based schemes, and multivariate cryptographic systems. These methods offer a new foundation for secure communication in the quantum era, relying on complex mathematical structures that are not easily solved by quantum algorithms like Shor's, which could efficiently break RSA and ECC encryption.

---

[110] https://www.linkedin.com/pulse/future-quantum-cryptography-securing-data-world-intro-act-p4pre,
   https://www.archonsecure.com/blog/quantum-resistant-cryptography,
   https://www.healthcareitnews.com/news/nist-releases-draft-algorithms-quantum-resistant-cryptography, and https://www.cisa.gov/news-events/alerts/2022/07/05/prepare-new-cryptographic-standard-protect-against-future-quantum-based-threats

The National Institute of Standards and Technology (NIST) has been at the forefront of this transition, conducting a multi-year project to standardize post-quantum cryptographic algorithms. This initiative has already resulted in the selection of several quantum-resistant algorithms that are set to replace vulnerable public-key cryptographic systems. The ongoing standardization process is crucial not only for ensuring the security of future communications but also for guiding global efforts in adopting these new technologies.

However, the shift to quantum-resistant cryptography is not without challenges. One of the major hurdles is the integration of these new algorithms into existing technological infrastructures. Many current systems are deeply entrenched in public-key cryptography, and transitioning to new standards will require significant updates to software and hardware, as well as comprehensive testing to ensure compatibility and security. Additionally, there is the challenge of ensuring that these new cryptographic methods are as efficient and user-friendly as their predecessors to facilitate widespread adoption.

Moreover, the concept of "harvest now, decrypt later" has added urgency to these efforts. Adversaries could potentially collect encrypted data today, with the intention of decrypting it in the future using quantum computers. This threat makes it imperative for organizations to start implementing quantum-resistant solutions sooner rather than later to protect sensitive data that needs to remain secure for many years to come.

In conclusion, the future of quantum-resistant cryptography is a dynamic field that holds the key to securing our digital world against the quantum threat. As research continues to evolve, it will be crucial for governments, industries, and the academic community to collaborate on developing and deploying these technologies. By proactively addressing the challenges and embracing the new cryptographic landscape, we can safeguard our information assets and ensure that our digital society remains secure in the face of quantum advancements.

9. Monitoring, Detection, and Response

In today's ever-evolving digital landscape, the stakes have never been higher. The proliferation of cyber threats, from sophisticated state-sponsored attacks to opportunist cybercriminals, has emphasized the indispensable role of monitoring, detection, and response. These are the crucial triad of activities that ensure digital assets, infrastructures, and user data remain safeguarded against the relentless threats they face daily.

As we plunge deeper into the realm of artificial intelligence, AI's role in these activities is becoming increasingly prominent. Not only does AI introduce its unique set of vulnerabilities, but it also offers transformative solutions, revolutionizing how organizations detect, respond to, and mitigate threats. AI-driven systems can process vast datasets, identify patterns imperceptible to human analysts, and initiate rapid response actions—all in real time.

Moreover, as threat actors also harness advanced technologies, the challenge of defending digital domains escalates exponentially. Traditional cybersecurity strategies, reliant on manual processes and heuristic-based solutions, often fall short in the face of highly sophisticated, AI-assisted cyber threats. Thus, modern cybersecurity demands a paradigm shift, one that seamlessly integrates AI capabilities into its core functions.

Real-time monitoring powered by AI, for instance, doesn't just oversee system activities—it learns from them. By continuously analyzing network traffic, user behaviors, and system interactions, AI can establish a dynamic 'normal' baseline, making anomaly detection far more accurate. Anomalous behaviors, even subtle ones, can be flagged instantaneously, paving the way for quicker, more informed response actions.

As we delve deeper into this section, we will explore the manifold ways in which AI is reshaping the fields of threat intelligence, real-time monitoring, anomaly detection, and incident response. The symbiosis of human expertise and AI's computational prowess heralds a new dawn for cybersecurity, promising a future where digital defenses are more robust, adaptive, and resilient than ever before.

9.1.   AI in Threat Intelligence[111]

Artificial intelligence has increasingly become the backbone of modern threat intelligence efforts. In a world inundated with data, the human capability to analyze and derive actionable insights from raw information is often outpaced by the sheer volume of threats emerging daily. Enter AI—a tool that not only augments human analysis but, in many cases, surpasses it by identifying hidden patterns, predicting threat evolutions, and automating the otherwise tedious task of sifting through terabytes of data.

Threat intelligence powered by AI does more than just streamline processes. It revolutionizes them. With machine learning algorithms, neural networks, and other AI models at its disposal, AI-enhanced threat intelligence provides dynamic, real-time insights. It can forecast threat trajectories, discern between genuine threats and benign anomalies, and prioritize risks based on their potential impact. The ability to offer proactive, predictive intelligence makes AI an indispensable asset in the modern cybersecurity toolkit.

As we transition into exploring the key areas where AI bolsters threat intelligence, it becomes evident that its application is vast and multifaceted. From its role in cyber threat hunting, a proactive approach to identifying hidden threats, to enriching threat intelligence feeds, ensuring data integrity in threat databases, and automating threat analysis, AI's contributions are both profound and transformative. Let's delve deeper

---

[111] http://connections-qj.org/article/cyber-threat-prediction-machine-learning and
     https://www.linkedin.com/pulse/how-predictive-analytics-could-change-cybersecurity-john-giordani

into these subareas to gain a holistic understanding of AI's pivotal role in modern threat intelligence.

9.1.1.   Predictive Analysis: Forecasting Cyber Threats

In the ever-evolving realm of cybersecurity, reacting to threats after they occur is no longer sufficient. The sophisticated nature of modern cyber-attacks, combined with their rapid proliferation, demands a proactive stance, and that's where predictive analysis enters the picture. Predictive analysis, in the context of cyber threat intelligence, refers to the utilization of statistical algorithms and machine learning techniques to identify the likelihood of future threats based on historical data. It's like a weather forecast but for cyber threats, giving organizations a heads-up to prepare and defend against potential breaches.[112]

Harnessing the power of AI, predictive analysis can sift through enormous sets of data in mere seconds, identifying patterns and trends that might be invisible to the human eye. These patterns, when extrapolated, can predict the trajectory of a potential cyber threat. For instance, if a particular type of malware has been observed to evolve in a certain manner over the past months, AI can forecast its next iteration, helping cybersecurity teams prepare their defenses in advance. Moreover, predictive analysis can detect subtle anomalies in network traffic, hinting at a possible reconnaissance activity by adversaries and allowing security teams to reinforce vulnerable points before an actual attack materializes.

However, while predictive analysis offers an advanced warning system, it's essential to approach its predictions with a degree of caution. No forecasting method, no matter how advanced, is infallible. Thus, while AI-enhanced predictive tools provide valuable insights, they should complement, not replace, other threat detection and defense mechanisms. In our journey to understand AI's role in threat intelligence, we'll now move to its utility in cyber threat hunting, another proactive approach but with a more hands-on touch.

---

[112] http://connections-qj.org/article/cyber-threat-prediction-machine-learning, https://www.linkedin.com/pulse/how-predictive-analytics-could-change-cybersecurity-john-giordani, and https://www.athreon.com/predictive-analytics/amp/

9.1.2.   *Phishing Detection: Automating the Identification Process*

Phishing attacks have become a ubiquitous cyber threat, capitalizing on human psychology and ever-evolving digital lures to compromise personal information and corporate data. The classic approach to combating phishing has been a mix of end-user education and traditional signature-based detection mechanisms. However, the sheer volume of phishing attempts and the creative tactics employed by adversaries are outpacing traditional defenses. This is where AI steps in, offering an agile, adaptive, and faster response to the changing phishing landscape.[113]

The beauty of AI lies in its ability to learn and adapt. AI models can develop an acute sense of discernment by training on vast datasets of both legitimate and malicious emails. They scrutinize various email aspects, such as the sender's details, content, embedded links, and attachment types, to determine the likelihood of a message being a phishing attempt. Modern AI models can even analyze the visual components of a web page link in an email, comparing it to a known set of legitimate sites. This method is especially useful for detecting web pages that visually impersonate popular sites to steal credentials.

Additionally, AI algorithms are particularly proficient at detecting spear-phishing attempts. These are tailored phishing emails designed for a specific individual or organization. Because of their personalized nature, spear-phishing emails often bypass traditional defenses. AI models, by continually learning from the communication patterns within an organization, can detect anomalies—like an unusual request for a funds transfer or a sudden email from a high-ranking officer with a dubious attachment.

The dynamic capabilities of AI in phishing detection underline the transformative effect AI has on cybersecurity. Yet, as with all tools, it's paramount to ensure the AI models remain up-to-date, reflecting the latest in phishing tactics. This ensures that the AI remains a step ahead of the adversaries. Continuing our exploration, the next domain where AI is leaving its mark is in real-time threat monitoring, bringing a paradigm shift in how we perceive and respond to cyber threats.

---

[113] https://www.proquest.com/docview/2455786156, https://dl.acm.org/doi/10.1155/2017/5421046, and https://www.mdpi.com/2073-8994/12/10/1681

9.1.3.   *Dark Web Monitoring: Keeping Tabs on the Underbelly of the Internet*

The dark web, a part of the deep web inaccessible through conventional search engines, is a notorious hub for illegal activities. From selling stolen personal and corporate data to trading in malware tools, it's a marketplace for cybercriminals. Given its encrypted nature and the utilization of specialized browsers for access, conventional monitoring tools often fall short. However, with the advent of AI, the tides are turning, enabling organizations to proactively scour the dark web's hidden alleys and detect potential threats.[114]

One of the significant challenges with dark web monitoring is the sheer volume of data and the speed at which information changes. Traditional methods require substantial manual effort, and by the time potential threats are identified, the damage may have already been done. AI-driven monitoring tools, however, can process vast amounts of data in real-time. They're trained to look for specific markers or patterns related to an organization, such as mentions of a company's name, executive details, proprietary software names, and more. By doing so, they provide early warning signs of potential data breaches or upcoming targeted attacks.

Furthermore, the language barrier is another issue in the dark web. With forums and marketplaces operating in multiple languages and often using coded language or jargon, manual monitoring can be arduous. AI, with natural language processing (NLP) capabilities, transcends this barrier. Not only can it quickly translate content, but it can also understand context, decipher slang, and even spot-coded communication, highlighting potential threats that might be missed by human analysts.

However, while AI-driven dark web monitoring offers an edge, it's essential to note its limitations. The dark web's decentralized and ever-changing nature means that there will always be areas that are difficult to penetrate, even for the most advanced AI systems.

Nevertheless, integrating AI into dark web monitoring tools provides organizations with a significantly enhanced level of protection and situational awareness. As we delve

---

[114] https://cyberint.com/blog/dark-web/a-new-approach-to-dark-web-monitoring/, https://bolster.ai/glossary/dark-web-monitoring, and https://typeset.io/questions/what-are-the-limitations-of-dark-web-monitoring-3jr48sidl0

deeper into the domain of AI-augmented cybersecurity, the next sub-area showcases how AI elevates real-time monitoring to new pinnacles of efficiency and accuracy.

- **Nature of the Dark Web:**
    - Part of the deep web, hidden from conventional search engines.
    - Hub for illegal activities, including data theft and malware trade.

- **Challenges in Monitoring:**
    - Rapid changes in data and vast volumes make manual monitoring inefficient.
    - Language barriers, with content in various languages and use of coded jargon.
    - Decentralized and encrypted nature creates zones hard to penetrate.

- **AI-Driven Monitoring Advantages:**
    - Ability to process extensive data in real-time.
    - Identifies specific markers or patterns, such as mentions of proprietary names.
    - Natural Language Processing (NLP) overcomes language and jargon barriers.

- **Considerations:**
    - Despite AI capabilities, some areas of the dark web remain challenging to access.
    - Essential to stay updated with evolving dark web structures and languages for efficient monitoring.

9.1.4.   *Automated Threat Ranking: Prioritizing Threats for Effective Response*

In a world bursting at its digital seams with data, not all cyber threats are created equal. The importance of effectively ranking these threats cannot be overstated, as it allows security professionals to allocate resources wisely, ensuring that the most detrimental threats are addressed first. Modern cyber-attack landscapes are incredibly diverse, and they evolve constantly. In the face of this dynamism, relying solely on manual processes for threat ranking is no longer viable, if it ever was. This is where the power of AI-driven automated threat ranking comes into play.[115]

AI's capabilities in data processing and pattern recognition enable it to sift through vast troves of data, identifying anomalies and potential threats. But beyond mere identification, these AI systems can rank threats based on various factors, including potential impact, the likelihood of occurrence, and the value of the assets at risk. By analyzing historical data, as well as real-time data feeds, these systems can predict which threats are likely to cause the most significant harm, allowing cybersecurity professionals to focus on them with urgency.

The implications of effective threat ranking are profound:

- **Efficiency and Resource Allocation:** Organizations can deploy their resources more efficiently, ensuring that the highest-risk vulnerabilities or threats are addressed as a priority. This can result in significant cost savings and better overall cyber hygiene.

- **Proactive versus Reactive Security Posture:** Rather than constantly playing catch-up, organizations can switch to a proactive security stance, anticipating and mitigating threats before they become full-blown attacks.

- **Improved Incident Response:** By knowing which threats are the most pressing, incident response teams can better prepare and execute their strategies, leading to faster containment and resolution times.

- **Stakeholder Communication:** Automated threat ranking also offers a standardized way to communicate threats to stakeholders. A clear threat hierarchy can guide decision-making at all organizational levels, from the IT department to the boardroom.

- **Continuous Learning and Adaptation:** As AI-driven systems encounter and rank new threats, they continuously learn and refine their ranking algorithms, ensuring their ongoing relevance and accuracy.

---

[115] https://ontic.co/resources/article/prioritizing-threat-actors-3-steps-to-uncovering-and-concentrating-on-your-most-significant-risks/, https://www.mimecast.com/blog/ushering-in-ai-to-automate-cyberthreat-intelligence/, and https://www.isaca.org/resources/isaca-journal/issues/2021/volume-6/evidence-based-prioritization-of-cybersecurity-threats

In conclusion, automated threat ranking embodies the confluence of AI's computational power with the intricacies of cybersecurity. As the cyber realm becomes even more complex, such intelligent automation will be advantageous and essential. Moving forward, the next section delves into real-time monitoring, illustrating AI's transformative effect on live threat detection and mitigation.

9.2.   Real-time Monitoring and Anomaly Detection

The world of cybersecurity is a perpetually active arena. As organizations become increasingly interconnected and data-dependent, the frequency and sophistication of cyberattacks have skyrocketed. Real-time monitoring is no longer a luxury but an imperative. While traditional security systems relied on static rules and known signature-based detection, the sheer volume of data and the evolving nature of threats have made it evident that more dynamic and adaptive approaches are necessary. This is where real-time monitoring combined with AI-driven anomaly detection shines.[116]

Anomaly detection, at its core, involves identifying patterns in data that do not conform to an expected behavior. These "anomalies" can be indicative of a security breach, data exfiltration, or even system malfunction. In the past, detecting such anomalies was akin to finding a needle in a haystack. AI transforms this process by bringing in a magnifying glass, highlighting potential points of concern.

One significant advantage of AI in this realm is its ability to process vast amounts of data at unparalleled speeds. It can concurrently analyze multiple data streams, ensuring that no potential threat slips through. Moreover, AI systems can learn over time, adapting to new data patterns and evolving with the changing dynamics of the cyber environment.

Some pivotal aspects and benefits of AI-driven real-time monitoring and anomaly detection include:

- **Self-learning Systems:** These AI models can learn from past data, recognize patterns, and even predict potential future threats. Over time, they become

---

[116] https://www.toptal.com/cybersecurity/questions-about-ai-cybersecurity, https://www.immuta.com/guides/data-security-101/user-behavior-analytics/, and https://gurucul.com/blog/how-behavior-analytics-improves-cybersecurity

more efficient, reducing false positives and ensuring that genuine threats are swiftly identified.

- **Scalability:** AI solutions can easily scale with the organization's growth. Whether it's an increase in network endpoints, user devices, or data volume, AI-driven systems can handle the surge without compromising on efficiency.

- **User Behavior Analytics (UBA):** By analyzing the typical behavior of users, AI can detect unusual patterns that might indicate a compromised account. This is especially useful in identifying insider threats or compromised insider credentials.

- **Multifaceted Data Analysis:** AI doesn't just look at one dimension of data. It considers multiple facets, including network traffic, user access logs, transaction records, and more, to provide a holistic view of the system's security posture.

- **Reduced Response Time:** With real-time analysis, potential threats are detected almost instantly, allowing for immediate action. This swift detection drastically reduces the window of opportunity for attackers.

- **Adaptation to Zero-Day Threats:** Traditional security tools may falter against unknown threats or zero-day exploits. In contrast, AI-driven systems can identify unusual patterns, flagging potential zero-day attacks even if the specific signature is unknown.

Organizations embarking on their AI-driven cybersecurity journey should be cognizant of the challenges. While these systems offer unparalleled benefits, they also require continuous training and updates. Ensuring the AI models remain updated with the latest threat intelligence is crucial. Additionally, while AI can aid in detection, the human element remains invaluable in decision-making and response strategies. In subsequent sections, we'll explore the nuances of incident response in a world increasingly influenced by AI.

9.2.1.   *Behavioral Analysis: Understanding User Patterns*

User behavior plays a pivotal role in the cybersecurity ecosystem. Traditional security systems, designed to combat known threats, often miss subtle, unusual activities that may indicate a breach. Behavioral analysis, fortified by AI, transcends these limitations by deeply understanding and monitoring user patterns. It transforms the nature of cybersecurity from merely being reactive to proactive, preempting threats before they escalate.

Behavioral analysis revolves around constructing a comprehensive user profile based on routine activities. This profile includes metrics such as frequently accessed files, regular login times, commonly used devices, and typical data transfer patterns. Once this baseline is established, AI-driven systems continuously compare real-time user activity against the baseline. Anomalies, such as accessing sensitive files at odd hours or sudden massive data transfers, trigger alerts.

Several aspects make behavioral analysis an invaluable asset in the cybersecurity armory:

- **Insider Threat Detection:** Often, security threats don't originate from faceless hackers in distant lands. Disgruntled employees, negligent staff, or compromised insider credentials can pose as much, if not more, of a threat. Behavioral analysis can flag unusual internal activities, offering an additional layer of protection against insider threats.

- **Reduced False Positives:** One of the chronic issues plaguing traditional security systems is the high rate of false positives. By deeply understanding user behavior, AI-driven behavioral analysis reduces these, ensuring that security teams can focus on genuine threats.

- **Adaptability:** As employees evolve in their roles, so do their access patterns. Behavioral analysis isn't static. The AI models continually learn, adapting to the user's changing behavior and ensuring that the system remains both secure and user-friendly.

- **Account Takeover Detection:** Even if attackers gain credentials, their behavior post-access is likely to diverge from the legitimate user's patterns. Behavioral analysis can detect such inconsistencies, triggering alerts for potential account takeovers.

- **Enhanced Data Loss Prevention:** By monitoring data transfer patterns, behavioral analysis can identify potential data exfiltration attempts, whether they're subtle trickles of information or massive data dumps.

Incorporating behavioral analysis into the cybersecurity framework does necessitate some considerations. The privacy of users is paramount. Monitoring must strike a balance between ensuring security and respecting individual privacy rights. Transparent policies, clear communication with employees, and strict data handling protocols can help navigate this delicate balance. As we delve deeper into real-time monitoring, it becomes evident that a multi-pronged approach, combining various AI-driven techniques, provides the most robust defense against evolving cyber threats. Here are some real-world examples:

- **Exabeam:** This SIEM solution leverages user and entity behavior analytics (UEBA) to detect and flag anomalous behavior based on historical patterns.

- **Aruba IntroSpect:** HPE's tool utilizes AI to determine changes in user behavior, continuously analyzing network actions to detect threats and rank risks.

- **Splunk UBA:** It uses unsupervised machine learning to detect anomalies, thereby identifying potential threats based on unusual patterns of behavior.

- **Gurucul:** This platform offers behavior-based security analytics, identifying insiders, account compromise, and data exfiltration attempts based on predictive risk-scored evidence.

9.2.2. Network Traffic Insights: Monitoring Data Flow

In the digital age, the pulse of an organization can often be measured by the flow of its data. Monitoring this data flow, especially on a network scale, has thus become critical for both operational efficiency and security. With the surge in the volume of data and the complexities of modern networks, manual oversight has become increasingly untenable. AI-driven network traffic analysis has emerged as a beacon of hope, offering granular insights and instant alerts about potential vulnerabilities or breaches.

The crux of network traffic monitoring lies in inspecting data packets as they traverse across the network. By examining these packets, security systems can glean invaluable insights about the nature of data being transferred, the devices involved, and any potential irregularities. However, with the sheer volume of data in modern networks, merely inspecting packets isn't enough. The ability to interpret, categorize, and act upon this data is where AI truly shines.

Several focal points make network traffic analysis central to a holistic cybersecurity strategy:

- **Baseline Establishment:** Just as with behavioral analysis of users, AI systems begin by understanding the 'normal' flow of data in the network. This involves recognizing peak traffic times, understanding regular data transfer volumes, and even identifying the typical nature of data being transferred.

- **Intrusion Detection Systems (IDS):** These are AI-powered systems specifically tailored to detect any anomalies in data flow. Be it sudden spikes in traffic, unauthorized access attempts, or uncharacteristic data requests, IDS offers real-time alerts, ensuring immediate response.

- **Intrusion Prevention Systems (IPS):** Going a step further than IDS, IPS not only detects anomalies but also takes pre-defined corrective actions. This might involve blocking certain IP addresses, quarantining affected devices, or even shutting down parts of the network temporarily.

- **Distributed Denial of Service (DDoS) Prediction:** DDoS attacks involve overwhelming a network with an immense volume of data requests, often rendering the system unusable. By monitoring network traffic and identifying patterns typical of DDoS initiation, AI systems can alert administrators even before the attack fully manifests.

- **Third-party Integrations:** Often, companies employ various software solutions for different aspects of operations. Each of these can have its own data flow pattern. Network traffic insights can identify any third-party software behaving erratically, thereby preventing potential vulnerabilities at their source.

- **Enhanced Visibility:** With the proliferation of IoT devices and remote working tools, the boundaries of organizational networks have become increasingly porous. AI-driven network traffic insights offer a bird's-eye view of the entire network, ensuring that no device, however peripheral, escapes scrutiny.

With the promise of AI in network traffic analysis also comes the responsibility of using it judiciously. It's imperative to ensure that while monitoring traffic, the privacy and integrity of the data remain uncompromised. As the cyber landscape becomes more intricate, the amalgamation of AI tools, including network traffic insights and other real-time monitoring strategies, will be the cornerstone of resilient cyber defense mechanisms. Here are some real-world examples:

- **Darktrace:** By learning 'normal' behavior over time, Darktrace can promptly respond to deviations, ensuring swift threat detection and mitigation.

- **Cisco Stealthwatch:** Uses telemetry data from the enterprise network and advanced analytics to detect abnormal patterns, ensuring threats are recognized in real-time.

- **Flowmon:** This tool monitors and analyzes network traffic, leveraging AI to detect anomalies and potential threats.

- **ExtraHop Reveal(x):** This provides real-time insights into network operations and performance, using AI to detect, investigate, and respond to threats.

9.2.3.   *Endpoint Security: Keeping Devices Safe in Real-time*

Endpoint security, a pillar of modern cybersecurity frameworks, ensures that individual devices (endpoints) connecting to a network are secure from potential threats. As organizations grow and become more interconnected, so does the assortment of devices—from desktops and laptops to smartphones and IoT devices. Each of these devices presents potential entry points for cyber attackers. With the advancements in AI, the methods to safeguard these entry points have revolutionized, moving from mere device protection to real-time threat intelligence and response.

Traditionally, endpoint security was centered around antivirus software and firewalls. However, the current digital ecosystem demands a more proactive and adaptive approach. Modern cyber threats often bypass traditional defenses, employing sophisticated methods like zero-day exploits or advanced malware. AI assists in plugging these gaps, leveraging machine learning models to continuously learn from cyber threat data and thus identify and counteract threats almost instantaneously.

Here's how AI is reshaping the domain of endpoint security:

- **Behavioral Analytics:** Instead of solely relying on signature-based threat detection, AI systems study the behavioral patterns of devices. This means that even if a piece of malware or a hacker technique hasn't been previously identified (and thus doesn't have a "signature"), the system can detect it based on its anomalous behavior.

- **Automated Threat Hunting:** AI can proactively scan networks for signs of potential threats, rather than waiting for an intrusion to take place. This active approach helps organizations stay one step ahead of potential attackers.

- **Real-time Malware Analysis:** With the rapid creation and mutation of malware strains, AI-powered systems can dissect and understand these threats in real-time, updating their defense mechanisms instantaneously.

- **Fileless Attack Detection:** Traditional endpoint security might miss attacks that don't involve downloading malicious files. AI can detect these fileless, memory-based attacks by closely monitoring system processes and memory usage.

- **Patch Management:** AI tools can predict which software vulnerabilities are most likely to be exploited in real-world attacks and prioritize patching those first, ensuring efficient use of resources.

- **Response Automation:** Beyond detection, AI-driven endpoint solutions can take corrective actions, such as quarantining a compromised device or blocking a malicious connection, without human intervention, thereby reducing response time.

- **Integrative Defense Mechanisms:** Modern endpoint security solutions, powered by AI, are designed to seamlessly integrate with other security tools in the organizational infrastructure. This allows for a unified and more robust defense strategy.

The enhancement of endpoint security using AI isn't just about staying ahead of cybercriminals. It's about building a dynamic, adaptive, and resilient security posture that can withstand the constantly evolving threat landscape. With devices becoming more ubiquitous and integral to organizational operations, ensuring their safety in real-time is not just a necessity—it's a mandate for sustainable growth and trustworthiness. Here are some real-world examples:

- **CrowdStrike Falcon:** This endpoint protection platform deploys AI to detect and thwart malware and other sophisticated threats.

- **Symantec Endpoint Protection:** Harnesses a vast cyber intelligence network to detect threats across various endpoints, providing integrated response capabilities.

- **SentinelOne:** This tool operates on a behavioral AI model, focusing on behavior patterns to detect threats, ensuring protection even against zero-day exploits.

- **Carbon Black (now part of VMware):** A cloud-native endpoint protection platform leveraging behavioral analytics to detect malicious activities.

9.2.4.   AI-powered Intrusion Detection Systems: Advanced Threat Recognition

Intrusion Detection Systems (IDS) have been a cornerstone of network security for years. Their primary role is to identify suspicious activities within a system by continuously monitoring network traffic and subsequently alerting administrators of any detected anomalies. With the advent of AI and machine learning, IDS have undergone a significant transformation, evolving from rule-based alerts to intelligent systems capable of understanding, learning from, and even predicting security breaches.

Traditionally, IDS relied heavily on signature-based methods, where known patterns of malicious activity, or "signatures," were fed into the system. Once matched, alerts were generated. However, this method posed limitations. For instance, it would only detect previously recognized threats and was prone to a high number of false positives. Enter the age of AI. With its capacity to process vast amounts of data and its inherent learning capabilities, AI has amplified the proficiency of IDS in unparalleled ways.

Here's a deeper dive into how AI has bolstered IDS:

- **Anomaly-based Detection:** Beyond just matching signatures, AI-driven IDS uses machine learning to establish a 'baseline' of normal network behavior. Any deviation from this baseline, which could indicate a potential security breach, triggers an alert. This is particularly effective against zero-day vulnerabilities and advanced persistent threats.

- **Reduced False Positives:** By understanding network behavior more holistically, AI can discern between genuine threats and benign irregularities. This reduction in false positives ensures that security teams can focus their attention on genuine security alerts rather than chasing down false alarms.

- **Scalability and Efficiency:** With the increasing complexity and volume of network traffic, manual analysis becomes almost impossible. AI can quickly analyze vast datasets in real-time, making it viable for organizations with large-scale network operations.

- **Predictive Analysis:** AI doesn't just respond to threats–it can predict them. By analyzing patterns and trends, AI-powered IDS can forecast potential attack vectors, giving organizations a head start in bolstering their defenses.

- **Automated Responses:** Beyond mere detection, some advanced AI-powered IDS are equipped to take immediate action upon threat detection. This can range from blocking malicious IP addresses to isolating affected network segments, ensuring swift containment of potential threats.

- **Integration with Other Systems:** AI-driven IDS can seamlessly integrate with other security tools, such as SIEM (Security Information and Event Management) systems, creating a cohesive security environment where information and insights are shared across platforms.

- **Continuous Learning:** The AI models within IDS are not static. They learn and evolve, adapting to new threats and understanding the ever-changing network behavior, ensuring that the system remains effective over time.

In the hyperconnected era, where threats are becoming more sophisticated and pervasive, AI-driven intrusion detection offers a beacon of hope. By fusing the analytical prowess of AI with traditional detection mechanisms, organizations can safeguard their assets more effectively, ensuring that breaches are not just detected but predicted and prevented. Here are some real-world examples:

- **Vectra Cognito:** Automates the detection of cyber attackers in real-time network traffic, ensuring rapid incident response.

- **McAfee Network Security Platform:** A next-generation IPS that incorporates AI to discern complex attack patterns and respond accordingly.

- **Snort:** While it might be one of the older IDS tools, continuous updates and community-generated rules allow it to remain relevant. Recent iterations have seen increased utilization of AI and machine learning for threat detection.

- **AlienVault USM (Unified Security Management):** Integrates multiple essential security capabilities within one platform, with AI and machine learning at its core, facilitating threat detection and response.

9.3.   Incident Response in an AI-Driven World

In the rapidly evolving cyber landscape, incident response has taken on a new dimension with the advent of AI. As networks become more complex and threats more sophisticated, organizations are confronted with the herculean task of not just detecting but also efficiently responding to these challenges. Traditional incident response strategies, reliant on human intervention and static rule-based systems, are increasingly seen as inadequate. The sheer volume of data and the velocity at which threats propagate necessitate a transformative approach, and this is where AI-driven incident response proves its mettle.

AI brings to the table the dual capabilities of speed and precision. With the capability to analyze vast troves of data at lightning speed, AI-powered tools can detect anomalies and initiate countermeasures much faster than human teams could. More than just a first line of defense, they augment human responders by filtering out false positives, focusing on genuine threats, and suggesting optimal response strategies based on historical and contextual data.

However, with this automation comes an increased responsibility. AI models, as robust as they might be, are still not infallible. They rely on vast datasets for training, and the quality of their response is only as good as the data they've been fed. The emergence of adversarial attacks designed to confuse and mislead AI models is a stark reminder that these systems can be gamed. Therefore, a careful balance needs to be struck between automation and human oversight to ensure that the incident response is not just swift but also accurate.

Additionally, as AI continues to be integrated into cyber defense frameworks, there's an inevitable learning curve for security professionals. Incident response in an AI-driven world requires teams to not only understand the intricacies of the threats they face but also the workings of the AI tools at their disposal. Training and continuous learning become paramount. As AI models evolve and adapt, so too must the human operators overseeing them.

In this section, we'll delve deeper into the nuances of AI-enhanced incident response, exploring how it's reshaping the cyber landscape, the challenges it presents, and the strategies organizations can adopt to harness its full potential. As we move forward, it's evident that AI is not just an adjunct to incident response—it's set to become its cornerstone.

9.3.1. Automated Responses: Swift Action Against Threats

In the boundless digital realm, time is of the essence. With the frequency and sophistication of cyberattacks surging, a delayed response—even by mere seconds—can amplify the adverse impacts manifold. Recognizing this, organizations are increasingly pivoting towards automated responses as part of their incident response toolkit. These automated systems, augmented by artificial intelligence, not only detect threats but also take predefined actions without necessitating human intervention. This swift, autonomous reaction to threats often means the difference between a minor security hiccup and a major data breach.

Automated responses have several distinct advantages. Foremost among them is the ability to respond to threats at machine speed. Traditional incident response, which hinges on human analysts reviewing and reacting to alerts, can't compete with the pace at which AI-powered tools operate. By the time an analyst discerns the nature of a threat, it might have already penetrated deeper layers of the network. Automated systems nip this problem in the bud by instantly recognizing malicious patterns and responding to them. For instance, upon detecting suspicious activity, an AI-driven system might instantly isolate the affected endpoint or block a dubious IP, stemming the threat's spread.

Yet, with these advantages come new challenges. Blind reliance on automated responses can lead to unintended consequences. There's the risk of false positives—legitimate activities being flagged and acted upon as threats. Such overzealous responses can disrupt regular operations, leading to downtime and potential revenue loss. Hence, the design of these systems demands precision. The AI models underpinning them must be trained on comprehensive and updated datasets to minimize errors. They must also be integrated seamlessly into the broader cybersecurity infrastructure, ensuring that automated actions align with the organization's overall security posture.

Real-world applications of automated response mechanisms are already evident in solutions like Endpoint Detection and Response (EDR) platforms and Next-Generation Firewalls (NGFWs). These tools, backed by AI algorithms, not only identify but also remediate threats in real-time, often without human operators even being aware of the intrusion.

As cyber threats continue to evolve, the adoption of automated responses will likely become more pervasive. However, organizations must proceed with caution, continuously refining their systems to ensure they're both swift and accurate. Balancing automation with discerning human oversight will remain crucial as we navigate this new frontier of cybersecurity.

These tools exemplify the ongoing transformation in cybersecurity. By leveraging AI's capabilities, they're ensuring threats are not just detected but also acted upon with minimal delay. However, while their efficacy is proven, it's paramount that organizations using such tools have a clear understanding of their functionalities to optimize their benefits and reduce false positives. Here are some real-world examples:

- **CrowdStrike Falcon:** CrowdStrike's Falcon platform is an EDR solution that utilizes AI to provide real-time threat detection and automated incident response. When Falcon detects malicious activities, it can autonomously quarantine affected systems or terminate malicious processes, ensuring rapid reaction to threats. This allows security teams to intervene promptly and conduct a more in-depth analysis.[117]

- **Cisco Threat Response:** Part of Cisco's integrated security portfolio, Cisco Threat Response, automates integrations across select Cisco Security products. When a threat is detected, it not only provides detailed intelligence but can also automatically enforce policies to contain the threat. This reduces the window of opportunity for attackers and minimizes the manual workload for security teams.[118]

- **Palo Alto Networks Cortex XDR:** A detection, investigation, and response product, Cortex XDR breaks down the silos of traditional security products and uses AI and machine learning to automatically uncover and address threats across the network, cloud, and endpoints. It can also take a series of actions based on predefined rules, such as blocking command and control traffic or quarantining infected hosts.[119]

- **Darktrace Antigena:** A product of Darktrace, Antigena acts as a "digital antibody." Relying on machine learning, it understands 'self' for your enterprise. That is, it knows normal behavior. When it detects deviations that

---

[117] https://www.crowdstrike.com/falcon-platform/artificial-intelligence-and-machine-learning/

[118] https://www.cisco.com/c/dam/m/en_uk/events/2016/securityexperts/pdf/rapid_threat_containment_sept_8th_2016.pdf

[119] https://www.paloaltonetworks.co.uk/cortex/xdrvscybereason

indicate potential threats, Antigena takes proportionate, measured actions to neutralize the threat without affecting routine operations.[120]

These tools exemplify the ongoing transformation in cybersecurity. By leveraging AI's capabilities, they're ensuring threats are not just detected but also acted upon with minimal delay. However, while their efficacy is proven, it's paramount that organizations using such tools have a clear understanding of their functionalities to optimize their benefits and reduce false positives.

9.3.2. Human-AI Collaboration: Merging Intuition with Algorithms

In an age dominated by cyber threats, solely relying on automated solutions or human intervention is no longer sufficient. The symbiosis of human intelligence with machine-driven insights can elevate cybersecurity to new heights. While AI can process vast datasets quickly, identifying patterns and anomalies, the human brain's ability to understand context, infer motives, and deduce complex scenarios remains unmatched. Thus, merging human intuition with the speed and precision of AI creates a potent defense against cyber threats.

AI tools, particularly in the realm of cybersecurity, can be likened to high-powered telescopes. They magnify and highlight potential threats, making them easier to spot. However, interpreting these threats, especially in complex scenarios, requires the human touch. For instance, while an AI might flag an unusual data access pattern as a potential breach, a human analyst can determine whether this was due to a legitimate one-off event or a genuine security concern.

Moreover, a collaborative approach aids in refining AI models. As security experts interact with AI-driven insights, they can provide feedback, helping the AI adapt and learn. This continuous learning loop ensures that the AI model remains updated and can more accurately reflect the ever-evolving threat landscape.

Several initiatives and tools are being developed to foster this collaboration:

- **IBM Watson for Cyber Security:** IBM Watson for Cyber Security utilizes the cognitive computing capabilities of Watson to process vast amounts of security research and data, which would be beyond human capacity. It integrates AI's

---

[120] https://darktrace.com/news/darktrace-antigena-launched-new-era-as-cyber-ai-fights-back

data processing power with human security analysts' inputs, analyzing unstructured data such as blogs, websites, and research papers to uncover sophisticated threats. Watson for Cyber Security augments security analysts' ability to identify and understand threats by correlating this data with local security offenses, thereby revolutionizing how security analysts work.[121]

- **Microsoft Azure Sentinel:** Azure Sentinel is Microsoft's cloud-native SIEM solution that employs machine learning to assist security analysts in threat detection. It provides a scalable, cloud-native platform that offers security information and event management (SIEM) and security orchestration, automation, and response (SOAR) capabilities. Azure Sentinel delivers intelligent security analytics and threat intelligence across the enterprise, enabling attack detection, threat visibility, proactive hunting, and threat response. It allows security professionals to customize threat detection algorithms through a user-friendly interface, ensuring that AI findings are aligned with the organization's unique needs and contexts.[122]

- **Google Chronicle:** Chronicle, part of Google Cloud's security services, focuses on delivering high-speed analytics to enable security teams to investigate alerts and incidents more efficiently. It ingests, analyzes, and searches all security telemetry at Google scale and speed, providing threat intelligence and intelligent security analytic capabilities. Chronicle uses machine learning to sift through massive datasets and offers an interface designed to help human analysts understand the threat narrative, thereby improving SOC productivity and combating modern threats.[123]

- **Splunk Phantom:** Phantom, developed by Splunk, is a security orchestration, automation, and response (SOAR) tool that integrates AI-driven analysis with human-led security operations. It enables security teams to codify their workflows into "playbooks," allowing the AI to handle repetitive tasks while

---

[121] https://www.ibm.com/blogs/nordic-msp/watson-cyber-security/ and https://cyberagility.academy/the-top-10-ai-cybersecurity-products/

[122] https://learn.microsoft.com/en-us/azure/sentinel/overview and https://www.bluevoyant.com/knowledge-center/what-is-azure-sentinel-renamed-to-microsoft-sentinel

[123] https://chronicle.security/solutions/chronicle-security-solution-partners/ and https://cybriant.com/the-ultimate-guide-to-google-chronicle-siem/

humans focus on complex decision-making. Phantom supports automated responses to threats using machine learning and AI capabilities, and its integration with AWS and other platforms makes it a versatile tool for automating security incident analysis workflows.[124]

These platforms, among many others, underscore the industry's understanding of the importance of human-AI collaboration. As cyber threats become more sophisticated, a harmonized approach ensures that defenses are both rapid and nuanced, making them significantly more effective.

9.3.3. Post-Incident Analysis: Learning from Breaches Using AI

Post-incident analysis, often referred to as a post-mortem, is a critical step in understanding the vulnerabilities and shortcomings of an organization's security infrastructure. It is not just about identifying what went wrong—it's about drawing lessons, strengthening security protocols, and ensuring that similar breaches do not recur. In the face of increasing cyber threats, AI is now playing an indispensable role in bolstering post-incident analysis, offering an unprecedented depth of insight and predictive capabilities.

At the core of post-incident analysis is the painstaking task of sifting through logs, understanding the sequence of events, and piecing together the attacker's trail. Traditionally, this would take considerable time, often hampered by the volume of data and the intricacies of advanced threats. AI, with its prowess in handling vast datasets and pattern recognition, considerably speeds up this process. It can quickly correlate disparate pieces of information, identifying unusual patterns and presenting a comprehensive view of the breach.

Furthermore, as cyberattacks grow in sophistication, they often leave behind subtle traces that might be overlooked by a manual review. AI-driven tools can pinpoint these faint signals, illuminating the attacker's methodologies, tools used, and possible objectives. This granular understanding is crucial in developing robust countermeasures and fortifying defenses against future threats.

---

[124] https://pages.awscloud.com/rs/112-TZM-766/images/Global_PTNR_AWS_Splunk_Ebook_09252019.pdf and https://www.crestdatasys.com/solutions/splunk/splunk-phantom/

Another burgeoning application of AI in post-incident analysis is its ability to simulate attacks. By recreating the attack in a controlled environment, AI can predict potential future threats and variations of the same attack, enabling organizations to be proactive in their defense strategies.

Several tools and platforms exemplify the leverage of AI in post-incident analysis:

- **Endgame's Artemis:** Artemis is an AI-driven chatbot that provides an interactive chat experience for security analysts. It enables them to use natural language to perform analytics on endpoint data, helping to streamline the investigation process. Artemis can offer expert recommendations and rapid contextualization, guiding analysts through data in response to events or alerts, and suggesting logical and effective next steps or actions.[125]

- **Darktrace's Antigena:** Darktrace's Antigena is an autonomous response solution that acts in real-time to combat cyber threats. It is designed to calculate the best action to mitigate threats as they are detected. Post-incident, Antigena can provide a detailed analysis of the threat, including the steps taken by the AI to mitigate the incident, which can be invaluable for manual review and understanding the nature of the attack.[126]

- **Elastic (ELK) Stack:** The ELK Stack, which includes Elasticsearch, Logstash, and Kibana, is a powerful log management tool that also offers AI-driven analytics capabilities. It can handle large volumes of log data, identify patterns and anomalies, and provide visualization tools that help analysts understand the sequence of events during a breach. Elastic's machine learning features can automatically detect anomalies and categorize log events, aiding in root cause analysis and reducing the time to resolution.[127]

---

[125] https://www.elastic.co/blog/artemis-intelligent-assistant-cyber-defense and https://www.elastic.co/blog/open-security-impact-elastic-ai-assistant

[126] https://www.devoteam.com/expert-view/darktrace-the-future-of-cyber-security/, https://comport.com/resources/it-services/what-is-darktrace-how-can-its-cyber-ai-platform-leave-you-less-vulnerable/, and https://www.datalinknetworks.net/dln_blog/using-ai-to-protect-your-business-with-darktrace

[127] https://logz.io/learn/complete-guide-elk-stack/ and https://www.ibsscorp.com/resources/log-analysis-with-a-special-look-at-elastic-stack

- **Recorded Future:** Recorded Future provides real-time threat intelligence by analyzing the web across all languages and scanning for malicious activity. It can alert security teams to potential threats involving their domains, IPs, and leaked credentials. In post-incident analysis, Recorded Future can offer insights into the threat landscape by correlating data from various sources, including the dark web, and providing intelligence summaries that help analysts understand the context and significance of the threats they face.[128]

Harnessing AI for post-incident analysis is not merely about efficiency–it's about enhancing the depth, breadth, and precision of the analysis. As cyber threats continue to evolve, organizations that utilize AI's capabilities to understand and learn from past breaches will be better positioned to fend off future attacks.

9.3.4.   AI in Digital Forensics: Unraveling Complex Cyber Crimes

The digital realm has transformed the landscape of criminal activities. While technological advancements have made our lives more interconnected and efficient, they have also paved the way for sophisticated cybercrimes, ranging from data breaches to intricate ransomware attacks. As the complexity of these crimes intensifies, the traditional methodologies of digital forensics can sometimes fall short. Enter AI, which, with its unparalleled data analysis and pattern recognition capabilities, is revolutionizing the field of digital forensics, enabling experts to decode even the most convoluted cybercrimes.

Digital forensics is essentially the art and science of extracting and analyzing electronic data to reconstruct events or actions that have led to specific digital security incidents. Given the vast amounts of data typically involved in these analyses, manual investigations can be like searching for a needle in a haystack. AI, however, can sift through enormous datasets at lightning speed, pinpointing anomalies and offering investigative leads that humans might overlook.

Moreover, the modus operandi of cybercriminals is ever-evolving. They employ new techniques, hide their tracks better, and use advanced tools to evade detection. AI's machine learning algorithms are continually trained with new data, allowing them to

---

[128] https://go.recordedfuture.com/hubfs/data-sheets/threat-monitor.pdf,
https://www.devopsschool.com/blog/what-is-recorded-future-and-use-cases-of-recorded-future/,
and https://www.recordedfuture.com/products/threat-intelligence

adapt and recognize emerging patterns of cybercrimes. For instance, steganography, the practice of hiding malicious codes within legitimate-looking files, can be challenging to detect with traditional tools. Still, machine learning models can be trained to recognize subtle alterations in such files, unmasking concealed threats.

AI's capabilities in digital forensics are not just limited to detection. They extend to proactive defense. By understanding the methodologies of past attacks, AI tools can predict and prevent potential future cybercrimes, marking a shift from reactive to proactive digital forensics.

Several innovative tools and platforms are leveraging AI for digital forensics:

- **Cellebrite:** Known for its mobile forensic solutions, Cellebrite's Pathfinder tool uses AI to analyze digital evidence from mobile devices. It employs text and image analytics and can reveal connections from up to 100 extractions per case. Cellebrite's tools are designed to uncover leads with greater speed and accuracy, optimizing the investigation process.[129]

- **Autopsy:** Autopsy is a digital forensics platform that includes a suite of modules for various tasks, such as file type identification, keyword search, and email parsing. While the search results do not explicitly mention the use of machine learning for identifying explicit content, Autopsy does include modules like the Picture Analyzer, which could potentially use such technologies to aid in cybercrime investigations.[130]

- **Magnet Forensics:** Magnet Forensics offers tools that use AI to prioritize and categorize digital evidence. Their Magnet.AI feature within AXIOM scans artifacts, including chat and email attachments, web cache data, and video thumbnails, to identify content such as child sexual abuse, nudity, weapons, and

---

[129] https://h11dfs.com/cellebrite-pathfinder-a/, https://cellebrite.com/en/pathfinder/, and https://cellebrite.com/en/home/

[130] https://www.classcentral.com/course/youtube-starting-a-new-digital-forensic-investigation-case-in-autopsy-4-19-125853

drugs. This allows investigators to rapidly sort through data and focus on the most relevant information for a case.[131]

The integration of AI into digital forensics represents a pivotal moment for cybersecurity. As the line between the digital and physical worlds continues to blur, the onus is on forensic experts to stay ahead of the curve. By harnessing the power of AI, they can ensure a robust, adaptive, and comprehensive response to the multifaceted challenges posed by modern cybercriminals.

---

[131] https://www.reddit.com/r/computerforensics/comments/tfigdg/autopsy_sample_images_to_ learn_practice/ and https://www.forensicfocus.com/articles/industry-roundup-image-recognition-and-categorization/

10. The Ethical Dimensions of AI and Data Management

The meteoric rise of artificial intelligence and data-driven technologies has not only brought about unparalleled advancements in various sectors but has also thrust the conversation of ethics into the limelight. As these technologies shape our society, they inherently touch upon profound philosophical, moral, and ethical questions that have concerned humanity for centuries. These questions are not just academic in nature—they are essential in guiding the responsible development and deployment of AI and data management systems.

AI's capacity to process vast datasets and make autonomous decisions, while impressive, can sometimes result in unintended consequences that challenge our traditional notions of fairness, privacy, and justice. Such decisions, even if made in nanoseconds by algorithms, can have lasting impacts on individuals, communities, and societies. From facial recognition systems that may perpetuate racial biases to predictive policing algorithms that could reinforce existing prejudices, the interplay between AI and societal norms is intricate and often fraught with complications.

Moreover, data, the lifeblood of AI, is intimately intertwined with personal identities, histories, and narratives. The ways in which organizations collect, store, and utilize this data must be scrutinized through an ethical lens. Mismanagement or misuse of personal data not only violates privacy norms but can also lead to societal harms, such as identity theft, discrimination, or even the erosion of trust in digital systems.

Beyond the immediate societal implications, the development of AI rekindles age-old debates about the nature of consciousness, autonomy, and free will. As machines begin to exhibit behaviors that we associate with human intelligence—learning, reasoning, and even creativity—the boundaries between human and machine blur, pushing us to reevaluate our understanding of sentience and the moral obligations that come with it.

In diving deep into this section, we will endeavor to unpack the multifaceted ethical concerns surrounding AI and data management. We will look into real-world instances, philosophical underpinnings, and actionable guidelines to navigate this intricate landscape. The goal is not just to highlight challenges but to foster a holistic understanding that paves the way for more ethical, just, and inclusive AI technologies.

10.1.   Addressing Bias in AI Security Solutions

In the rapidly evolving realm of artificial intelligence, a pressing concern that often takes center stage is the issue of bias. Bias, simply put, refers to the unfair and often unintended favoring of one group or outcome over others. In AI, biases in data or algorithms can produce results that reflect those biases, leading to skewed, unfair, or even harmful outcomes. However, when this bias infiltrates security solutions powered by AI, the implications can be even more severe. Unlike applications in marketing or entertainment, where bias might result in mis-targeted content or slight user dissatisfaction, in security, bias can cause threats to be overlooked, produce false positives, or even fail to protect certain user groups effectively.

The presence of bias in AI security solutions can stem from various sources. Often, it's the training data that inadvertently introduces a slant. If an AI system is trained predominantly on data from one type of network, user base, or threat environment, it may not perform as effectively in different settings. For example, an AI system primarily trained on cyber threats from financial databases might struggle to identify nuanced threats in a healthcare setting. Similarly, if threat data is predominantly from one geographic region, the system might not recognize threats emerging from new areas.

Addressing bias is not just about ensuring fairness but also about optimizing the efficacy of AI security solutions. A biased system, by definition, is not seeing the full picture and is therefore less effective. As we delve deeper into this section, we will explore the nuances of bias in AI-powered security, its potential consequences, and strategies to minimize its impact. By understanding and mitigating bias, organizations can build more robust, reliable, and fair AI-driven security mechanisms, paving the way for safer digital ecosystems.

10.1.1.   Origins of Bias: Understanding Root Causes

Artificial intelligence, while profoundly transformative, is fundamentally a tool—one that processes data and learns from patterns. But like any tool, its outcomes are only as unbiased as its inputs and its creators. As such, it's pivotal to understand the root causes behind the biases in AI security solutions. Understanding these origins is the first step toward effective mitigation.[132]

- **Data-Driven Bias:** At the core of every AI model lies its training data. If this data contains inherent biases, either from underrepresented groups or overrepresented patterns, the AI will absorb and propagate them. For instance, if an AI security system is trained on datasets that predominantly feature malware attacks targeting a specific operating system, it may be less effective at recognizing threats to alternative systems. The inherent inclinations in the data can skew the AI's perception, making it less effective in diverse environments.

- **Algorithmic Bias:** While data is a significant source of bias, the algorithms themselves can sometimes introduce bias, especially if they're not designed to account for disparities in data. Certain algorithms might amplify existing prejudices in data or even favor certain data patterns over others. As an example, an algorithm designed to weigh recent cyber threats more heavily might overlook slower-evolving, but equally crucial, security challenges.

- **Human Bias:** Behind every AI system is a team of human developers. Unconscious biases from these developers can inadvertently be translated into the models they design. This includes choices about which data to use for training, which features to prioritize, and how to structure the AI's learning process.

- **Feedback Loops:** AI systems often learn continuously from new data. If they begin with a slight bias, and actions are taken based on that bias, new data generated can further reinforce this bias, creating a feedback loop. For instance, if an AI-powered security system disproportionately flags activities from a certain geographical region as suspicious and subsequently focuses more on

---

[132] https://feministai.pubpub.org/pub/the-algorithmic-origins-of-bias/release/3, https://www.datacamp.com/blog/what-is-algorithmic-bias, and https://arxiv.org/pdf/2305.06055.pdf

monitoring that region, it might continually reinforce its bias against that region.

Recognizing these root causes of bias is pivotal. It not only promotes awareness but also helps in devising targeted strategies to rectify them. As AI continues to shape the future of cyber security, ensuring its impartiality is paramount. Not only does this uphold ethical standards, but it also ensures that AI-driven tools provide comprehensive protection against an array of threats, irrespective of their origin or nature.

10.1.2.   Consequences of Untreated AI Biases

While the technological advancements of AI offer a vast array of benefits, the consequences of untreated biases within AI systems can have far-reaching and detrimental effects. This is especially poignant in the realm of cybersecurity and data management, where the stakes are particularly high. Overlooking or underestimating biases could result in both operational inefficiencies and severe ethical dilemmas:[133]

- **Compromised Security Measures:** An AI system that operates under bias might not detect threats accurately. For instance, if a security system is biased towards certain types of threats due to its training data, it could potentially overlook other equally harmful threats. This selective vision can lead to dangerous vulnerabilities, making networks and systems more susceptible to attacks.

- **Erosion of Trust:** For AI systems to be widely adopted and effective, there's a fundamental need for user trust. When biases, especially those that lead to discriminatory actions, become evident, they can quickly erode stakeholder and public trust. In the realm of security, this mistrust can deter users from relying on AI-driven solutions, pushing them towards less efficient or less secure alternatives.

- **Legal and Regulatory Repercussions:** As society becomes more aware of the ethical implications surrounding AI, regulations are evolving to hold companies accountable for discriminatory or biased outcomes. Companies that fail to

---

[133] https://www.thomsonreuters.com/en-us/posts/technology/ai-bias-report-duke-law/, https://cybersecurity-magazine.com/4-unexpected-ways-ai-bias-can-jeopardize-cybersecurity/, and https://www.cnbc.com/2019/07/17/ai-has-a-bias-problem-that-can-be-a-big-challenge-in-cybersecurity.html

address AI biases can face significant legal penalties, not to mention the reputational damage such incidents can inflict.

- **Ethical Implications:** Beyond the technical and operational consequences, untreated biases raise serious ethical concerns. Discriminating against certain user groups or neglecting particular threat vectors can lead to a disproportionate impact on certain populations, thereby further entrenching societal inequalities.

- **Increased Operational Costs:** Continuously rectifying the mistakes of a biased AI system can be resource-intensive. Whether it's responding to false positives, mitigating unanticipated threats, or addressing user grievances, the operational costs associated with untreated AI biases can quickly add up.

- **Feedback Loop Amplification:** As previously discussed, unchecked biases can create feedback loops, where the system's biases get constantly reinforced. Over time, this can make the underlying bias more pronounced, making mitigation efforts increasingly challenging and time-consuming.

Addressing biases isn't just a technical necessity—it's a moral imperative. Understanding the profound consequences of untreated biases underscores the need for proactive measures. It serves as a clarion call for developers, policymakers, and users alike to prioritize unbiased AI systems, ensuring that they are both effective in their intended purpose and ethical in their operations.

10.1.3. *Strategies for Debiasing AI Systems*

In the realm of AI, where biases can have profound implications, the need to establish strategies for debiasing systems becomes paramount. Addressing biases isn't solely about refining algorithms–it encompasses a holistic approach that involves various stakeholders, from data scientists to ethicists. While the challenge is multifaceted, with each AI application demanding a tailored solution, several generalized strategies can guide organizations in their pursuit of equitable AI systems:

- **Diverse Training Data:** One of the foremost causes of bias is the data on which AI systems are trained. Ensuring a diverse and representative dataset helps create a more balanced AI system. This involves gathering data from various sources and ensuring it captures the broad spectra of scenarios the AI might encounter.

- **Regular Audits and Evaluations:** Continuous monitoring and regular audits can help identify and rectify biases. Tools and frameworks like Fairness Indicators or AI Fairness 360 offer insights into how an AI model performs and help pinpoint areas of potential bias.

- **Transparent Algorithm Design:** Adopting a transparent approach to algorithm development allows for a clearer understanding of how decisions are made. Explainable AI (XAI) models, for instance, can offer insights into the decision-making process, making it easier to identify and rectify biased pathways.

- **Engage Ethicists and Diverse Teams:** The inclusion of ethicists in AI development teams can provide valuable perspectives on potential ethical dilemmas. Furthermore, cultivating a diverse team of developers and data scientists ensures multiple viewpoints are considered, leading to a more balanced system.

- **Feedback Mechanisms:** Implementing feedback loops where users can report potential biases or discrepancies allows for real-world validation. Such mechanisms help in refining the system based on real-world experiences and provide valuable data for ongoing improvement.

- **Bias Mitigation Algorithms:** Certain algorithms are specifically designed to reduce bias. Techniques like adversarial debiasing, for instance, introduce a secondary adversarial model during training to challenge the primary model's decisions, promoting fairness.

- **Ethical Guidelines and Frameworks:** Adopting ethical guidelines and frameworks specifically tailored for AI can help developers ensure fairness. These guidelines serve as a roadmap, detailing best practices and ethical considerations vital for unbiased AI development.

- **User Education:** Educating end-users about the potential biases in AI systems allows them to be more critical and discerning. This not only empowers users but also provides an additional layer of oversight.

Addressing biases in AI is an ongoing challenge, one that evolves with the technology and societal understanding of fairness. It requires consistent effort, collaboration across disciplines, and, most importantly, the will to prioritize ethics over convenience. By adopting these strategies and remaining vigilant, we can move towards a future where AI not only augments our capabilities but does so in a manner that upholds the ideals of fairness and equity.

10.1.4.   Best Practices: Designing Fair AI Security Solutions

As AI technologies continue to embed themselves within security systems and strategies, ensuring that they operate without inherent biases becomes a top priority. The stakes are particularly high in the security domain, where biased decisions can lead to skewed threat perceptions, flawed risk assessments, and misguided action plans. Ensuring fairness isn't just about meeting ethical guidelines—it's about optimizing the performance, reliability, and trustworthiness of AI security solutions. Here are best practices to ensure the design of fair AI security systems:

- **Stakeholder Collaboration:** Assembling a cross-functional team that includes domain experts, ethicists, user representatives, and data scientists ensures that a wide range of perspectives and expertise is brought to the design table. Collaborative efforts can help in spotting potential pitfalls and biases that might be overlooked by a homogenous team.[134]

- **Ethical Charters:** Organizations should adopt and adhere to ethical charters that explicitly outline commitments to fairness, transparency, and non-discrimination. This not only provides a guiding framework but also emphasizes the organization's dedication to ethical AI practices.[135]

- **Holistic Training Data Review:** Rather than a piecemeal assessment, the entire data pipeline—right from data collection to preprocessing—should be reviewed. This will ensure that biases aren't introduced inadvertently at any stage.[136]

---

[134] https://blog.iil.com/the-impact-of-artificial-intelligence-on-stakeholder-relations-management-practices/

[135] https://www3.weforum.org/docs/WEF_A_Holistic_Guide_to_Approaching_AI_Fairness_Education_in_Organizations_2021.pdf

[136] https://www.ncbi.nlm.nih.gov/pmc/articles/PMC10764412/

- **Continuous Monitoring and Feedback Loops:** Establish mechanisms that allow users and stakeholders to provide feedback on any biases they observe. This continuous monitoring system, combined with automated checks, can ensure that biases are identified and addressed promptly.

- **Open Source and Peer Review:** By open-sourcing AI models or algorithms, or at least subjecting them to third-party audits and peer reviews, organizations can benefit from the scrutiny of the wider AI and cybersecurity communities.[137] This uncovers latent biases and provides insights into potential improvements.

- **Fairness Metrics:** Incorporate fairness metrics into the testing and validation phases. Tools like Fairness Indicators can quantify biases, providing a clear picture of where interventions are needed.

- **Diversity in AI Training:** Beyond the data and algorithms, it's essential to ensure diversity in those who develop and train AI models. This includes promoting gender, racial, and experiential diversity within AI teams to get a broad range of insights and perspectives.

- **Scenario Testing:** Implement real-world scenario testing to understand how the AI system behaves in diverse situations. This not only tests the system's fairness but also its overall effectiveness in dynamic environments.

- **Transparent Documentation:** Ensure that there's comprehensive documentation available for every AI system, detailing how it works, the kind of data it was trained on, the fairness metrics used, and any known biases or limitations.

- **Ethical Training for Developers:** Provide regular training sessions on ethics and bias for all those involved in the AI development process. Awareness is the first step towards addressing and mitigating biases.

As AI security solutions become more intricate and influential, the responsibility to ensure fairness becomes ever more critical. Adhering to these best practices can pave the way for not only ethically-sound AI security solutions but also more effective and trustworthy systems. The end goal is a digital environment where security decisions made by AI are as fair, if not fairer, than those made by humans.

---

[137] https://www.mdpi.com/2413-4155/6/1/3

10.2.　Ethical Data Collection and Management

In the digital age, data has ascended to become one of the most valuable resources, often termed the "new oil." From optimizing business operations to driving innovative solutions like AI, data has anchored itself as the fulcrum upon which modern technological advancements pivot. Yet, with great power comes great responsibility. As businesses increasingly collect, store, and process vast amounts of data, concerns over its ethical management have come to the fore.[138]

The process of data collection and management isn't merely a technical or logistical challenge—it is fundamentally an ethical dilemma. Ethical data practices are more than just compliance with privacy laws or data protection regulations. They're about treating the data of individuals with respect, understanding the profound implications of misuse, and ensuring that every piece of information is gathered with consent, used responsibly, and stored securely. Ethical considerations are paramount, especially in the age of AI, where biased or improperly handled data can lead to skewed algorithms with wide-reaching consequences.

Furthermore, as society becomes increasingly data-driven, there's a growing realization that ethical lapses in data management can erode public trust. For companies, this means not only reputational damage but also potential economic repercussions. Thus, ethical data practices are not just a moral imperative but also a business necessity.

The crux of ethical data management is to prioritize individual rights and societal good above all. It's about recognizing that every data point represents a real person with rights, feelings, and aspirations. Therefore, every data-driven decision, whether made by humans or AI, should be approached with the utmost care, empathy, and responsibility.[139]

As we delve deeper into this section, we will uncover the critical aspects of ethical data collection and management, from understanding the nuances of informed consent to ensuring data minimization and purpose limitation. It's a journey towards constructing

---

[138] https://ukdataservice.ac.uk/learning-hub/research-data-management/ethical-issues/consent-for-data-sharing/

[139] https://www.ncbi.nlm.nih.gov/pmc/articles/PMC8662857/

a digital ecosystem where the rights of individuals are upheld and respected, and where data serves as a force for good.

10.2.1.   *Informed Consent: Respecting User Rights*

Informed consent is a foundational principle in both medical ethics and data privacy. It underscores the basic human right of autonomy, granting individuals control over their own information and decisions about how it's used. In the realm of data collection and management, informed consent is not merely a formality but a reflection of genuine respect for the individuals from whom data is sourced.

When individuals provide their data, whether it's personal information for a social media profile or health metrics for a research study, they often do so with certain expectations. They anticipate that their data will be used for the reasons they've been informed about and that it won't be misappropriated for other purposes. The key here is clarity. Often, companies hide behind legalese, lengthy terms of service, or opaque data practices, leaving users unaware of how their data might be used. This approach runs counter to the very spirit of informed consent.

Real informed consent in the digital realm involves:

- **Transparency:** Providing clear, concise, and jargon-free explanations about how the data will be used, stored, and potentially shared.

- **Voluntariness:** Ensuring that users aren't coerced into sharing data and that they understand they have the right to withdraw consent at any time.

- **Specificity:** Clearly specifying the purposes for which the data is being collected, ensuring that there's no ambiguity.

- **Revocability:** Allowing users to retract their consent, and putting mechanisms in place to delete or anonymize their data if they choose to do so.

Moreover, informed consent is an ongoing process. As data practices and business objectives evolve, it's essential that companies regularly reassess their consent mechanisms, ensuring they remain relevant and genuinely informative.

By prioritizing informed consent, organizations not only safeguard themselves against potential legal and reputational risks but also strengthen the bond of trust with their users. It lays the foundation for an ethical relationship between data collectors and individuals, ensuring that the digital landscape remains user-centric and respects individual autonomy. As we progress, we'll explore other dimensions of ethical data collection and management, understanding that each is interlinked and essential for creating a truly ethical data ecosystem.

10.2.2. Data Minimization: Collecting Only What's Needed

In an age where data is often equated with gold, the urge to amass vast amounts of information can be tempting for organizations. However, from both a security and an ethical standpoint, this "collect it all" mentality can be problematic. Data minimization, a cornerstone principle of many data protection frameworks, advocates for collecting only the data that's directly relevant and necessary for specific purposes.

The benefits of data minimization are manifold. Firstly, from a purely pragmatic viewpoint, less data means a smaller target. When breaches occur, organizations that have practiced data minimization expose less information, reducing potential harm to users and lessening the reputational damage. Secondly, by collecting only the essentials, organizations can more efficiently manage and protect the data they hold. It becomes easier to categorize, analyze, and store data when there's less of it, and redundancy is reduced.

Several key practices encompass the principle of data minimization:

- **Clear Purpose Definition:** Before collecting data, organizations should have a clear understanding of why they need it. Each piece of information should correlate with a specific business or operational need.

- **Regular Data Audits:** Regular assessments of stored data can help organizations identify and dispose of any unnecessary or outdated information.

- **Limiting Data Retention:** Establishing clear policies on data retention ensures that information is not kept indefinitely. Once data has served its purpose or is no longer relevant, it should be deleted or anonymized.

- **User-Centric Collection:** Giving users the option to decide what information they're comfortable sharing. Often, users might not be aware of the granular details being collected about them. By providing clear options and opt-outs, organizations can ensure they respect user boundaries.

Data minimization also reflects a broader ethical commitment. It signifies that an organization respects the privacy of its users, valuing it over potential data-driven insights that might be gleaned from excessive data hoarding. It's a recognition that in the vast landscape of data, quality and relevance supersede sheer quantity.

The conversation about data minimization naturally leads us to ponder other ethical facets of data management. How do we ensure, for instance, that the data we've ethically collected is also used and shared in ethical ways? The journey through data ethics is complex, but each principle, like data minimization, illuminates a part of the path.

10.2.3.   Ethical Handling of Sensitive Data

Sensitive data, by its very definition, implies information that can have profound implications if misused. This category often includes data like financial records, medical histories, personal identification details, and other unique identifiers that can be tied back to an individual or entity. Ensuring the ethical handling of such information isn't just about maintaining trust or adhering to regulations—it's a moral responsibility that underscores the integrity of an organization.[140]

At the heart of the ethical handling of sensitive data is the understanding of the potential harm that could ensue if this data were to be misused or accessed without authorization. Identity theft, financial fraud, discrimination, or even threats to personal safety can arise from mishandled sensitive data. Therefore, the stakes are incredibly high, demanding meticulous care in both collection and management.

Some key considerations in the ethical handling of sensitive data include:

- **Clear Classification:** Properly classifying data according to its sensitivity helps in laying down specific access controls. Not everyone in an organization needs access to all pieces of data. By delineating who gets access to what, the potential for accidental or deliberate misuse diminishes.

---

[140] https://studentprivacy.ed.gov/sites/default/files/resource_document/file/checklist_data_breach _response_092012_0.pdf, https://www.oaic.gov.au/privacy/privacy-guidance-for-organisations-and-government-agencies/preventing-preparing-for-and-responding-to-data-breaches/data-breach-preparation-and-response/part-2-preparing-a-data-breach-response-plan, https://esoftskills.com/healthcare/ensuring-data-privacy-and-ethical-handling-of-patient-digital-information/, and https://www.travelers.com/resources/business-topics/cyber-security/data-breach-incident-response-plan

- **Encryption and Secure Storage:** Sensitive data should be encrypted both at rest and in transit. This ensures that even if there were unauthorized access or data leaks, the information remains unintelligible without the proper decryption keys.

- **Purpose Limitation:** Sensitive data should be used solely for the purpose for which it was collected. For instance, medical data collected for health monitoring should not be repurposed for targeted advertising without explicit consent.

- **Transparency with Users:** Organizations need to be upfront about how they'll use sensitive data. Comprehensive privacy policies, clear terms of service, and user-friendly prompts are crucial in ensuring that users are aware of how their data will be handled.

- **Incident Response Plans:** Despite best efforts, data breaches can happen. Organizations need to have a clear incident response plan in place for such scenarios, focusing on swift containment and notification to the affected parties.

To further emphasize the criticality of this topic, we can look to numerous real-world incidents where the mishandling of sensitive data led to significant repercussions, both for individuals and for companies. It's a cautionary reminder that ethical considerations aren't abstract concepts—they have real-world implications and require proactive measures.

As we progress in our exploration of AI and data management's ethical dimensions, the interplay of technology and ethics becomes even more intricate. As AI systems become more adept at processing and analyzing vast datasets, the lines between general and sensitive data can blur, making the debate around transparency and accountability all the more pivotal.

10.2.4.   The Role of Privacy by Design in Ethical Data Management

The modern digital landscape, saturated with sophisticated tools and technologies, commands an evolved approach to data privacy—one that's integrated right at the foundational stages of product or system design. This proactive approach is captured by the paradigm of "Privacy by Design" (PbD). Rooted in the belief that privacy is not a luxury or an add-on but a fundamental right, PbD ensures that privacy is embedded intrinsically within technology, operational processes, and business practices.[141]

PbD was developed in the 1990s by Dr. Ann Cavoukian, the former Information and Privacy Commissioner of Ontario, Canada. It was conceptualized as a framework that businesses could implement throughout the life cycle of their data processing activities, from the earliest design stages right through to the operational stages. At its core, PbD challenges the long-standing dichotomy between privacy and security, positing that the two can and should co-exist.

Here are the key principles and the relevance of Privacy by Design:

- **Proactive not Reactive–Preventative not Remedial:** Instead of being an afterthought, privacy considerations are central from the outset. This translates to fewer privacy breaches and lessens the need for damage control, resulting in both cost savings and enhanced user trust.

- **Privacy as the Default Setting:** Users shouldn't have to jump through hoops to ensure their privacy is safeguarded. By making privacy the default setting, organizations assure users that their data will not be shared without explicit consent.

- **Privacy Embedded into Design:** Privacy isn't a standalone feature but is integrated into the system and design architecture. This holistic approach ensures that privacy is an inherent aspect of the product or service.

- **Full Functionality—Positive-Sum, not Zero-Sum:** The idea is to avoid trade-offs between privacy and security. Systems designed with PbD in mind achieve both objectives without compromising on either.

- **End-to-End Security—Lifecycle Protection:** Data is protected throughout its entire lifecycle, from initial collection to eventual disposal. This comprehensive approach ensures gaps aren't left open at any stage.

---

[141] https://formiti.com/why-privacy-by-design-is-essential-for-ai-projects/, https://en.wikipedia.org/wiki/Privacy_by_design, https://privacy.ucsc.edu/resources/privacy-by-design---foundational-principles.pdf, and https://iapp.org/resources/article/oipc-privacy-by-design-resources/

- **Visibility and Transparency:** Operations remain visible and transparent to both users and providers, ensuring accountability at all levels. This fosters trust and encourages more users to engage with the system.

- **Respect for User Privacy:** Ultimately, the user's interests are at the forefront, ensuring data minimization, strong security measures, and easy-to-understand privacy terms.

With the proliferation of AI and machine learning tools, which often require vast amounts of data to function optimally, the principles of Privacy by Design become even more critical. Implementing PbD in AI-driven environments ensures that while machines learn and evolve, the sanctity of personal data remains uncompromised.

As we move forward to explore transparency and accountability in AI systems, it's worth noting how Privacy by Design plays a pivotal role in setting the stage for ethical considerations, paving the way for more user-centric AI solutions.

10.3. Transparent and Accountable AI

As we delve deeper into the digital age, it becomes increasingly evident that while artificial intelligence systems possess the potential to reshape industries, influence economies, and alter personal experiences, they also come with the inherent obligation of being transparent and accountable. These traits are not just ancillary qualities–they represent the very bedrock upon which public trust in AI will be built or shattered.[142]

Transparency in AI refers to the clarity and openness with which these systems operate, ensuring that their workings are interpretable and understandable, not just by experts but also by the broader public. A transparent AI makes its decision-making processes clear, demystifying the layers of computations that go into producing a specific output. This is particularly pertinent when decisions made by AI systems have substantial ramifications, such as in healthcare, finance, or judicial systems.

Conversely, accountability in AI speaks to the responsibility and ownership of outcomes produced by these systems. As the adage goes, "With great power comes great

---

[142] https://link.springer.com/article/10.1007/s00146-023-01635-y and
https://blog.hubspot.com/marketing/ai-transparency

responsibility." AI developers, operators, and stakeholders must be ready to answer for the results of their systems, especially when unintended biases, errors, or malfunctions occur. In essence, there should be a mechanism in place to hold entities accountable for the consequences of AI decisions.

The intertwined notions of transparency and accountability have a shared purpose: they collectively ensure that AI systems serve humanity effectively and ethically. As AI grows more pervasive, the urgency to institute transparent and accountable mechanisms cannot be understated. With these principles as our compass, we will explore the facets and intricacies of making AI not just smart but also open and responsible.

10.3.1.   The Need for Transparency in AI Algorithms

Artificial intelligence, in its multifaceted forms, promises transformational change across industries. Yet, as with all tools of profound influence, it becomes imperative to ensure that its operations are clear and understandable. Transparency in AI algorithms is not merely a theoretical or philosophical desire—it is a practical necessity for multiple reasons.

Firstly, transparency fosters trust. As AI systems increasingly influence critical sectors like healthcare, finance, and law enforcement, understanding how these systems arrive at decisions becomes paramount. If an AI system, for instance, denies a loan application or recommends a medical procedure, stakeholders—from end-users to professionals— must have confidence in the decision-making process.

> *Without clarity on the "how" and "why" of algorithmic decisions, trust deteriorates rapidly.*

Secondly, transparency is key to addressing biases. Only when an algorithm's workings are transparent can biases, intentional or otherwise, be detected and rectified. An opaque system remains a black box, with its decisions unquestioned and unchecked, potentially perpetuating harmful stereotypes or erroneous assumptions. For instance, a recruitment AI that consistently sidelines applications from certain demographics may be unknowingly relying on biased historical data. Transparency helps identify and correct such tendencies.

Additionally, transparency facilitates regulatory compliance. As governments and institutions move to regulate AI, ensuring algorithmic transparency becomes a requirement, not just an option. Regulations, such as the European Union's General Data Protection Regulation (GDPR), grant individuals the right to explanations when subjected to automated decisions. Meeting such requirements necessitates an inherent level of transparency in AI systems.[143]

Lastly, transparent algorithms enable continuous learning and improvement. An open system invites scrutiny, feedback, and collaboration. When AI researchers, developers, and users can understand and analyze an AI's operations, they can suggest refinements, innovations, and adaptations, making the AI system more robust and effective over time.

In essence, while the technical marvel of AI is undeniably captivating, its long-term success and societal acceptance hinge on its transparency. As we navigate deeper into the realms of AI, ensuring this clarity becomes our collective responsibility.

10.3.2.   Accountability in AI Decision-making

Accountability, often considered a cornerstone of ethical systems, becomes even more pivotal when navigating the intricate world of artificial intelligence. While AI's capabilities to analyze vast data sets and derive insights are unparalleled, the autonomous nature of many AI systems has raised concerns over responsibility, especially when things go awry. In the realm of AI, accountability isn't just about assigning blame, but also about understanding, correcting, and improving:[144]

- **Defining Responsibility:** One of the first challenges in AI accountability is determining who (or what) should be held responsible. Is it the algorithm, the developers, the deployers, or the users? For example, if an autonomous vehicle malfunctions and causes an accident, identifying where the responsibility lies is vital. Traditional systems often have a linear flow of responsibility, but with AI, this flow is more complex due to the self-learning nature of many AI models.

---

[143] https://www.sciencespo.fr/public/sites/sciencespo.fr.public/files/SIMSEK%20Can.pdf and
https://www.brookings.edu/articles/the-ai-regulatory-toolbox-how-governments-can-discover-algorithmic-harms/

[144] https://link.springer.com/article/10.1007/s00146-022-01481-4 and https://chiefexecutive.net/who-is-accountable-when-ai-fails/

- **Traceable Decision Pathways:** Accountability requires the ability to retrace an AI system's decision-making pathways. It's not enough to know that an AI system made a decision–understanding the how and why is crucial. This traceability ensures that when AI-driven decisions impact individual rights or societal norms, they can be audited and assessed.

- **Corrective Measures:** Merely identifying errors is not sufficient–accountability also encompasses taking corrective action. If a financial AI system, for instance, inadvertently indulges in unethical trading practices, corrective measures might involve not just addressing that specific instance but also refining the algorithm to prevent future missteps.

- **Legal and Regulatory Frameworks:** Accountability in AI is also shaped by legal norms and regulatory frameworks. As legislators around the world grapple with the nuances of AI, laws are being drafted to ensure accountability. These laws often demand clear documentation, rigorous testing, and regular audits to ensure that AI systems adhere to ethical and legal standards.

- **Open Communication Channels:** To promote accountability, organizations must establish open channels of communication. These channels allow stakeholders, be they end-users, regulators, or affected parties, to raise concerns, seek clarifications, or challenge AI-driven decisions. In a healthcare setting, for example, if an AI recommends a particular treatment pathway, patients and physicians should have a mechanism to understand and potentially contest that decision.

- **Ethical Training and Awareness:** Lastly, cultivating a culture of accountability requires consistent training and awareness. AI developers, data scientists, and operators should be well-versed in ethical considerations, ensuring that they remain vigilant to potential pitfalls and proactive in addressing them.

As AI systems become more autonomous, the emphasis on accountability becomes paramount. AI, given its profound influence, should not operate unchecked. Instead, it should function within a framework that respects human values, societal norms, and legal mandates, with accountability being at the very heart of this framework.

10.3.3.   Guidelines for Ethical AI Audits

As artificial intelligence gains ground across diverse sectors, ensuring that its applications are ethical becomes crucial. AI audits, in this context, emerge as an effective mechanism to evaluate and ensure that AI systems are designed, developed, and deployed ethically. Much like financial audits aim to guarantee fiscal integrity, ethical AI audits are designed to vouch for the moral and ethical soundness of AI systems. Here's a closer look at the guidelines for conducting these audits:[145]

- **Comprehensive Scope:** At the outset, define a comprehensive scope for the audit. This should encompass the entire lifecycle of the AI system, from its inception and design phase to its deployment and feedback loop. Ensure that all critical aspects, such as data sourcing, algorithm design, output interpretation, and real-world application, are included.

- **Multidisciplinary Teams:** Ethical AI audits should be performed by teams that bring together a range of expertise. This could include data scientists, ethicists, sociologists, and industry-specific experts. A diverse team ensures a holistic evaluation, accounting for technical, ethical, societal, and practical considerations.

- **Transparent Evaluation Criteria:** Establish clear and transparent criteria against which the AI system will be assessed. These criteria should be based on universally recognized ethical principles, industry best practices, and any relevant regulatory guidelines. The criteria should be made public to foster trust and clarity.

- **Active Stakeholder Involvement:** Engage with a broad spectrum of stakeholders throughout the audit process. This includes the AI's intended users, those potentially affected by its decisions, developers, and even critics. Their feedback can offer invaluable insights and help identify blind spots.

- **Real-world Testing:** Go beyond theoretical evaluations. Test the AI system in real-world scenarios to gauge its ethical implications on the ground. Such

---

[145] https://www.law.com/legaltechnews/2023/10/20/navigating-the-ai-audit-a-comprehensive-guide-to-best-practices/ and https://www.isaca.org/resources/news-and-trends/industry-news/2022/ai-ethics-and-the-role-of-it-auditors

testing can reveal unforeseen challenges or biases that may not emerge in controlled or simulated environments.

- **Continuous Auditing:** AI systems, especially those that learn and evolve over time, should be subject to periodic ethical audits. These recurring audits will account for the system's evolution and any changing external factors, ensuring its continued adherence to ethical standards.

- **Transparent Reporting:** Upon completion of the audit, publish a detailed report outlining the audit's findings, recommendations, and any corrective measures taken. This promotes transparency, builds trust among stakeholders, and serves as a benchmark for future audits.

- **Feedback Mechanisms:** Post-audit, set up mechanisms for continuous feedback. Stakeholders should have channels to report any ethical concerns or discrepancies they observe as the AI system operates, ensuring that the audit's outcomes are consistently implemented and monitored.

- **Ethical Training for Auditors:** Ensure that auditors are well-versed in both the technical nuances of AI and the ethical considerations pertinent to its deployment. Training programs can equip auditors with the necessary skills to discern and address complex ethical dilemmas in AI applications.

In essence, ethical AI audits are not mere formalities but are instrumental in fostering AI systems that respect and uphold human values. By following these guidelines, organizations can instill trust, ensure compliance, and pave the way for AI applications that truly benefit society.

10.3.4. Real-world Case Studies: Successes and Failures in AI Transparency

Transparency in AI has been a topic of rigorous debate and concern, with various stakeholders advocating for clarity in how AI systems make decisions. Delving into real-world case studies offers rich insights into the practical ramifications of transparency, or the lack thereof, in AI. Here are some prominent instances highlighting both the successes and failures in the realm of AI transparency.

IBM's Watson for Oncology: Success[146]

- **Background**: IBM's Watson for Oncology was developed to assist doctors by suggesting cancer treatment options based on the analysis of vast amounts of medical literature.
- **Transparency Achievement**: IBM made it clear that Watson's suggestions were based on the literature it had been trained on and should be treated as recommendations rather than final decisions. This transparency helped physicians understand the basis of Watson's suggestions and use them as a complementary tool in their decision-making process.

Amazon's Recruiting Tool: Failure[147]

- **Background**: Amazon developed an AI-driven recruiting tool meant to review job applications and shortlist candidates.
- **Transparency Issue**: The system was discovered to be biased against female candidates, leading to a public relations setback for Amazon. Lack of transparency into how the AI made its decisions and the kind of data it was trained on became a significant concern. Amazon eventually disbanded the tool.

DeepMind's AlphaGo: Success[148]

- **Background**: AlphaGo, developed by Google's DeepMind, defeated the world champion of the game Go in a landmark achievement for AI.
- **Transparency Achievement**: DeepMind was quite open about how AlphaGo was trained using both supervised learning from historical games and reinforcement learning from playing against itself. This transparency demystified the AI's strategies and capabilities, making its achievements more understandable to the general public.

---

[146] https://www.statnews.com/2017/09/05/watson-ibm-cancer/ and https://spectrum.ieee.org/how-ibm-watson-overpromised-and-underdelivered-on-ai-health-care

[147] https://www.businessinsider.com/amazon-built-ai-to-hire-people-discriminated-against-women-2018-10

[148] https://github.com/Zeta36/chess-alpha-zero

COMPAS in the U.S. Criminal Justice System: Failure[149]

- **Background**: COMPAS (Correctional Offender Management Profiling for Alternative Sanctions) is an algorithm used in the U.S. to predict the likelihood of a defendant becoming a repeat offender.
- **Transparency Issue**: Concerns arose when it was discovered that the system might be biased against certain racial groups. The proprietary nature of the algorithm made it difficult for third parties to analyze or understand its decision-making processes, raising significant ethical and transparency concerns.

OpenAI's GPT-4: Success[150]

- **Background**: OpenAI's GPT-4 is one of the most advanced language models, capable of producing human-like text.
- **Transparency Achievement**: OpenAI has been forthright about its goals, development methodologies, and the potential risks and limitations of GPT-4. Their transparency initiatives, including research publications and detailed blogs, offer users and researchers valuable insights into the model's workings.

Facial Recognition Misidentifications: Failure[151]

- **Background**: Several facial recognition systems have been deployed in public spaces and for law enforcement purposes.
- **Transparency Issue**: Numerous instances have come to light where these systems have wrongly identified individuals, especially from certain ethnic groups. The lack of transparency in how these models are trained and the data sets they're based on has led to calls for stricter regulations or outright bans in certain jurisdictions.

Drawing lessons from these case studies, it becomes evident that transparency in AI isn't just an ethical imperative but also a practical necessity. A transparent approach not only wins public trust but also allows for constructive feedback, leading to better and more reliable AI systems.

---

[149] https://afraenkel.github.io/fairness-book/content/04-compas.html

[150] https://community.openai.com/t/no-access-to-api-with-gpt-4-model-although-there-is-a-history-of-successful-payments/298980 and https://hexaviewtech.com/blog/openai-gpt-4/

[151] https://news.utdallas.edu/science-technology/racial-bias-facial-recognition-2020/ and https://www.frontiersin.org/journals/psychology/articles/10.3389/fpsyg.2020.00208/full

10.4. The Broader Societal Impacts of AI

Artificial intelligence, as a frontier technology, does more than merely reconfigure the algorithms and databases at the heart of digital systems. It holds the transformative power to reshape societies, sculpt economies, and redefine human roles in profound ways. As AI systems become more deeply embedded in our daily lives, the ripple effects of their influence transcend mere technological advancement and raise fundamental questions about societal values, economic equity, and the essence of human experience.

The implications of AI are multifold and complex. From automating jobs to reshaping how we consume information, AI is a double-edged sword that presents both tremendous opportunities and notable challenges. For instance, while AI has the potential to address pressing global issues, such as climate change and healthcare delivery, it also risks amplifying existing social disparities, encroaching on privacy, and undermining democratic principles.

Moreover, the integration of AI into society fosters new dynamics in human-machine interactions. As AI agents become our collaborators, caregivers, and even companions, we are compelled to reconsider the nature of empathy, trust, and relationships. What does it mean to form bonds with non-human entities? How do we ensure that our ethical and emotional compass isn't skewed in an AI-augmented world?

Furthermore, as AI starts to make decisions traditionally reserved for humans, it challenges the established notions of accountability, autonomy, and moral responsibility. When an AI-driven vehicle makes a life-altering decision in a split second, who is to be held accountable? When an AI system inadvertently perpetuates bias, who shoulders the blame?

Moving forward, it's paramount for technologists, policymakers, and society at large to engage in collective introspection. As we stand on the cusp of an AI revolution, it's essential to approach the broader societal impacts of AI with a balance of enthusiasm, caution, and responsibility. This section delves deeper into these multifaceted consequences and explores the broader canvas of AI's influence on society.

10.4.1.   The Dual-use Dilemma: Beneficial and Harmful AI Applications

Every technological innovation throughout history, from the printing press to nuclear energy, has carried with it the duality of being a tool for progress or a weapon for destruction. AI is no exception to this dual-use paradigm. Its profound capabilities promise to revolutionize countless sectors, from healthcare to education, by introducing efficiencies, personalization, and predictive insights. Yet, these same capabilities can be and are being, weaponized in ways that challenge ethical norms and societal structures.[152]

The promise of AI for beneficial applications is evident. In medicine, AI-driven tools can identify diseases at early stages, even before symptoms manifest, enabling timely intervention. In the realm of environmental science, AI models predict climate changes with unparalleled precision, informing policymakers about necessary measures. In education, personalized learning models cater to the unique needs of each student, ensuring no one is left behind. These are just a few of the myriad ways AI contributes positively to society.

However, the darker side of AI's dual-use potential cannot be ignored. Take, for instance, the domain of information dissemination. AI-driven "deepfakes" can fabricate hyper-realistic video content, placing words into the mouths of public figures they never uttered. This capability threatens to undermine the very nature of truth in our digital age, offering tools for misinformation campaigns that can sway public opinion or even influence elections. Similarly, AI can be harnessed by malicious actors to automate cyber-attacks, bypass security measures, or engage in surveillance on an unprecedented scale.

It's essential to acknowledge that the line between beneficial and harmful applications isn't always clear-cut. A technology designed with noble intentions can inadvertently create harm when placed in the wrong hands or when unforeseen consequences emerge. Consider AI-driven social media algorithms: initially designed to keep users engaged and connected, they've come under scrutiny for potentially promoting echo chambers and polarizing content.

The dual-use dilemma of AI necessitates robust frameworks for governance, ethics, and oversight. Decision-makers must walk a fine line, fostering innovation and reaping the

---

[152] https://www.veltris.com/blogs/digital-engineering/8-applications-of-artificial-intelligence-in-education/, https://www.v7labs.com/blog/ai-in-education, and https://link.springer.com/article/10.1007/s10676-023-09703-z

benefits of AI while concurrently implementing safeguards against its malicious applications. As AI's capabilities continue to grow, society will be continually tasked with reevaluating its relationship with this powerful tool, ensuring that its vast potential is harnessed for the greater good and not for harm.

10.4.2.   Ethical Considerations in AI's Global Reach

In an increasingly interconnected world, the innovations and challenges posed by AI are not confined to individual countries or cultures. They spill over borders, affecting global economies, political landscapes, and socio-cultural dynamics. AI's global reach, however, is not uniform. Its proliferation varies across nations, governed by technological infrastructure, socio-economic factors, and political will. As AI continues to weave into the fabric of our global society, it brings forth a plethora of ethical considerations that require multinational deliberation and action.[153]

First and foremost is the issue of AI's accessibility. While developed nations, with their robust tech infrastructures and ample resources, surge ahead in the AI race, many developing countries risk being left behind. This digital divide has profound implications, as those without access to advanced AI tools might miss out on its potential benefits in healthcare, education, agriculture, and more. Over time, this could exacerbate existing socio-economic disparities on a global scale. Ensuring equitable access to AI technologies is, therefore, an ethical imperative that calls for collaborations between governments, industries, and international bodies.

Another ethical quandary emerges in the form of cultural biases embedded within AI algorithms. AI models, especially those developed in Western nations, might inadvertently contain biases that reflect the cultural, socio-economic, or political perspectives of their place of origin. When deployed globally, these biases can lead to misinterpretations or even reinforce harmful stereotypes. For instance, facial recognition systems trained predominantly on one racial or ethnic group might falter when recognizing others, leading to significant implications in areas like law enforcement or surveillance.

---

[153] https://uxdesign.cc/bias-in-ai-is-a-mirror-of-our-culture-3607bd795c57?gi=e744006b82dc, https://solutionsreview.com/data-management/how-to-plan-for-data-sovereignty-in-the-age-of-ai/, and https://www.forbes.com/sites/forbestechcouncil/2023/07/19/unveiling-the-role-of-ai-algorithms-unmasking-societal-inequities-and-cultural-prejudices/?sh=58da9c982f60

Then there's the matter of data sovereignty and privacy. As companies and governments deploy AI systems across borders, questions arise about who owns the data, where it's stored, and how it's used. Different nations have varying standards and regulations concerning data privacy. Ethical challenges emerge when AI systems, designed per one country's regulations, are deployed in another with more stringent or differing privacy norms. This can lead to potential misuse or misinterpretation of data, infringing on individual rights and national interests.

Lastly, the global nature of AI means that its negative implications, like job losses due to automation, might be felt more acutely in certain sectors or regions than others. A factory's automation in one country might lead to unemployment in another where parts were manually assembled. Such scenarios demand international dialogues and potentially even compensatory mechanisms to ensure that the benefits and burdens of AI are distributed fairly.

In summary, as AI's tendrils extend globally, it becomes imperative for nations to engage in cooperative and comprehensive dialogues, sharing best practices and jointly addressing the ethical challenges posed. Only through collective action can we ensure that AI's global reach is both beneficial and just.

10.4.3.   The Future of Work: AI's Role and Ethical Implications

The rapid evolution of AI has redefined the landscape of the global workforce. With automation and AI-driven solutions taking center stage, traditional job roles are undergoing transformation, leading to a radical shift in the nature of employment. The future of work under the influence of AI holds immense promise, but it is also intertwined with a multitude of ethical concerns that need meticulous attention.

At the outset, AI's ability to enhance efficiency and productivity is commendable. Tasks that once consumed substantial time and resources can now be executed swiftly and accurately by algorithms. From automating mundane administrative chores to performing intricate data analyses, AI is revolutionizing industries. This surge in productivity could potentially fuel economic growth, pave the way for innovative job roles, and even allow humans to engage more deeply in creative, strategic, or human-centric tasks, where empathy and interpersonal skills are paramount.

However, on the flip side, there's an undeniable concern: job displacement due to automation. As machines take over repetitive tasks, certain job roles, especially in sectors like manufacturing, customer service, and transportation, face the threat of becoming obsolete. This raises pertinent questions about the future of those employed in these roles. Will they be rendered jobless or can they be retrained and absorbed into new roles? The ethical challenge here is ensuring a just transition for these workers. Companies and governments bear a responsibility to provide education, training, and support to aid this workforce in adapting to the AI-augmented landscape.

Additionally, AI's influence extends to the very nature of work itself. The rise of AI-powered tools facilitates remote work and flexible schedules, potentially leading to a more diverse and inclusive work environment. But it also raises questions about work-life balance, surveillance in the workplace, and the potential erosion of personal boundaries as AI systems track productivity and efficiency, sometimes encroaching on personal time or space.

Moreover, AI's predictive capabilities, while valuable in talent acquisition and employee assessment, pose ethical dilemmas related to privacy and bias. AI-driven recruitment tools might inadvertently favor certain demographics over others or might make predictions based on data that's not truly indicative of an individual's potential or capabilities. Such biases, if unchecked, could perpetuate inequality and hamper diversity in the workplace.[154]

In envisioning the future of work, it's clear that while AI offers transformative potential, it's also a double-edged sword. Balancing the advantages of AI-driven efficiencies with the ethical considerations of job displacement, privacy, and fairness is a challenge that businesses, governments, and civil society must collaboratively address. As we stand at this pivotal juncture, our choices will shape not just the future of work but the very fabric of our societies.

10.4.4. Long-term Considerations: AI, Ethics, and Humanity's Future

As AI technologies advance at an unprecedented pace, humanity faces pivotal decisions about the ethical and societal implications of integrating such powerful tools into our daily lives and broader systems. While short- and mid-term concerns focus largely on areas like job displacement or algorithmic fairness, the long-term considerations delve into the very essence of human existence, our values, and our place in the cosmos.

---

[154] https://www.servicedeskinstitute.com/five-ethical-issues-of-ai-in-the-modern-workplace/ and
https://www.infosecurity-magazine.com/opinions/navigating-ai-job-losse/

Firstly, there's the matter of superintelligent AI. Should we eventually create machines that surpass human intelligence in all domains, we'll be faced with profound questions about control and alignment. How can we ensure that such an entity's goals align with ours, especially when its cognitive capabilities outstrip our own? What measures do we take now to avoid potential pitfalls or existential threats that could arise from misaligned superintelligent systems in the future? The ethical considerations here touch upon safeguarding the very future of human civilization.

Beyond existential risks, there's the philosophical debate about consciousness and sentience in AI. If, in the distant future, we create machines that claim to have experiences, feelings, or a sense of self, how do we ethically respond? The moral consideration of potentially sentient AI delves into uncharted territory, prompting discussions about rights, responsibilities, and the nature of consciousness itself. Such debates would fundamentally challenge our understanding of entities deserving of moral consideration.

Furthermore, as AI becomes more integrated into our lives, the boundary between human and machine might blur, leading to complex questions about identity and augmentation. Brain-computer interfaces, for instance, could merge the biological with the digital, enhancing human capabilities but also raising ethical questions about autonomy, consent, and the nature of human experience. In a world where our thoughts could potentially be read, altered, or even shared, the very essence of privacy and individuality will be redefined.

There's also the broader societal aspect to consider. As AI systems increasingly shape our cultures, economies, and politics, how do we ensure that they do so in a way that upholds our collective values? How can we avoid potential dystopias where AI-driven surveillance states limit human freedoms or where algorithms dictate the course of human history without meaningful human input?

In the grand narrative of human history, the advent of AI is a seminal moment that demands foresight, wisdom, and a deep reflection on our values. As we chart this course into the unknown, the choices we make will resonate not just through the immediate decades but potentially for millennia.

Balancing innovation with ethical restraint, and technological prowess with philosophical insight, is the formidable challenge that lies ahead. Embracing this challenge is imperative, for it will define our legacy as stewards of a world on the cusp of an AI-driven evolution.

10.5.   Ethical Frameworks and AI Governance

In the unfolding tapestry of the AI era, where the dazzling promises of technology intertwine with intricate ethical dilemmas, the need for robust ethical frameworks and AI governance structures becomes paramount. These structures don't merely act as constraints but serve as guiding compasses, ensuring that the journey of AI evolution is anchored in human values, societal well-being, and long-term sustainability.

Ethical frameworks are not just academic exercises–they translate our shared values and philosophical foundations into actionable principles and guidelines. When constructed diligently, they help technology designers, policymakers, and users navigate the complex decision-making landscape associated with AI's development and deployment. By examining both the micro-level interactions (like algorithm design or data handling) and the macro-level implications (like societal impacts or global dynamics), ethical frameworks provide a holistic view that helps to anticipate challenges and mitigate risks.

AI governance, on the other hand, operationalizes these frameworks. It establishes the processes, institutions, and norms necessary to enforce ethical principles in real-world AI applications. Governance encompasses a wide range of activities, from the creation of regulatory policies and industry standards to the setting up of oversight bodies and community-driven initiatives.

The goal is to create an ecosystem where AI thrives but is also kept in check, ensuring its alignment with the broader interests of humanity.

In this rapidly advancing domain, one size does not fit all. Different regions, cultures, and communities might have varying perspectives on what ethical AI entails. Hence, the challenge is to create flexible governance structures that respect diversity while upholding universal human rights and freedoms. This delicate balance requires continuous dialogue, iterative learning, and the collective wisdom of stakeholders from all sectors of society.

As we delve into the intricacies of ethical frameworks and AI governance in this section, it's essential to remember the core intent: to shape a future where AI amplifies human potential, enriches our societies, and serves the greater good. While undoubtedly complex, this endeavor is a testament to our commitment to ensuring that the AI-driven future remains firmly rooted in our shared human heritage and aspirations.

10.5.1.   Existing Ethical Frameworks for AI and Their Limitations

The proliferation of AI technologies has catalyzed a concurrent surge in the development of ethical frameworks aimed at guiding AI's responsible growth. These frameworks, springing from diverse sources such as academia, tech giants, governments, and international organizations, often share common ground on principles but differ in nuances and approaches.

Among the most widely recognized is the set of guidelines proposed by the Organisation for Economic Co-operation and Development (OECD), which emphasizes values such as transparency, robustness, and respect for human rights. Similarly, companies like Google, Microsoft, and IBM have rolled out their own ethical principles for AI, highlighting aspects like fairness, accountability, and safety. The convergence around these broad themes indicates a shared realization of AI's potential pitfalls and the collective endeavor to sidestep them.[155]

However, the translation of these high-level principles into actionable practices remains a significant challenge. For instance, while most frameworks champion transparency, the practicality of making a complex deep learning model entirely transparent remains debated. Additionally, while fairness is universally touted, defining and measuring it in diverse cultural contexts is far from straightforward. The AI community still grapples with the multidimensionality of fairness, and one solution might inadvertently exacerbate bias in another context.

Furthermore, many existing ethical frameworks, while rich in ideals, often lack enforcement mechanisms. Voluntary adherence, though commendable, is hardly a guarantee, especially when economic incentives might push companies in the opposite direction. The absence of global consensus on some issues, combined with the intricacies of international law and geopolitics, further complicates the establishment of universally binding norms for AI ethics.

Lastly, while these frameworks have undeniably advanced the discourse on AI and ethics, they often stem from a predominantly Western perspective, sometimes overlooking non-Western ethical traditions and viewpoints. This Eurocentrism can inadvertently propagate biases and miss out on holistic solutions that diverse philosophical traditions might offer.

---

[155] https://ethicalgeo.org/ethics-board-at-ibm/ and https://www.oecd-ilibrary.org/science-and-technology/the-state-of-implementation-of-the-oecd-ai-principles-four-years-on_835641c9-en

While the existing ethical frameworks for AI have laid the essential groundwork, they are not without limitations. The journey ahead requires refining these principles, grounding them in practical realities, and fostering a more inclusive, global dialogue to ensure AI's ethical development across different socio-cultural landscapes.

10.5.2. *Establishing Robust AI Governance Structures*

AI governance refers to the combination of tools, policies, and procedures that organizations put in place to ensure that their AI systems operate effectively, ethically, and in compliance with relevant laws and regulations. A robust AI governance structure doesn't just provide oversight—it helps ensure that AI deployments align with organizational objectives, ethical commitments, and broader societal concerns.

The need for governance in AI is evident. As AI systems become increasingly integrated into various facets of society—from healthcare and finance to entertainment and transportation—the potential for harm, misuse, or unintended consequences also grows. Without proper governance, these tools can exacerbate social inequalities, expose vulnerabilities, and facilitate the misuse of technology in harmful ways.

Here are the key components of a robust AI governance structure:

- **Guidelines and Principles:** This is often the starting point for many organizations. Establishing clear ethical guidelines and principles offers a roadmap for AI developers and users. It sets the tone for what is acceptable and what isn't. However, principles alone aren't sufficient–they need to be paired with actionable guidelines that can be applied in real-world scenarios.

- **Review and Oversight Bodies:** Creating internal oversight committees or review boards comprising both technical and non-technical members can ensure that AI projects align with the organization's ethical commitments. These bodies can review AI projects at various stages of development, from inception to deployment, offering feedback and ensuring alignment with established guidelines.

- **Transparency Mechanisms:** Transparency in AI doesn't just involve making the code or algorithm public. It's about providing clarity on how decisions are made, the data sources, the potential biases in the data, and the potential impacts of AI decisions. This requires documentation standards and practices that capture the reasoning behind specific AI decisions.

- **Feedback Loops:** Effective governance is iterative. Organizations must establish mechanisms to gather feedback from AI system users and those affected by the system's decisions. This feedback provides insights into how the system operates in real-world conditions and where it might be falling short of its ethical or functional objectives.

- **Continuous Monitoring and Audit Trails:** AI systems, once deployed, need continuous monitoring to ensure they are operating as intended. This includes both performance monitoring and ethical monitoring. Audit trails, which log decisions and the rationale behind them, can be instrumental in case a decision needs to be reviewed or challenged.

- **Redress Mechanisms:** Even with the best intentions and robust governance, AI systems can and will make mistakes. Organizations must establish mechanisms through which individuals can challenge AI decisions, seek redress, or even receive compensation if harmed.

- **Stakeholder Engagement:** AI doesn't operate in a vacuum. Its impacts ripple across various stakeholders, from end-users and customers to broader society. Engaging with these stakeholders, understanding their concerns, and adjusting governance structures in response is crucial for comprehensive oversight.

Establishing these governance structures might seem daunting, but they are essential. Not only do they protect organizations from potential pitfalls and liabilities, but they also ensure that AI is harnessed for the collective good, striking a balance between innovation and responsibility. As AI continues to reshape the world, strong governance structures will be the anchor that keeps its vast potential grounded in ethical and responsible use.

10.5.3.   The Role of Regulatory Bodies and International Cooperation

In the age of AI, the ethical and regulatory landscape is increasingly complex. With AI systems breaking conventional boundaries and operating on a global scale, the role of regulatory bodies and international cooperation has never been more critical. These entities set the standards for how AI systems are developed, deployed, and maintained, ensuring that they adhere to globally recognized ethical and legal norms. The pivotal role of regulatory bodies involves:

- **Standard Setting:** Regulatory agencies, whether they are national bodies like the U.S. Federal Trade Commission (FTC) or international ones like the European Union's European Commission, play a vital role in establishing the standards and guidelines for AI. By setting baseline requirements for AI systems, regulatory bodies ensure that organizations are held accountable for the ethical implications of their AI tools.

- **Oversight and Auditing:** Beyond just setting standards, regulatory bodies often have the authority to conduct audits, ensuring that organizations are complying with the established guidelines. This can be especially crucial in industries where AI has significant implications, such as healthcare or finance.

- **Sanctioning and Enforcement:** When organizations or individuals violate regulatory guidelines or standards, these bodies have the authority to impose penalties, ranging from fines to stricter sanctions. This deters unethical AI practices and holds violators accountable.

Navigating a global landscape requires:

- **Shared Guidelines and Norms:** As AI systems become increasingly interconnected across borders, there's a growing need for shared guidelines and norms. International bodies like the United Nations or World Trade Organization can spearhead efforts to create these shared norms, ensuring that AI systems are consistently ethical, irrespective of their country of origin.

- **Collaborative Research:** The challenges of AI are vast, complex, and not limited to any single nation. By fostering international collaboration in research, countries can pool resources, share insights, and collaboratively address some of the most pressing AI challenges.

- **Harmonizing Regulations:** A major challenge for global corporations is navigating the patchwork of AI regulations across different countries. International cooperation can help harmonize these regulations, making it easier for companies to operate globally while still adhering to ethical and regulatory standards.

The broader implications of international AI governance include:

- **Geopolitical Considerations:** As nations race to become AI superpowers, there's a risk that competitive dynamics overshadow the shared challenges posed by AI. International cooperation encourages nations to view AI as a shared frontier, not just a competitive arena.

- **Shared Ethical Foundations:** Different cultures might have varying perspectives on ethics. International collaboration fosters a dialogue, enabling the creation of AI systems that respect diverse viewpoints while adhering to shared ethical principles.

- **Tackling Global Challenges:** AI has the potential to address some of the world's most pressing issues, from climate change to healthcare. International cooperation ensures that nations can leverage AI collaboratively, maximizing its benefits for humanity as a whole.

In conclusion, while individual nations and their regulatory bodies play an indispensable role in AI governance, the global nature of AI underscores the importance of international collaboration. By working together, nations can ensure that the AI revolution is not only technologically transformative but also ethically sound and beneficial to all.

10.5.4. Ethical Training and Education in AI and Security

The rapid evolution and integration of AI into every sphere of life, particularly in the realm of security, makes it imperative to emphasize the ethical dimensions of technology at every stage of its development and implementation. However, understanding the ethical nuances of AI and security isn't innate—it requires structured learning, continuous training, and a multidisciplinary approach. Here, we delve into the importance of ethical training and education in the AI and security sector and highlight its crucial components.

The rationale behind ethical education in AI and security includes:

- **Preventing Unintended Consequences:** A foundational understanding of ethical principles can help AI professionals anticipate potential pitfalls and avoid unintentional harm. This knowledge acts as a safeguard against biases, unauthorized surveillance, or other inadvertent misuses of technology.

- **Building Trust in AI Systems:** For AI systems, especially those related to security, to gain widespread acceptance and trust, users and stakeholders need assurance that these systems operate within established ethical boundaries.

- **Fostering Ethical Innovation:** While innovation is crucial, it shouldn't come at the cost of ethics. Training helps technologists strike a balance, ensuring advancements respect human rights, privacy, and other ethical considerations.

Core components of ethical training in AI include:

- **Introduction to Ethical Principles:** This encompasses the basics of ethics, discussing topics like justice, fairness, and rights, contextualized for the AI and security domain.

- **Hands-on Case Studies:** Practical sessions where learners analyze real-world AI scenarios, dissecting the ethical considerations and potential ramifications of different decisions.

- **Multidisciplinary Perspectives:** Encouraging engagement with philosophy, sociology, and other disciplines to provide a holistic view of ethics in technology.

- **Scenario Planning and Ethical Decision-making:** Simulations or role-playing exercises that place individuals in positions to make decisions, allowing them to witness the outcomes of their choices.

The need for continuous education is driven by:

- **The Evolving Landscape of AI:** AI, by its nature, is ever-evolving. As new algorithms, applications, and techniques emerge, the ethical challenges associated with them also shift. Continuous learning ensures professionals remain updated on these shifts.

- **Regularly Refreshing Ethical Standards:** Just as technology updates are frequent, so should refreshers on ethical standards. This helps internalize ethics as an integral part of the AI development process.

- **Engaging with Emerging Ethical Dilemmas:** As AI integrates deeper into society, new ethical challenges will emerge. Regular training sessions can help professionals proactively engage with and address these issues.

Collaboration with external entities allows for:

- **Engaging Ethical Experts:** Collaborations with philosophers, ethicists, and other experts can provide nuanced perspectives, enriching the training process.

- **Partnerships with Academic Institutions:** Tapping into academic expertise can help in crafting curriculum, conducting research, and ensuring training remains at the forefront of ethical considerations.

In wrapping up, it's clear that ethical training and education isn't merely an adjunct to the world of AI and security–it's an integral component. As we stride further into the AI-driven future, ensuring that professionals in this space are ethically equipped will not only shape the trajectory of technological developments but will also define the kind of digital world we're building for future generations.

11. Future Trends in AI-Proof Data Management

In the dynamic landscape of technology, where the horizon is constantly expanding and shifting, the intertwining of artificial intelligence and data management has ushered in a new era of innovation and challenges. From the nascent stages of machine learning algorithms to the now palpable effects of AI in everyday life, the relentless pace of AI evolution prompts a pertinent question: What does the future hold for AI-proof data management?

The answer lies at the intersection of technological advancement, security needs, and the ever-growing expanse of data. AI-proof data management isn't just about guarding against AI-powered threats—it's also about harnessing AI's potential to create more robust, adaptive, and resilient data management systems. As we envisage the future, several key trends are starting to emerge.

The rise of quantum computing threatens to unravel traditional cryptographic methods, prompting a rush towards post-quantum cryptography. Concurrently, the sophistication of AI-powered threats is also on the rise, challenging the very defenses that AI itself has helped to establish. Amid these technological races is a silver lining: a global collaborative effort aiming to create standardized defenses, share threat intelligence, and ensure that the benefits of AI are leveraged for the greater good.

Furthermore, the decentralization of data through technologies like blockchain and edge computing presents both opportunities and challenges for AI-proof data management. As devices at the edge grow smarter, so does the need to protect the data they generate and process.

In delving deeper into these trends, this section aims to provide a roadmap for understanding the trajectory of AI-proof data management. By identifying and analyzing these emerging patterns, organizations and individuals can better prepare for the challenges and opportunities that lie ahead.

11.1.　AI-Driven Quantum Encryption

The fusion of artificial intelligence and quantum encryption is nothing short of revolutionary. As the digital age continues to expand its horizons, the vulnerabilities and potential threats within cyberspace are also on the rise. The convergence of AI with quantum encryption offers a potent solution to these emerging challenges.[156]

Quantum encryption, inherently, is a product of the mind-boggling principles of quantum physics. Unlike classical encryption methods that rely on complex algorithms, quantum encryption banks on the properties of quantum bits or qubits. When a qubit is observed, it changes its state, making eavesdropping detectable instantly. This principle ensures a level of security that is, in theory, unbreakable by any computational means, including the might of quantum computers themselves.

Introducing AI into this mix adds another layer of sophistication. While quantum encryption ensures security, AI can optimize the encryption process, adaptively choose encryption keys based on the nature of the data, and foresee potential quantum threats based on patterns and anomalies. Moreover, AI can facilitate quantum key distribution, enhancing the speed and efficiency with which these keys are exchanged over vast networks.

But the journey of integrating AI with quantum encryption isn't without its challenges. The sheer novelty of quantum systems means that we're still in the early stages of understanding their full capabilities and potential pitfalls. AI algorithms need to be tailored specifically to operate in sync with the intricacies of quantum mechanics, ensuring that the two technologies complement rather than conflict with each other.

As we move forward, AI-driven quantum encryption stands as a beacon of hope for a future where our data remains secure in an increasingly interconnected world. Its

---

[156] https://quantumxc.com/blog/quantum-cryptography-explained/ and https://www.ibm.com/thought-leadership/institute-business-value/en-us/report/quantumsecurity

potential to redefine the very foundations of cybersecurity warrants close attention and investment from both the private sector and governmental bodies.

11.1.1.   Evolution of Quantum Technology and AI Synergy

The fusion of quantum technology with artificial intelligence marks a thrilling evolutionary journey in the world of computation and cybersecurity. While both fields, individually, have made astounding progress in recent decades, their integration represents a paradigm shift that could redefine the boundaries of what's technologically achievable.

Historically, quantum mechanics and its associated technologies were purely the domain of physicists and were perceived as abstract, distant from practical applications. The last couple of decades, however, have witnessed a surge in efforts to harness quantum mechanics for computational purposes, resulting in the birth and growth of quantum computers. Unlike classical computers, which rely on bits, quantum computers use qubits, granting them the potential for immensely superior computational power, especially for certain types of problems.[157]

Parallelly, the rise of artificial intelligence has been one of the defining narratives of the 21st century. Machine learning, deep learning, and neural networks have opened doors to tasks previously thought unattainable for machines, from nuanced natural language processing to advanced image recognition.

The convergence of these two behemoths began tentatively. Initial efforts sought to use quantum computers to accelerate machine learning processes, given their ability to handle vast datasets and complex computations at speeds unimaginable for classical computers. The term "quantum machine learning" started to gain traction, signaling the onset of algorithms that could potentially train on quantum data and provide results that classical algorithms would take ages to compute.

On the other hand, AI began playing a role in optimizing quantum computing processes. Advanced algorithms were employed to calibrate qubits, reduce quantum noise, and even design new quantum circuits. The synergy was evident: while quantum computing

---

[157] https://www.forbes.com/sites/jonathanreichental/2023/11/20/quantum-artificial-intelligence-is-closer-than-you-think/?sh=4057545f4318 and
https://kpmg.com/xx/en/home/insights/2024/03/quantum-and-cybersecurity.html

could provide AI with hitherto unparalleled processing capabilities, AI could help quantum computing become more stable and efficient.

This intertwined evolution is still in its nascent stages. Challenges abound, from the technical intricacies of quantum computing to the ethical and logistical concerns tied to AI. However, the trajectory indicates a future where the synergy between quantum technology and AI could underpin breakthroughs across sectors, from medicine and logistics to, of course, data security and encryption. The collaborative spirit of these two domains promises not just advancement, but a potential revolution in our technological landscape.

11.1.2.   Quantum Key Distribution: A New Frontier in Secure Communication

In the ever-evolving landscape of cyber threats and the increasing demand for secure communication, Quantum Key Distribution (QKD) emerges as a groundbreaking solution, signaling the dawn of an almost unbreachable cryptographic era.

Quantum Key Distribution, at its core, relies on the principles of quantum mechanics, particularly the behavior of individual quantum particles like photons. The most enchanting property leveraged in QKD is the 'no-cloning theorem.' This principle dictates that it's impossible to create an exact copy of an arbitrary unknown quantum state. In the realm of secure communication, this means that any eavesdropper trying to intercept the quantum keys would inevitably disturb the original quantum state, thereby alerting the communicating parties to the presence of an intrusion.

Let's consider a practical scenario. Alice and Bob want to communicate securely. Using QKD, they can exchange quantum keys, which are essentially sequences of qubits. If an eavesdropper, Eve, tries to intercept this key, the very act of her measurement disturbs the quantum states. When Alice and Bob later compare parts of their keys, these disturbances become apparent, signaling potential eavesdropping. If no such disturbances are observed, they can be confident in the security of their communication.

The BB84 protocol, proposed by Charles Bennett and Gilles Brassard in 1984, is one of the pioneering and most well-known QKD schemes. The protocol uses polarized photons to transmit information and has proven to be robust against various forms of attacks, making it a foundational piece in the realm of quantum cryptography.

Another crucial advantage of QKD lies in its future-proof nature. With the impending rise of quantum computers, traditional cryptographic methods, like RSA, become obsolete as quantum computers could, in theory, factorize large prime numbers in polynomial time, breaking the encryption. QKD, on the other hand, remains secure regardless of the computational power thrown at it, because its security arises from the fundamental laws of physics and not computational complexity.

In recent years, companies and governments worldwide have been investing heavily in QKD research, with pilot projects for quantum-secured bank transactions and governmental communications already in play. Moreover, endeavors like the Micius satellite by China have showcased the potential for space-based QKD, marking the first steps towards a global quantum-secure communication network.[158]

In essence, Quantum Key Distribution paints a promising picture for the future of secure communication, offering a robust shield against both contemporary and futuristic cyber threats. As quantum technology becomes more accessible, the fusion of QKD with mainstream communication channels may become the gold standard in data protection.

11.1.3. Quantum Key Distribution: Attacks Capable of Defeating

Quantum Key Distribution (QKD) is often hailed as a secure communication method that is theoretically impervious to any computational attack due to its foundation in the laws of quantum mechanics. However, practical implementations of QKD systems have shown vulnerabilities that can be exploited through various attacks. These attacks do not undermine the principles of quantum mechanics themselves but rather exploit engineering imperfections in the actual devices used for QKD.[159]

One such attack is the "Trojan-horse" attack, which is a sophisticated strategy that can be used to defeat QKD systems. In this type of attack, an eavesdropper, often referred to as Eve, sends bright light pulses into the quantum communication equipment of the legitimate users, Alice and Bob. These pulses are reflected off components within the equipment, such as modulators, and carry information about the settings or the state of the device. Eve can then intercept these reflected pulses and gain information about the secret key generation process without being detected.

---

[158] https://aerospace.org/sites/default/files/2020-07/Touch-Gordon_QKD_20200715.pdf, https://crypto.stackexchange.com/questions/86139/has-anyone-implemented-the-bb84-protocol, and https://www.aliroquantum.com/blog/quantum-network-security-protocols-bb84

[159] https://www.cryptomuseum.com/covert/bugs/thing/

The "Trojan-horse" attack is a strategy where attackers use deception to breach a secure system, and the incident involving "The Thing" serves as a classic example of this technique in the realm of espionage and cybersecurity. "The Thing," also known as the Great Seal bug, was a sophisticated listening device concealed within a wooden carving of the Great Seal of the United States. This carving was presented as a gift to the U.S. Ambassador to the Soviet Union, W. Averell Harriman, by the Soviet Union in 1945. Unbeknownst to the recipients, the carving contained a passive covert listening device invented by Léon Theremin, a Russian inventor.

The device was ingeniously designed to be entirely passive, meaning it had no power source of its own and could remain undetected during conventional sweeps for electronic bugs. It was activated by an external radio signal sent from a distance, which would "illuminate" the device, causing it to resonate and retransmit sound from the ambassador's office back to the Soviets. The Thing utilized a tiny capacitive membrane connected to a small quarter-wavelength antenna, and it was only when illuminated by the correct frequency that it became an active transmitter of sound.

The discovery of The Thing in 1952, hidden inside the ambassador's office, was a stark revelation of the lengths to which espionage could be taken, using seemingly innocuous gifts as trojan horses to infiltrate secure communications. This incident underscores the concept of the trojan-horse attack by demonstrating how trust and normalcy can be exploited to achieve covert surveillance. The Thing's design and operation principles laid the groundwork for modern understanding of passive surveillance devices and the importance of physical security measures in diplomatic and sensitive environments.

The "Trojan-horse" attack is particularly concerning because it can be carried out without causing any noticeable increase in the quantum bit error rate (QBER), which is typically monitored to detect eavesdropping. This means that Eve can obtain a non-zero portion of the final secret key without raising any alarms. To counteract such attacks, QKD systems need to be carefully designed with appropriate shielding, filtering, or other countermeasures to prevent external light from entering or internal light from leaking out of the system.

Another vulnerability in QKD systems is related to the detectors used to measure quantum states. Attackers can exploit imperfections in these detectors to gain information about the key. For example, by using bright illumination attacks, an eavesdropper can blind the detectors and then control their responses to incoming quantum states, effectively bypassing the security of the system.

These practical attacks underscore the importance of not only relying on the theoretical security guarantees of QKD but also ensuring that the physical implementation of QKD systems is secure against known vulnerabilities. It is essential for researchers and engineers to continuously identify and mitigate such side-channel attacks to maintain the integrity of QKD systems in real-world applications. As the field of quantum cryptography advances, the development of new countermeasures and the refinement of existing ones will be crucial in safeguarding against these sophisticated attacks.[160]

11.1.4. Challenges and Opportunities in AI-Driven Quantum Encryption

In the thrilling convergence of quantum encryption and artificial intelligence, a realm full of promise is unfolding, offering enhanced security mechanisms never before thought possible. But with these groundbreaking advancements come a series of challenges that the scientific community, technologists, and policymakers must jointly navigate.

Challenges include:

- **Technical Complexity:** Quantum systems, by their very nature, are inherently delicate and challenging to maintain. The slightest environmental interference can disrupt a quantum state, known as quantum decoherence, potentially compromising data integrity. Integrating AI with its computational demands can add another layer of complexity to these systems.[161]

- **Scalability Issues:** As of now, quantum communication systems, particularly those used in QKD, have limited range capabilities. Creating a large-scale, global quantum network that can handle massive amounts of data transfer remains a formidable challenge.[162]

- **Integration with Classical Systems:** The majority of today's communication infrastructure is based on classical systems. Integrating quantum systems

---

[160] https://www.sciencedirect.com/science/article/pii/S0304397514006938 or https://iopscience.iop.org/article/10.1088/1367-2630/16/12/123030.

[161] https://thequantuminsider.com/2024/03/26/is-q-day-closer-than-we-think-ibm-researchers-say-hybrid-quantum-ai-may-poses-near-term-threats/ and https://arxiv.org/html/2403.02240v1

[162] https://arxiv.org/html/2403.02240v1

smoothly, without causing disruptions or introducing vulnerabilities, especially when AI components are involved, is an ongoing challenge.[163]

- **Training and Expertise:** The interdisciplinary nature of AI-driven quantum encryption demands a new breed of experts knowledgeable in quantum mechanics, cryptography, and artificial intelligence. Current educational systems may not be adequately equipped to produce such multidisciplinary professionals.[164]

Opportunities include:

- **Enhanced Security:** AI can optimize quantum encryption protocols, dynamically adjust to environmental conditions to minimize quantum decoherence, or even predict and preemptively counteract quantum-based attacks.[165]

- **Dynamic Key Generation:** AI can help in real-time generation and management of quantum keys, making the QKD process more efficient and adaptable to changing threat landscapes.

- **Predictive Maintenance:** Using AI, it's possible to anticipate when a quantum system might face potential decoherence or other issues, allowing for proactive measures to ensure uninterrupted and secure communication.[166]

---

[163] https://arxiv.org/html/2403.02240v1

[164] https://www.journalofyoungphysicists.org/post/the-role-of-quantum-computers-in-the-future-of-ai-and-data

[165] https://thequantuminsider.com/2024/03/26/is-q-day-closer-than-we-think-ibm-researchers-say-hybrid-quantum-ai-may-poses-near-term-threats/

[166] https://www.journalofyoungphysicists.org/post/the-role-of-quantum-computers-in-the-future-of-ai-and-data

- **Interdisciplinary Innovation:** The intersection of AI and quantum encryption can lead to the birth of entirely new cryptographic methods and security protocols, catalyzing a new wave of research and innovation.[167]

- **Automated Quantum Networks:** AI can manage and operate large-scale quantum networks, ensuring optimal routing of quantum information, managing nodes, and guaranteeing the overall health of the network.[168]

As we stand at the cusp of this technological renaissance, the symbiosis of AI and quantum encryption will undoubtedly shape the future of secure communication. While the road ahead might be fraught with challenges, the potential benefits and breakthroughs promise a safer, more secure digital future. The task at hand for researchers, policymakers, and industry leaders is to collaboratively address these challenges, ensuring that as these technologies evolve, they do so in a manner that benefits society at large.

11.1.5. Case Studies: Leading Innovations in Quantum and AI Integration

The marriage between quantum technology and artificial intelligence is not just theoretical—it's becoming a reality. Several leading tech organizations and research institutions worldwide are diving into the uncharted waters of quantum-AI synergy. Let's look at a few notable examples that have made significant strides in this domain.

- **IBM's Quantum Experience:** IBM has been a forerunner in the field of quantum computing. With the launch of the IBM Quantum Experience, users have been given cloud-based access to quantum processors. By integrating AI into this platform, IBM is aiming to optimize quantum algorithms and make quantum simulations more efficient. The company believes that AI can be pivotal in

---

[167] https://thequantuminsider.com/2024/03/26/is-q-day-closer-than-we-think-ibm-researchers-say-hybrid-quantum-ai-may-poses-near-term-threats/

[168] https://www.pymnts.com/news/artificial-intelligence/2024/the-impact-quantum-powered-ai-could-have-on-payments/

managing quantum systems, reducing errors, and enhancing the overall quantum computation experience.[169]

- **Google's Quantum AI Lab:** Not to be outdone, Google's Quantum AI Lab focuses on building quantum processors and developing novel quantum algorithms to accelerate tasks, some of which include machine learning. Their experiments with quantum processors have led them to conclude that quantum computing can enhance certain machine learning tasks, potentially revolutionizing areas like image and speech recognition.[170]

- **Alibaba Cloud and CAS:** In a collaboration between Alibaba Cloud and the Chinese Academy of Sciences (CAS), a quantum computing cloud platform was launched, offering users access to an 11-qubit quantum processor. The integration of AI technologies aims to provide solutions for routing optimization problems, financial analysis, and drug discovery.[171]

- **Intel's Quantum Research:** Intel has been exploring quantum computing for AI tasks, emphasizing the development of quantum chips. By combining AI algorithms with quantum chips, Intel believes they can drastically reduce the time needed for data processing, making real-time data analysis and predictions more efficient than ever before.[172]

- **D-Wave Systems:** This company has been a pioneer in the realm of quantum annealing, a quantum computing technique. D-Wave's processors have been tested for various tasks, including optimization problems and machine learning

---

[169] https://newsroom.ibm.com/2023-12-04-IBM-Debuts-Next-Generation-Quantum-Processor-IBM-Quantum-System-Two,-Extends-Roadmap-to-Advance-Era-of-Quantum-Utility and https://newsroom.ibm.com/2023-12-04-IBM-Debuts-Next-Generation-Quantum-Processor-IBM-Quantum-System-Two,-Extends-Roadmap-to-Advance-Era-of-Quantum-Utility

[170] https://thequantuminsider.com/2023/05/08/google-quantum-computing/, https://quantumai.google/research, and https://quantumai.google/lab

[171] https://www.alibabacloud.com/en/press-room/alibaba-cloud-and-cas-launch-one-of-the-worlds-most?_p_lc=1 and https://coingeek.com/alibaba-shuts-down-quantum-computing-unit-to-focus-on-ai-research/

[172] https://thequantuminsider.com/2023/04/26/intels-quantum-computing-2023-2/ and https://www.allaboutcircuits.com/news/intel-makes-new-quantum-chip-available-to-research-community/

applications. Their ambition to integrate AI revolves around the idea of creating more intuitive quantum systems that can "learn" from their environments and "adapt" accordingly.[173]

These case studies depict just the tip of the iceberg. Many smaller start-ups and research teams globally are making advancements, each contributing a piece to the vast puzzle of quantum-AI integration. Their collective efforts hold the promise of ushering in a new era where problems once deemed insurmountable become tractable, and where the convergence of these two technologies propels us into an unforeseen age of innovation and discovery.

11.2. The Rise of AI-Powered Threats

In the vast expanse of the digital realm, as AI systems become more sophisticated and prevalent, there's an emerging shadow: the potential use of these systems for malicious purposes. AI, with its vast capabilities, holds the promise of transforming industries, revolutionizing medical research, and providing solutions to some of humanity's most daunting challenges. However, like all powerful tools, it can be wielded for both beneficial and harmful purposes.

AI-powered threats represent a new frontier in the world of cybersecurity. While traditional cyber threats involve human hackers attempting to infiltrate systems, exploit vulnerabilities, and disrupt digital infrastructures, AI-powered threats bring forth a new dimension where attacks can be carried out with increased speed, efficiency, and adaptability. These AI-driven cyber-adversaries can potentially learn from their mistakes, evolve their strategies in real-time, and operate at a scale that's unmanageable for human defenders alone.[174]

---

[173] https://en.wikipedia.org/wiki/D-Wave_Systems, https://thenewstack.io/d-wave-suggests-quantum-annealing-could-help-ai/, https://www.hpcwire.com/2024/01/30/eyes-on-the-quantum-prize-d-wave-says-its-time-is-now/, and https://www.dwavesys.com/learn/featured-applications/?items=all&thirdParty=0

[174] https://arxiv.org/ftp/arxiv/papers/2105/2105.00192.pdf and https://iopscience.iop.org/article/10.1088/1742-6596/1964/4/042072/pdf

Furthermore, these threats are not just limited to hacking. The proliferation of deepfakes, which utilize AI to create hyper-realistic but entirely fake content, poses challenges to information integrity. There's also the potential misuse of AI in surveillance, leading to unprecedented breaches of privacy. From automated phishing attempts that evolve based on user interaction to AI-driven malware that can adapt to different system defenses, the landscape of potential threats is rapidly expanding.[175]

While this may paint a grim picture, recognizing the potential challenges is the first step towards mitigation. Addressing AI-powered threats requires an in-depth understanding of AI's capabilities, a proactive approach to cybersecurity, and global cooperation. As we delve deeper into this section, we will explore the various facets of these emerging threats, understand their implications, and discuss potential countermeasures. The technological arms race between AI-driven threats and defenses is on, and staying informed is paramount.

11.2.1.   Understanding Deepfake Technologies and Their Implications

Deepfakes, a portmanteau of "deep learning" and "fake," are at the forefront of AI-powered threats. Enabled by deep learning algorithms, deepfakes have the capability to manipulate or generate visual and audio content that is nearly indistinguishable from the real thing. This level of realism poses both technical and ethical challenges, given the potential for misuse in areas ranging from misinformation campaigns to identity theft.

The underlying technology behind deepfakes is based on Generative Adversarial Networks (GANs). GANs consist of two neural networks – the generator, which creates images, and the discriminator, which evaluates them. These networks operate in tandem, continually refining the output until the generated content is of such quality that the discriminator can't tell if it's real or fake. Through countless iterations and training on vast datasets, GANs can produce convincingly realistic content.

The implications of deepfakes are vast and multi-dimensional:

- **Misinformation and Disinformation:** Deepfakes can be weaponized to spread false information, potentially leading to public panic, tarnishing reputations, or even affecting election outcomes. An authentic-looking video of a world leader

---

[175] https://link.springer.com/article/10.1007/s00500-023-08605-y

making controversial statements, for instance, can cause significant geopolitical ramifications.[176]

- **Identity Theft and Fraud:** Deepfakes can be used to impersonate individuals, potentially tricking biometric systems or convincing people to undertake actions based on fraudulent communications that appear to be from trusted sources.[177]

- **Privacy Concerns:** As deepfakes become more mainstream, there's a growing concern about consent. Using someone's likeness without permission, especially in potentially damaging or misleading scenarios, raises significant ethical and privacy concerns.[178]

- **Legal and Ethical Challenges:** Current legal frameworks may not be adequately equipped to handle disputes arising from the misuse of deepfakes. Determining responsibility and prosecuting creators of malicious deepfakes pose new challenges for the legal system.

However, it's crucial to note that deepfakes aren't inherently malevolent. Like any technology, they have benign applications. For instance, they can be used in filmmaking for special effects, or in voice synthesis for virtual assistants. It's the malicious or uninformed use of deepfakes that poses risks.

As deepfakes continue to advance, it's essential for individuals, companies, and governments to understand the technology and its potential implications, and to develop both technical and policy-based countermeasures. In the sections that follow, we will dive deeper into the challenges posed by AI-powered threats and explore strategies to counteract them.

---

[176] https://inspiredelearning.com/blog/examples-of-deepfake-technology/

[177] https://www.forbes.com/sites/jessedamiani/2019/09/03/a-voice-deepfake-was-used-to-scam-a-ceo-out-of-243000/?sh=58da68602241

[178] https://withpersona.com/blog/what-are-deepfakes and https://netmission.asia/2023/03/09/netmission-case-study-series-2023-the-dark-side-of-deep-fakes-its-dangerous-consequences-on-society/

11.2.2.   AI-Enhanced Malware: Redefining Cyber-Attack Paradigms

The landscape of cyber threats has seen a tectonic shift with the inception of AI-driven tactics. Among the most potent applications of AI in this domain is AI-enhanced malware. Traditional malware often operates under predefined conditions and scripts. However, with the integration of AI, these malicious software entities are capable of learning from their environment, adapting, and subsequently refining their attack techniques. They don't just act–they evolve.

- **Adaptive and Stealthy Attacks:** AI-enhanced malware can assess its environment and alter its behavior to avoid detection. For example, if the malware detects it's being run in a sandbox environment (a common technique used by security researchers to study malware), it can go dormant, displaying no malicious behaviors, only to activate later when it deems the environment safe.

- **Automated Exploit Generation:** Using AI, malware can automatically find vulnerabilities in software. This level of automation can drastically increase the speed at which new attacks can be deployed, giving defenders less time to respond and patch vulnerable systems.

- **Polymorphic and Metamorphic Malware:** While polymorphic malware changes its code to evade signature-based detection, metamorphic malware goes a step further by altering its underlying algorithms. AI can automate and enhance this transformation process, making each instance of the malware look and behave differently, thus rendering traditional antivirus tools less effective.

- **Smart Targeting:** AI-enhanced malware can be programmed to target specific organizations or individuals. By analyzing vast amounts of data, these malware variants can determine the most effective vectors of attack, whether that's targeting specific network vulnerabilities or using social engineering tactics tailored to specific individuals.

Examples of such threats are already emerging. The **DeepLocker** malware, for instance, employed AI to stay undetected until it reached its specific target, using facial recognition capabilities to ensure it only attacked its intended victim.[179]

---

[179] https://www.secplicity.org/2018/08/27/artificial-intelligence-part-2-cyber-criminals-get-smart-with-ai/

The integration of AI into malware represents a paradigm shift in cyber warfare. It's not just about making malware more effective—it's about fundamentally changing the way they operate. As these threats become more prevalent, it underscores the need for a new generation of cybersecurity solutions, ones that can anticipate, understand, and counteract AI-driven tactics. The arms race between cyber attackers and defenders is accelerating, with AI at its core. The next segments delve into further AI-powered threats and the proactive measures that the cybersecurity community is taking to combat them.

11.2.3.   Countermeasures: Leveraging AI to Detect AI-Powered Threats

The cat-and-mouse game between cyber attackers and defenders is entering a new era, as both sides harness the power of artificial intelligence. As threat actors employ sophisticated AI-driven strategies, the cybersecurity community is in a race to develop countermeasures that can detect and neutralize these threats. The integration of AI into our defense mechanisms is not just a novel trend but an imperative:

- **Behavior-based Detection:** Unlike traditional signature-based detection methods, behavior-based models analyze patterns and anomalies in behavior to identify malicious activities. For instance, while an AI-enhanced malware might alter its code to bypass signature checks, its behavior (such as trying to access a large number of files quickly) can still be flagged as suspicious. AI can be trained to recognize these abnormal patterns, even if they've never been seen before.

- **AI-Enhanced Threat Hunting:** Proactive threat hunting is about identifying threats before they cause damage. With AI, threat hunters can analyze vast amounts of data, sift through false alarms, and pinpoint genuine threats. It can identify patterns and correlations that would be impossible for humans to discern, making the threat-hunting process more efficient and effective.[180]

- **Deep Learning for Deepfakes:** Deepfakes, as previously discussed, use neural networks to create hyper-realistic but entirely fake content. Ironically, similar deep learning models can be employed to detect them. By training on vast

---

[180] https://www.forbes.com/sites/forbestechcouncil/2023/07/21/how-ai-enabled-threat-intelligence-is-becoming-our-future/?sh=58d47498727e

datasets of both genuine and manipulated content, AI models can become adept at spotting the subtle inconsistencies present in deepfakes.[181]

- **Self-Adapting Security Systems:** One of the significant advantages of AI-enhanced threats is their ability to adapt. However, this advantage isn't exclusive to the attackers. Defense systems, powered by AI, can also adapt in real-time, learning from each attack and refining their defenses. Such systems can update their threat models without human intervention, ensuring that they are always prepared for the latest strategies employed by attackers.[182]

- **Automated Incident Response:** When a potential threat is detected, time is of the essence. AI can automate many aspects of the incident response process, from isolating affected systems to gathering forensic data. Such automation ensures that threats are dealt with promptly, minimizing potential damage.[183]

Real-world implementations of these strategies are becoming increasingly prevalent. Companies like **Darktrace** utilize AI to model a 'pattern of life' for every user and device in a network, enabling it to spot unusual behavior that might indicate a threat.[184] Another example is **Cylance**, which uses machine learning to predict, with high accuracy, where threats might come from, even if those threats have never been encountered before.[185]

In this ever-evolving battleground, AI stands as both a weapon and a shield. The challenge for the cybersecurity community is to stay one step ahead, continually refining and reimagining their defenses in the face of increasingly intelligent threats. This ongoing struggle underscores the importance of understanding the broader landscape of AI-driven cyber warfare, as explored in the upcoming sections.

---

[181] https://www.mdpi.com/2079-9292/13/1/95

[182] https://clue.ch/en/managed-services/ai-based-threat-detection/

[183] https://atlanticdatasecurity.com/blog/ai-cybersecurity-threat-detection/

[184] https://www.summitpartners.com/resources/darktrace-pioneering-ai-in-the-cyber-security-space

[185] https://adapture.com/artificial-intelligence-and-anti-virus-the-cylance-cybersecurity-approach/

11.2.4.   *The Next Decade: Predicting the Trajectory of AI-Powered Cyber Threats*

Integrating artificial intelligence into the cyber realm represents an inevitable paradigm shift. With every technological advance, there are always those who will seek to exploit it, and AI is no exception. As we look to the future, it becomes increasingly crucial to anticipate the nature and scope of AI-powered threats that organizations and individuals might face in the coming decade. Here's an exploration of the potential trajectory of these threats:

- **Self-evolving Malware:** The malware of the future will not just be AI-enhanced—it will possess the ability to evolve. By leveraging advanced machine learning algorithms, these malicious programs will adapt in real-time to countermeasures, refining their tactics, techniques, and procedures (TTPs) to remain undetected and enhance their propagation and impact.[186]

- **Autonomous Attack Swarms:** Imagine a coordinated attack not by a group of hackers, but by a swarm of AI-driven bots. These swarms will be able to split tasks, communicate in encrypted channels, and adjust strategies based on feedback, making them incredibly difficult to detect and neutralize.[187]

- **AI-driven Social Engineering:** With the increasing sophistication of AI-driven natural language processing and generation, the coming decade could see a surge in AI-powered phishing or spear-phishing attacks. These systems could craft highly convincing and personalized messages, targeting users based on their online behaviors and preferences.[188]

- **Adaptive Ransomware:** Future ransomware will not just encrypt your data and demand a ransom. By leveraging AI, it might analyze the importance and sensitivity of your files and adjust its ransom amount accordingly.[189] Such threats could even negotiate with victims, altering demands based on user reactions and desperation levels.

---

[186] https://cyberpedia.reasonlabs.com/EN/self-replication.html

[187] https://www.ncbi.nlm.nih.gov/pmc/articles/PMC10030838/

[188] https://www.tripwire.com/state-of-security/navigating-new-waters-ai-powered-phishing-attacks

[189] https://www.veeam.com/blog/cyber-security-trends.html

- **Deepfake Escalation:** While deepfakes currently pose significant threats in terms of misinformation, their potential misuse extends far beyond creating fake news clips. They might be used for identity theft, falsifying evidence in legal settings, or manipulating stock markets by impersonating CEOs in fake announcement videos.[190]

- **AI as an Insider Threat:** As organizations increasingly incorporate AI solutions into their internal processes, there's a risk that these systems could be turned against them. Malicious entities might corrupt these AI systems to act as insider threats, bypassing traditional security mechanisms.[191]

Global cybersecurity firms like **FireEye** and **CrowdStrike** have already started releasing periodic reports that touch upon the evolving nature of AI-driven threats. These insights not only serve as warnings but guide the direction of research and development in cybersecurity defenses.

In understanding the potential threats of the future, organizations and individuals can better prepare and fortify their cyber defenses. The intertwining of AI with cyber threats may pose novel challenges, but it also drives innovation and resilience in the face of adversity. The following sections will explore more trends and shifts, shedding light on how we might shape a secure cyber landscape in the AI era.

11.3. Collaborative Global Data Protection Initiatives

In an era characterized by increasing digital interconnectivity, the protection of data has never been more pivotal. As the challenges associated with AI and cybersecurity expand beyond borders, it becomes clear that isolated strategies and siloed efforts can only go so far in ensuring comprehensive data protection. The demand for collaborative global data protection initiatives is an inevitable outcome of our interconnected world, marked by shared threats and common vulnerabilities.

---

[190] https://www.forbes.com/sites/forbestechcouncil/2024/01/23/deepfake-phishing-the-dangerous-new-face-of-cybercrime/?sh=6c04fe4b4aed

[191] https://www.forbes.com/sites/forbestechcouncil/2023/07/21/how-ai-enabled-threat-intelligence-is-becoming-our-future/?sh=58d47498727e

Historically, data breaches, cyber threats, and privacy violations have not confined themselves to geographical boundaries. The repercussions of major cyber-attacks, such as WannaCry or NotPetya, reverberated globally, revealing that cybersecurity isn't merely a domestic concern but a global one. As AI intensifies these cyber threats, the collective defense, marked by international cooperation, becomes more than just a strategic move—it's a survival imperative.

The rise of transnational corporations and cloud-based services means that data constantly flows across borders. This complicates jurisdictional oversight and creates potential loopholes for malicious entities to exploit. Collaborative initiatives aim to bridge these jurisdictional divides by harmonizing data protection standards, ensuring that data remains secure irrespective of where it's stored or processed.

Moreover, global collaborations can pool resources, expertise, and insights, leading to more effective countermeasures against threats. Shared intelligence, coordinated responses, and joint research ventures can elevate the collective cyber defense capabilities, far surpassing what individual nations or organizations could achieve on their own.

However, while the advantages of these collaborations are clear, actualizing them isn't straightforward. Differences in political ideologies, economic priorities, and cultural perspectives on privacy can become barriers.

Nevertheless, the path forward is unmistakable: in a world dominated by AI and complex cyber threats, global collaboration is the linchpin of a resilient digital future. The subsequent sections will delve deeper into the various facets of these collaborative efforts, their achievements, challenges, and potential future directions.

11.3.1. The Importance of Global Cooperation in Cybersecurity

The digital realm has seamlessly intertwined itself with the global fabric, rendering borders porous in the face of cyber threats. The traditional, compartmentalized approach to cybersecurity, which focuses exclusively on domestic concerns, is increasingly insufficient in a hyper-connected era. Global cooperation in cybersecurity, thus, emerges not as a mere good-to-have but as an essential paradigm in maintaining the stability and security of the digital ecosystem.[192]

At the heart of this importance lies the recognition that cyber threats are universally shared. The vulnerabilities exploited in one corner of the globe can be identical to those in another, and threat actors often don't discriminate based on geography. When the WannaCry ransomware spread in 2017, for instance, it didn't target a specific country—it affected systems worldwide, from the UK's National Health Service to factories in France and enterprises in Asia. A coordinated international response could have mitigated some of the extensive damage caused by such a threat.

Furthermore, global cooperation in cybersecurity fosters the sharing of best practices, insights, and intelligence. Nations and organizations with advanced cyber defenses can provide valuable insights to others, elevating the global cybersecurity baseline. When countries pool their knowledge and resources, the resulting synergy can lead to more potent defenses and proactive strategies, outpacing the evolving techniques of cyber adversaries.

Another pivotal aspect of international collaboration is the development of harmonized legal and regulatory frameworks. As data moves fluidly across borders, a mismatch in regulations can create inadvertent loopholes or hurdles for businesses. Uniform cybersecurity standards and regulations can not only simplify international business but also ensure that there are no weak links in the global data protection chain.

Lastly, a cooperative approach can yield innovations in threat mitigation through collaborative research and development. Nations and organizations can jointly fund and spearhead research projects, leveraging diverse talents and perspectives. Such endeavors can lead to breakthroughs in cyber defense technologies, encryption methods, and AI-driven protective solutions, offering robust safeguards against emerging threats.

In summation, as the digital realm grows and intertwines further with every facet of our lives, isolated efforts in cybersecurity will fall short. Global cooperation isn't just a strategic move—it's the bulwark that will determine the resilience and security of our shared digital future.

---

[192] https://www.csis.org/analysis/shared-responsibility-public-private-cooperation-cybersecurity

11.3.2.   International Frameworks for AI and Data Management

As the digital age progresses, AI and data management have emerged as two critical pillars of modern technology, influencing sectors ranging from healthcare to finance. Their profound impact on individuals, societies, and economies makes it essential to establish international frameworks that guide their usage and evolution. These frameworks serve multiple purposes, ensuring ethical deployment, harmonized regulations, and setting the stage for collaborative advancements.

One of the most notable international efforts in this domain is the General Data Protection Regulation (GDPR) introduced by the European Union. The GDPR is a comprehensive data protection framework aiming to empower individuals by giving them more control over their personal data. Its principles, such as data minimization, right to erasure, and stringent consent requirements, have set the tone for many subsequent national data protection regulations across the world. GDPR's influence is palpable outside the EU as businesses globally adapt to its standards to ensure compliance and maintain operations in the European market.[193]

Similarly, the OECD (Organisation for Economic Co-operation and Development) has put forth its principles on artificial intelligence, stressing transparency, robustness, safety, and fairness. These principles are designed to promote trust in AI systems, and they urge member nations to ensure that AI respects human rights and democratic values. Though non-binding, the principles provide a foundational guideline for countries to shape their AI policies and regulations.[194]

The UNESCO's draft recommendation on the ethics of AI is another pivotal effort, focusing on the universal values that AI systems should uphold. It emphasizes ensuring AI respects human rights, promoting transparency and accountability, and safeguarding data privacy. Furthermore, it accentuates the need to prepare society for AI's implications by promoting digital literacy and educating the public on the nuances of AI.[195]

---

[193] https://gdpr-info.eu/

[194] https://www.oecd.org/science/forty-two-countries-adopt-new-oecd-principles-on-artificial-intelligence.htm

[195] https://www.unesco.org/en/articles/recommendation-ethics-artificial-intelligence

The Global Partnership on Artificial Intelligence (GPAI) also deserves mention. Initiated by the G7, the GPAI seeks to bridge the gap between theory and practice by supporting the responsible development and use of AI, grounded in human rights, diversity, and innovation. It brings together experts from various fields to collaborate on AI challenges, ensuring that the benefits of AI are shared universally.[196]

The establishment of such international frameworks and cooperative bodies is paramount for several reasons. Firstly, they pave the way for a level playing field, where companies and nations operate under consistent standards, fostering global business and innovation. Secondly, they ensure that as AI and data management technologies evolve, they do so ethically, with humanity's broader interests in mind. Lastly, they foster a culture of shared knowledge and resources, accelerating advancements while mitigating potential pitfalls.

In essence, as AI and data management continue their ascension as cornerstone technologies of our era, international frameworks play a pivotal role in guiding their trajectory. They ensure that while we harness their immense potential, we remain cognizant of the responsibilities and challenges they introduce.

11.3.3.   Successful Cross-border AI Security Collaborations

The modern digital landscape is inherently global, and threats to its stability and security often disregard national boundaries. As cyber threats become increasingly sophisticated, aided by the rapid advancements in AI, addressing them in silos is neither feasible nor effective. This realization has led to numerous cross-border collaborations focusing on AI-driven cybersecurity solutions. These collaborations not only pool resources and expertise but also allow for the swift dissemination of threat intelligence and best practices.

One of the standout examples of such collaborations is the collaboration between NATO (North Atlantic Treaty Organization) and the European Union.[197] Both entities have repeatedly stressed the importance of AI in the future of defense and security. To this end, they've embarked on joint research initiatives, shared best practices in AI-driven cybersecurity, and held regular dialogues to harmonize their AI security postures. By

---

[196] https://dig.watch/actor/global-partnership-on-artificial-intelligence

[197] https://www.politico.eu/article/nato-ai-artificial-intelligence-standards-priorities/

unifying their approaches, they present a formidable front against potential AI-driven threats.

Another notable collaboration can be found in the CyberGreen initiative. It's a global effort focused on improving the overall health and resilience of the digital ecosystem. Through partnerships with various nations, this initiative employs AI and machine learning to identify vulnerabilities in global digital infrastructure, providing stakeholders with actionable insights to address potential threats proactively.

The Financial Services Information Sharing and Analysis Center (FS-ISAC) is an embodiment of sector-specific collaboration.[198] Bringing together financial institutions from around the globe, FS-ISAC serves as a hub for sharing threat intelligence. With AI-driven tools, the center analyzes vast amounts of data to identify emerging threats, ensuring member institutions are always a step ahead of potential cyber adversaries.

Lastly, the Global Research and Analysis Team (GReAT) from Kaspersky is an exemplary model of a private sector-driven cross-border collaboration.[199] With experts hailing from various parts of the world, GReAT employs advanced AI tools to dissect complex cyber threats, subsequently publishing their findings for the broader cybersecurity community. Their research has been instrumental in unmasking several high-profile cyber espionage campaigns.

These collaborations underscore the significance of unified action against common digital adversaries. When countries and organizations join forces, they not only magnify their defensive capabilities but also send a clear message to threat actors about the collective resolve to safeguard the digital realm. The continuous evolution of AI tools further amplifies these collaborative efforts, ensuring that defenders are always equipped with cutting-edge solutions to counter emerging threats.

11.3.4.   The Role of Non-Governmental Organizations (NGOs) and Think Tanks

In the global effort to understand and navigate the challenges of AI-driven security, Non-Governmental Organizations (NGOs) and think tanks have emerged as pivotal actors. Unlike government agencies or commercial entities, these organizations often operate

[198] https://www.fsisac.com/newsroom/pr-ai-risk-papers

[199] https://carnegieeurope.eu/2022/09/15/artificial-intelligence-and-cybersecurity-nexus-taking-stock-of-european-union-s-approach-pub-87886

with a level of independence that enables them to produce unbiased research, advocate for international standards, and foster collaborations across borders.

1. *Research and Policy Recommendations:* Think tanks, with their vast pool of experts from various fields, play a crucial role in researching the nuances of AI-driven threats and defenses. Their interdisciplinary approach provides comprehensive insights into the multifaceted challenges of AI in cybersecurity. The Carnegie Endowment for International Peace, for instance, has made significant contributions in the realm of cyber policy, suggesting norms and frameworks that countries can adopt.

2. *Advocacy for Ethical AI Use:* NGOs often stand at the forefront of advocating for ethical considerations in AI development and deployment. Organizations like Human Rights Watch and Amnesty International regularly highlight the misuse of AI in surveillance and other areas, emphasizing the need for ethical guidelines and international standards.

3. *Bridging the Gap:* Both NGOs and think tanks play a bridging role between the public, private sectors, and the general public. They organize conferences, seminars, and workshops, bringing together experts, policymakers, industry leaders, and civil society to discuss challenges and brainstorm solutions. The annual RSA Conference, though more commercial, is an example of how various stakeholders can come together to address global cybersecurity challenges.

4. *Capacity Building:* NGOs often focus on capacity building in countries that lack the resources or expertise in AI-driven cybersecurity. By organizing training sessions, developing educational materials, or even providing direct support, these organizations ensure that no country is left behind in the global effort against cyber threats. The Global Cyber Security Capacity Centre (GCSCC) at the University of Oxford, for example, focuses on enhancing cybersecurity capabilities across different nations.

5. *Promoting Global Standards:* Think tanks and NGOs are often instrumental in promoting global standards. They provide platforms where experts from different countries can discuss and develop common norms and best practices. The World Economic Forum's Centre for Cybersecurity is one such initiative that aims to build a safe and secure global digital space through collective action.

In conclusion, as the cyber landscape continues to evolve with AI innovations, the role of NGOs and think tanks becomes even more crucial. Their unique position, free from commercial or political pressures, allows them to foster cooperation, conduct unbiased research, and drive initiatives that benefit the global community. Their efforts complement those of governments and private sectors, making them indispensable in the journey towards a secure and ethical digital future.

11.4. The Potential of Decentralized Data Systems

In the evolving landscape of AI and cybersecurity, a key transformation is the move towards decentralized data systems. As conventional centralized systems have shown vulnerabilities and are often targets for sophisticated cyberattacks, the concept of decentralization has garnered significant attention and exploration. Decentralized systems, often driven by blockchain technology and distributed ledger principles, promise enhanced security, improved privacy, and a more resilient infrastructure for data management:[200]

- **Resilience Against Attacks:** One of the most compelling advantages of decentralized data systems is their inherent resistance to single points of failure. Traditional centralized systems, if compromised, can lead to the breach of vast amounts of data. However, decentralized systems distribute data across multiple nodes, ensuring that even if a portion of the system is attacked, the entire network remains largely unaffected. This dispersion reduces the potential reward for cybercriminals, as hacking one node won't grant them full system access.

- **Enhanced Data Privacy:** Decentralization offers improved privacy controls for users. In many decentralized systems, users retain control over their personal data, deciding who can access it and for what purpose. This contrasts with centralized models where large corporations or entities hold vast amounts of user data, often leading to concerns about misuse, unauthorized access, or unsolicited data sharing.

---

[200] https://www.linkedin.com/pulse/blockchain-ai-powerful-duo-cybersecurity-varteq/

- **Immutable Records and Trust:** Distributed ledger technologies, like blockchain, provide an immutable record of transactions. Once data is stored on the blockchain, it cannot be easily altered without the consensus of the network. This immutability instills trust in the system, making it especially valuable for sectors like finance, real estate, and supply chain, where verifiable records are paramount.

- **Empowering End Users:** Decentralized systems often give more power to end users, both in terms of data control and in terms of participation in the system's governance. Through mechanisms like tokenomics and decentralized autonomous organizations (DAOs), users can have a direct say in the evolution and rules of the platform.

- **Potential Challenges:** While decentralized systems present numerous advantages, they are not without challenges. Issues related to scalability, energy consumption (especially in proof-of-work blockchains), and interoperability with existing systems are still being addressed. Moreover, while they offer enhanced security in many respects, they also introduce new attack vectors that experts need to understand and mitigate.

In the broader narrative of AI-proof data management, decentralized systems provide a promising avenue, harnessing the power of distributed networks and cryptography to offer a more secure and private digital ecosystem. As we navigate the future of cybersecurity, the integration of AI with decentralized technologies is poised to be a critical component in safeguarding our digital assets and privacy.

11.4.1.   *Understanding Blockchain's Role in Secure Data Management*

The concept of blockchain, often recognized as the underlying technology behind cryptocurrencies like Bitcoin and Ethereum, has far-reaching applications beyond the realm of finance. At its core, a blockchain is a decentralized and distributed ledger that records transactions across numerous computers in a way that ensures the data's security and immutability. Its potential in secure data management is profound, and here we delve into its various facets:

- **Immutable Transaction Records:** Once a transaction is added to a blockchain, it becomes nearly impossible to alter. Every block in the chain contains a cryptographic hash of the previous block, creating a chain of blocks that are interdependent. This structure ensures that if an individual attempts to alter information in one block, they would need to change the contents of all subsequent blocks, which is practically infeasible due to the consensus mechanisms in place.

- **Decentralized Validation:** Traditional data management systems often rely on a central authority to validate transactions, leading to potential vulnerabilities and a single point of failure. In contrast, blockchain operates on decentralized validation mechanisms. For a transaction to be added to the blockchain, it needs validation from multiple nodes (computers) in the network, ensuring a democratic and highly secure validation process.

- **Transparency with Privacy:** One of blockchain's unique features is its ability to offer transparency without compromising privacy. While all transactions are visible to every participant in the network, they are recorded using cryptographic pseudonyms or addresses. This ensures that while activities are transparent and verifiable, the identities of the participants remain concealed.

- **Smart Contracts:** Beyond mere transaction records, blockchain can automate complex processes using smart contracts. These are self-executing contracts with the terms directly written into code. Smart contracts automatically trigger actions when predefined conditions are met, reducing the need for intermediaries and introducing new levels of automation in data management.

- **Potential in Supply Chain, Healthcare, and More:** The secure and transparent nature of blockchain makes it invaluable in industries where data integrity and traceability are critical. In supply chain management, blockchain can track products from their origin to the consumer. In healthcare, it can ensure the secure and transparent storage and transfer of medical records. These are but a few examples of blockchain's potential in redefining secure data management across sectors.

As artificial intelligence continues to permeate various sectors, the integration of AI algorithms with blockchain can bring about new innovations. Predictive analytics on transparent and immutable data, automated decision-making through smart contracts, and enhanced security mechanisms are just the tip of the iceberg. Understanding the synergy between AI and blockchain is essential for any forward-looking organization or individual in the realm of data management and security.

11.4.2.   How AI Enhances Decentralized Systems

Decentralized systems, especially those based on blockchain technology, have sparked a revolution in secure data management. However, the infusion of artificial intelligence into these systems is amplifying their capabilities, creating an ecosystem where both technologies leverage each other's strengths. Here, we explore the ways in which AI augments decentralized systems and pushes the boundaries of what's achievable:

- **Improved Scalability and Efficiency:** One of the criticisms of early blockchain systems, particularly those like Bitcoin, is their limited scalability. AI, with its advanced algorithms and processing capabilities, can optimize the way transactions are verified, ensuring that decentralized systems can handle larger transaction volumes at faster speeds.

- **Advanced Data Analysis:** While blockchains store vast amounts of data securely, deciphering meaningful insights from this data can be a challenge. AI algorithms can sift through vast blockchain datasets, identifying patterns, anomalies, and actionable insights, enhancing decision-making processes and predictive capabilities.

- **Enhanced Security Protocols:** AI-driven security mechanisms can bolster the already robust security features of blockchain. By continuously learning from ongoing network activities, AI can predict potential vulnerabilities, detect irregularities, and even deploy countermeasures in real-time, further fortifying decentralized networks.

- **Smart Contract Optimization:** While smart contracts have automated many processes on blockchain, there are still concerns about their potential vulnerabilities or flawed logic. AI can assist in the automatic generation, verification, and optimization of smart contracts, ensuring they execute as intended and without errors.

- **Resource Management:** Mining, especially in proof-of-work blockchain systems, can be resource-intensive. AI can optimize the mining process by predicting the best times to mine, optimizing resource allocation, and even reducing the energy footprint, making the entire process more sustainable and cost-effective.

- **Personalized User Experiences:** AI can analyze user behaviors and preferences within decentralized systems to create more personalized and efficient user experiences. From optimizing wallet management to recommending specific blockchain-based services, AI can tailor the decentralized experience to individual users.

- **Interoperability and Integration:** As the digital world becomes more interconnected, there's a need for different blockchain systems and traditional databases to interact seamlessly. AI can facilitate this integration, ensuring data flows smoothly and securely between disparate systems.

The symbiotic relationship between AI and decentralized systems exemplifies how emerging technologies can complement and enhance each other. As these technologies continue to evolve, their convergence will pave the way for innovative solutions that redefine data management, security, and the broader digital landscape.

11.4.3. Challenges in Integrating AI with Decentralized Systems

The fusion of AI and decentralized systems, particularly blockchain, holds enormous promise. Nevertheless, blending two revolutionary technologies is not without its set of challenges. This section delves into the complexities and hurdles of integrating AI with decentralized systems and the considerations that stakeholders must be aware of:

- **Data Privacy Concerns:** One of the core principles of decentralized systems is the assurance of data immutability and transparency. AI, on the other hand, requires vast amounts of data to train, refine, and implement models. Striking a balance between making data available for AI processes and preserving user privacy is a challenge. There's a risk of exposing sensitive information or creating vectors for data linkage attacks.

- **Computational Overhead:** AI algorithms, especially deep learning models, demand significant computational resources. When combined with the already resource-intensive nature of some decentralized systems (like proof-of-work blockchains), there can be substantial overhead, leading to potential inefficiencies or bottlenecks.

- **Consensus Mechanism Complications:** Decentralized systems rely on consensus mechanisms to validate transactions. Incorporating AI processes into these mechanisms can introduce complexities, especially if nodes in the network interpret data or run algorithms inconsistently, leading to potential disputes or forks.

- **Quality and Integrity of Data:** For AI to produce reliable outcomes, it needs high-quality data. In decentralized systems, ensuring the accuracy and integrity of data being fed into AI models becomes crucial. Erroneous data can lead to flawed AI decisions, which can be hard to reverse given the immutable nature of blockchains.

- **Smart Contract Limitations:** While AI can optimize and enhance smart contracts, the static nature of some smart contract platforms can be limiting. The inability to update or change a contract once deployed might hinder the integration of dynamic AI models that evolve over time.

- **Interoperability Issues:** As previously mentioned, interoperability is a significant advantage when AI is integrated with decentralized systems. However, achieving this seamless interaction between different blockchain platforms, traditional databases, and AI models presents technical and standardization challenges.

- **Economic and Incentive Misalignments:** The integration of AI might necessitate changes in the incentive structures of decentralized systems. For instance, rewarding nodes for contributing computational power for AI processes or penalizing malicious behavior might require rethinking traditional blockchain reward mechanisms.

- **Regulatory and Compliance Hurdles:** As AI and blockchain technologies are relatively new, the regulatory landscape is still evolving. Ensuring that AI-driven decentralized applications comply with regional and international regulations, especially concerning data protection and privacy, adds another layer of complexity.

Integrating AI with decentralized systems is an ambitious undertaking, with both technical and ethical challenges. However, the potential benefits—enhanced security, efficiency, and novel applications—justify the efforts. By acknowledging and addressing these challenges head-on, stakeholders can pave the way for a harmonized and powerful convergence of AI and decentralization.

11.4.4.   Real-world Implementations and Innovations in Decentralization

The combination of AI and decentralized systems, especially blockchain technology, is more than just a conceptual discussion–there have been tangible implementations that demonstrate this convergence's potential. This section aims to provide a snapshot of real-world applications where AI and decentralized systems have synergistically come together to solve challenges or create innovations:

- **Decentralized Identity Systems:** Projects like Sovrin and uPort are working on providing users with self-sovereign identities, where individuals have full control over their personal data. AI can enhance such platforms by analyzing usage patterns, identifying potential threats, and offering recommendations for better data management and privacy.[201]

- **Decentralized Data Marketplaces:** Platforms like Ocean Protocol facilitate the secure sharing of datasets without compromising data ownership, enabling AI researchers and companies to access diverse datasets without privacy issues. Using smart contracts and tokenized incentives, AI models can securely train on a decentralized network with data from multiple sources.[202]

- **Predictive Analysis on Blockchains:** Augur and Gnosis are examples of decentralized prediction markets. They harness the power of AI to analyze vast amounts of data to predict outcomes, ranging from election results to market movements. This combination promotes trust, as predictions are based on transparent algorithms and recorded on immutable ledgers.[203]

- **AI-driven Smart Contracts:** Smart contracts on platforms like Ethereum can be enhanced using AI to make decisions based on external data points. Chainlink, for instance, provides reliable oracles that supply real-world data to smart

---

[201] https://hyscaler.com/insights/trust-revolution-self-sovereign-identity/

[202] https://blog.singularitynet.io/ocean-protocol-partners-with-singularitynet-de112ae68244, https://www.toolify.ai/ai-news/unlocking-the-potential-of-tokenized-data-and-ai-with-ocean-protocol-2294248, and https://iq.wiki/wiki/ocean-protocol

[203] https://www.bitcoinmarketjournal.com/smart-contracts-and-ai/ and https://www.diva-portal.org/smash/get/diva2:1306764/FULLTEXT01.pdf

contracts. The convergence allows for dynamic contracts that can adjust based on real-time data analyzed by AI.[204]

- **Decentralized Finance (DeFi) and AI:** The DeFi sector, with platforms like Aave and Compound, has witnessed rapid growth. AI can optimize lending rates, evaluate borrower reliability, and predict market fluctuations, ensuring better returns and reduced risks for users.[205]

- **AI-enhanced Supply Chain Management:** Projects like VeChain use blockchain to provide transparent and immutable records for supply chains. When AI is incorporated, it can predict delays, identify inefficiencies, and even authenticate products, ensuring genuine items reach consumers.

- **Decentralized AI Training Platforms:** Platforms like SingularityNET allow AI developers to upload their algorithms, and users can request custom AI model training. Such platforms democratize AI access and ensure transparent and fair compensation for developers.

- **AI in Decentralized Content Management:** Projects like Steemit use blockchain to reward content creators directly. AI can curate content, identify plagiarism, and provide insights into audience preferences, optimizing the content dissemination process.

- **Decentralized Healthcare Data Systems:** Platforms such as Nebula Genomics allow individuals to own their genomic data and decide how to share or monetize it. AI can analyze this data to provide personalized health insights, predict susceptibilities, and guide research, all while preserving data privacy.[206]

The synergy between AI and decentralized systems is still in its infancy, but the potential is enormous. As these technologies mature, we can anticipate an ecosystem where the transparency and immutability of decentralization complement AI's predictive power and intelligence, ushering in a new era of innovation and trust.

---

[204] https://blog.chain.link/blockchain-ai-use-cases/

[205] https://vegavid.com/blog/5-blockchain-projects-using-ai-that-are-shaping-the-future/

[206] https://vegavid.com/blog/5-blockchain-projects-using-ai-that-are-shaping-the-future/

11.5.   AI-Powered Data Management for Emerging Technologies

As we continue to advance into the digital age, emerging technologies are consistently reshaping the landscape of data management. These technologies, while novel and exciting, also introduce complex challenges that require sophisticated solutions. AI, with its unparalleled capabilities in data processing and pattern recognition, stands at the forefront of addressing these challenges and optimizing the functionalities of these emergent technologies. In this section, we explore how AI-driven strategies are being tailored to manage the data intricacies of some of the most prominent upcoming tech trends.

11.5.1.   AI-Proof Security for the Internet of Things (IoT) Ecosystem

The Internet of Things (IoT) represents a vast interconnected web of devices, ranging from smart refrigerators and wearable fitness trackers to advanced industrial machinery sensors. As IoT devices permeate every facet of our daily lives and industrial operations, they generate a colossal amount of data, presenting both opportunities and vulnerabilities. Each of these devices, while enhancing functionality and convenience, also acts as a potential access point for malicious actors.

With such an intricate network of devices continuously communicating, traditional security measures often fall short. The dynamic nature of the threats targeting IoT ecosystems necessitates a more adaptive and proactive approach. Enter AI. AI's capability to learn, predict, and respond in real-time makes it a formidable ally in ensuring the security of IoT devices and the data they manage.

However, integrating AI into IoT security is not without challenges. The sheer volume of data, diverse device protocols, and real-time processing demands require innovative solutions. In this section, we will delve into how AI-driven strategies are being developed and employed to fortify the IoT ecosystem, ensuring its resilience against an ever-evolving threat landscape. As we progress, the significance of AI's role in shaping the future of IoT security becomes unmistakably clear, laying the foundation for a secure, interconnected world.[207]

11.5.2.   Augmented Reality (AR) and Virtual Reality (VR): Pioneering Immersive Experiences Safeguarded by AI

Augmented Reality (AR) and Virtual Reality (VR) technologies have been game-changers in creating immersive digital experiences. They have found applications across sectors, from gaming and entertainment to healthcare, education, and industrial design. As AR and VR platforms evolve, offering users more intricate and deeply immersive experiences, the data they collect, process, and transmit becomes increasingly voluminous and sensitive. This massive influx of data requires heightened security protocols, especially since breaches in such environments could compromise user privacy, safety, and even their perception of reality.

AI plays a pivotal role in enhancing the security protocols of AR and VR systems. With graphics processing units (GPUs) pushing the limits of these digital realities, AI algorithms are simultaneously running in the background, ensuring data integrity and monitoring for any anomalies that might indicate a security threat. Given that AR and VR systems require real-time processing to deliver smooth experiences, the speed at which AI can detect and respond to threats becomes essential.

However, as with any technological integration, challenges emerge. The sheer computational demands of AR and VR systems mean that embedding AI security protocols can often strain resources. Moreover, the unique data types and the nature of user interactions in AR and VR environments necessitate tailored AI security solutions that are different from those used in more traditional computing settings. In this section, we'll explore the innovations at the intersection of AI, AR, and VR, understanding how they shape the future of immersive digital experiences while prioritizing user security and privacy. As we journey through this domain, the blend of realism and digital sophistication underscores the importance of robust, AI-driven security measures.[208]

---

[207] https://embeddedcomputing.com/technology/iot/data-analytics/a-comprehensive-approach-to-enhancing-iot-security-with-artificial-intelligence

[208] References: https://viso.ai/computer-vision/augmented-reality-virtual-reality/

11.5.3. Internet of Things (IoT): Navigating a Hyper-Connected World with AI-Driven Safeguards

The Internet of Things (IoT) has ushered in an era of unprecedented connectivity, weaving a complex tapestry of devices, from everyday household items to intricate industrial machines, into the vast expanse of the internet. Refrigerators, thermostats, wearables, and even light bulbs now boast internet connectivity, offering users convenience and advanced functionalities. By 2030, it's projected that over 32 billion cellular IoT devices will be online, signaling the expansive reach and transformative power of this technology.[209]

However, this hyper-connectivity brings with it a slew of security challenges. The diversity and volume of devices, each with its own set of vulnerabilities, provide cybercriminals with multiple entry points to exploit. Traditional security measures often fall short of adequately protecting the IoT landscape, given the scale and decentralized nature of its architecture. This is where AI enters the fray, offering dynamic and scalable solutions to monitor, detect, and respond to threats across the myriad of IoT devices.

Harnessing the power of machine learning and advanced analytics, AI algorithms can learn from the behavior of devices and networks, detecting anomalies and potentially harmful patterns in real-time. For instance, if a smart thermostat begins to communicate with an unfamiliar server, AI-driven systems could promptly recognize this anomaly and take corrective action. Beyond mere detection, AI can also predict potential vulnerabilities by analyzing trends and patterns, thereby fortifying IoT networks even before threats materialize.

Yet, the blend of AI and IoT is not without challenges. Concerns over data privacy, the computational demands of AI, and the vast heterogeneity of IoT devices mean that security solutions need to be constantly evolved and adapted. In this section, we delve deep into the confluence of AI and IoT, exploring the advancements, challenges, and the path forward in ensuring a secure and efficient IoT ecosystem. As the boundaries between the physical and digital realms blur, AI stands as a sentinel, ensuring that our hyper-connected world remains safe and resilient.

---

[209] https://transformainsights.com/research/forecast/highlights

11.5.4. 5G Technology: Turbocharging Connectivity and the Imperative for AI-Enhanced Security

The dawn of 5G technology is revolutionizing global communication networks, offering blistering speeds, near-zero latency, and an ability to handle an exponentially greater number of connected devices. This quantum leap from its predecessor, 4G, doesn't only mean faster downloads or smoother streaming–it's reshaping entire industries, from manufacturing and transportation to healthcare and entertainment. As autonomous vehicles, smart cities, telemedicine, and augmented reality become commonplace, 5G stands as the robust backbone supporting these advancements.

However, with great power comes great responsibility. The same features that make 5G transformative—its high speed, dense connectivity, and low latency—also open the door to novel security challenges. The vast and intricate network of devices and systems operating on 5G necessitates a more sophisticated approach to security, one that goes beyond the capabilities of traditional firewalls and encryption methods. Cyber threats, already evolving at an alarming pace, could potentially exploit the multi-layered architecture of 5G networks, leading to new attack vectors.

This is where AI emerges as a potent ally. By continuously monitoring data traffic, identifying unusual patterns, and making split-second decisions, AI can provide a dynamic defense against threats in a 5G environment. For example, in a 5G-powered smart city, an AI system can detect and mitigate potential DDoS attacks in real-time, safeguarding critical infrastructure from malfeasance. Furthermore, AI-driven security solutions can adapt and learn from every attempted intrusion, refining their defensive strategies and staying one step ahead of cyber adversaries.

However, the integration of AI into 5G security isn't without its complexities. The sheer volume of data processed in 5G networks requires robust AI algorithms capable of discerning genuine threats from false alarms. Additionally, as 5G facilitates the rise of edge computing, ensuring AI security at the "edge"—closer to where data is generated—becomes paramount.

11.5.5. Neuromorphic Computing: Bridging the Gap between Brain and Machine through AI-Proof Security

In our relentless quest for faster, more efficient computing paradigms, the concept of neuromorphic computing emerges as a tantalizing promise of the future. Drawing inspiration from the very structure and function of the human brain, neuromorphic computing aims to mimic our neural systems' intricate workings to create more energy-efficient, faster, and adaptive artificial neural networks. These systems aren't just about emulating the brain–they're about potentially revolutionizing fields ranging from real-time data processing to robotics, creating devices that can learn and adapt organically.

However, the power and adaptability of neuromorphic computing systems come with unique security challenges. Just as these systems learn and evolve from the data they're exposed to, they can be susceptible to malicious data inputs that could misguide their learning processes. This adaptability could be manipulated by malicious actors, leading to a myriad of security concerns.

AI becomes a natural ally in addressing these challenges. Traditional security protocols, designed for linear and predictable systems, are ill-suited to safeguard the dynamic nature of neuromorphic systems. AI-driven security solutions can monitor, in real-time, the behavior of neuromorphic circuits, flagging anomalies and potentially malicious adaptations. By applying AI's pattern-recognition capabilities, we can better ensure that neuromorphic systems remain uncompromised and function as intended.

The synergy between neuromorphic computing and AI doesn't end at security. AI algorithms, when run on neuromorphic hardware, can achieve unparalleled efficiency as they are executed on systems that mirror their neural-based designs. This marriage between hardware and software paves the way for innovations previously deemed as science fiction, from hyper-realistic simulations to truly autonomous robots that learn from their surroundings.

11.5.6. *Bioinformatics and Genomic Data Management: Harnessing AI's Potential While Safeguarding the Building Blocks of Life*

In the intricate world of biology, the sheer volume, complexity, and dynamic nature of genomic data present profound challenges and unprecedented opportunities. As we push the boundaries of what's possible in genetic engineering, precision medicine, and evolutionary studies, the field of bioinformatics stands as the linchpin, decoding the vast and intricate tapestry of genomic data. It offers tools and methodologies to understand, annotate, and make meaningful predictions based on genetic sequences. Yet, the staggering amount of data produced by high-throughput sequencing technologies requires computational firepower and analytical prowess beyond traditional means.

Enter artificial intelligence. With its capacity to sift through massive datasets, identify patterns, and make predictions, AI has rapidly found its footing in the realm of bioinformatics. Deep learning models can predict protein structures, identify genetic variations linked to specific diseases, and even simulate the evolutionary trajectories of certain genes. The potential applications are boundless, from tailoring medical treatments to an individual's genetic makeup to identifying and mitigating genetic diseases before they manifest.

However, the sensitive nature of genomic data brings forth a slew of ethical and security concerns. Genomic data is deeply personal–it's the very code that defines an individual. In the wrong hands, such data could be used maliciously, from discrimination based on genetic predispositions to biohacking attempts aimed at manipulating an organism's genetic structure. Ensuring the security, integrity, and confidentiality of this data is of paramount importance.

AI-driven security solutions offer a promising avenue in this regard. By leveraging AI's pattern recognition and anomaly detection capabilities, we can create systems that monitor genomic databases in real-time, flagging unauthorized access or suspicious activities. Furthermore, AI can aid in ensuring that genomic data shared for research purposes is effectively anonymized, stripping away identifiers without compromising the data's research value.

11.5.7. Smart Cities and Urban Planning: Streamlining Urban Life with AI-Powered Solutions

Cities, as we know them, have been constantly evolving organisms, reflecting the ebb and flow of societies, economies, and technologies. Today's urban environments, however, stand at an unprecedented cusp of transformation. With burgeoning populations and the ever-growing demands of modern life, cities must adapt swiftly, efficiently, and sustainably. The vision of a 'Smart City' emerges from this very need: a city that harnesses technology to enhance the quality of life, improve resource efficiency, and ensure equitable development.

The crux of this transformative vision lies in data. From traffic patterns to energy consumption, from waste management to public health, vast volumes of data are generated every moment in an urban ecosystem. But raw data, in isolation, isn't very useful. It's the analysis, insights, and actionable intelligence derived from this data that make all the difference. And this is where artificial intelligence takes center stage.

By leveraging AI, smart cities can predict traffic congestion and optimize routes in real time. They can monitor air quality, making informed decisions to curb pollution. AI-driven systems can optimize energy grids, reducing wastage and ensuring uninterrupted supply. Surveillance systems equipped with AI can bolster urban security, detecting threats and anomalies swiftly. The potential applications are numerous and transformative.

Yet, with the integration of AI in urban systems, new challenges arise. The very data that powers these AI models often encompass the personal details of citizens. Whether it's their movement patterns, their energy consumption habits, or their interactions with urban amenities, there's a fine line between useful data and invasive surveillance. Ensuring the privacy and security of this data becomes paramount.

11.6. Leveraging RPA, Intelligent Automation, and Low-Code Platforms for Enhanced Security

The adoption of RPA, intelligent automation, and low-code/no-code platforms is on the rise as organizations seek to enhance efficiency and drive innovation. However, the security implications of these technologies are a growing concern. Proper management can transform these potential vulnerabilities into opportunities to strengthen security defenses.[210]

Security risks include:

- **RPA Security Considerations**: RPAs can significantly enhance operational efficiency but also increase the attack surface by interacting with critical systems. Ensuring RPAs operate within the principle of least privilege and implementing robust access controls are essential for mitigating risks.[211]

- **Intelligent Automation Vulnerabilities**: AI components in intelligent automation may be vulnerable to data poisoning and model evasion attacks.

---

[210] "Security Implications of Emerging Tech," TechSecurity Magazine, 2022.

[211] "RPA and Security: Opportunities and Challenges," CyberSec Journal, 2021.

Continuous monitoring and adopting adversarial training are crucial for early identification and rectification of potential weaknesses.[212]

- **Low-Code/No-Code Security**: While empowering non-technical users to develop applications, these platforms may bypass traditional security reviews. Establishing a governance framework with security best practices is vital for ensuring developed applications are secure by design.[213]

We can enhance security through automation and low-code platforms:

- **Automated Security Workflows**: Utilizing RPA and intelligent automation for security operations, from threat detection to response, can free up security teams to address more complex threats.[214]

- **Custom Security Solutions with Low-Code**: Low-code platforms enable the rapid development of custom security tools, offering real-time visibility into security postures and facilitating quick adaptation to new threats.[215]

- **Compliance and Reporting**: Automation of compliance reporting and management tasks through these technologies reduces human error, ensuring up-to-date regulatory compliance.[216]

For example, a financial institution effectively used RPA to automate the monitoring and reporting of suspicious activities, substantially decreasing detection and response times to potential threats.[217] Another example, leveraging a low-code platform, a healthcare

---

[212] "Mitigating AI Vulnerabilities," AI Safety Review, 2023.

[213] "Governance in Low-Code/No-Code Development," DevSecOps Digest, 2022

[214] "Streamlining Security Operations with RPA," Security Innovations, 2023.

[215] "Rapid Security Tool Development with Low-Code Platforms," LowCode Today, 2021.

[216] "Automating Compliance for Efficiency," ComplianceTech Watch, 2022.

[217] "Case Study: RPA in Financial Security," Financial Security Insights, 2023.

provider developed a custom application for managing patient consent and access logs, significantly enhancing data privacy and regulatory compliance.[218]

Best practices for secure implementation include:

- **Security Assessments**: Regular evaluations of the security posture of RPA bots, AI models, and low-code applications are essential for identifying and mitigating vulnerabilities.[219]

- **Security Training for Citizen Developers**: It's critical that users of low-code/no-code platforms receive training on security best practices and the significance of data protection.[220]

- **Integration with Security Infrastructure**: APIs should be used to integrate RPA and low-code platforms with existing security tools, ensuring a unified approach to security.

[221]

---

[218] "Enhancing Healthcare Privacy with Low-Code," HealthTech Privacy Review, 2022.

[219] "Best Practices in Tech Security Assessments," SecureTech Journal, 2023.

[220] "Training Citizen Developers for Secure App Development," EduTech Security, 2023.

[221] "Integrating Automated Systems for Enhanced Security," API Security Trends, 2021.

12. The Board of Directors and AI

In the age of digital transformation, there is hardly a facet of business that remains untouched by artificial intelligence (AI). While the operational teams, developers, and data scientists grapple with the intricacies of AI on the ground, a broader, more strategic perspective is being sought in the boardrooms. The role of the board of directors, traditionally seen as guiding the ship through high-level oversight, is now entwined with understanding and directing AI strategy. As AI reshapes business models, disrupts industries, and redefines customer experiences, board members must responsibly understand, evaluate, and harness its potential.

However, the rapid rise of AI brings a distinct set of challenges. The technology itself can be complex and esoteric, often perceived as a realm exclusively for tech experts. Yet, for an organization to truly integrate AI into its fabric, this perception must be dispelled. The board of directors, though not expected to delve into the granular details, should possess a clear conceptual grasp of AI's capabilities and implications. By understanding the foundational elements of AI, the board can make informed strategic decisions, ensuring that the organization remains competitive and agile in an AI-driven world.

Furthermore, as stewards of organizational integrity, boards carry the ethical responsibility of ensuring AI's deployment aligns with societal values and norms. From concerns about data privacy to the potential biases AI systems can inherit, a myriad of ethical dilemmas arise that boards must confront. It's not just about maximizing profits or optimizing operations anymore–it's about pioneering responsible AI that upholds the values of stakeholders, customers, and society at large.

The board's engagement with AI also extends to matters of risk and governance. AI, for all its benefits, can introduce new vulnerabilities—both technical and reputational. Missteps in AI implementations can lead to significant financial and reputational losses. As such, boards need to ensure robust oversight mechanisms are in place and that AI strategies are both resilient and flexible, adapting to the rapidly changing landscape.

Additionally, there's an increasing realization that the board itself needs to evolve in this AI era. This means not only continuous education about AI's evolving role in business but also possibly integrating AI experts into board discussions or even board compositions. Such integration ensures that AI-related decisions are made with a blend of business acumen and technical expertise.

In essence, the relationship between the board of directors and AI is not just one of oversight but of engagement, understanding, and evolution. As we navigate further into this chapter, we'll delve deeper into each facet of this relationship, illuminating the board's pivotal role in guiding organizations through the challenges and opportunities presented by AI.

12.1.   Introduction to AI for Board Members

AI is no longer just a buzzword but an integral component of modern business dynamics. For board members, individuals often selected for their expertise in governance, finance, and broader industry trends, understanding the essence of AI might seem daunting. Yet, in today's competitive business environment, a basic grounding in AI's foundational principles isn't just beneficial—it's crucial. As strategic decision-makers, board members need a coherent understanding of how AI can influence business trajectories, reshape industries, and redefine stakeholder values.

At its core, AI refers to machines programmed to mimic human intelligence processes, such as learning, reasoning, and problem-solving. It isn't about creating robots that think like humans but rather about devising algorithms that can process vast amounts of data far quicker and more accurately than humans ever could. Machine Learning (ML), a subset of AI, allows systems to automatically learn and improve from experience. This capability is what often gives AI its seemingly "magical" quality.

For board members, the allure of AI isn't in its technical intricacies but in its transformative potential. AI can be the catalyst for new product lines, more efficient operational workflows, novel customer experiences, and even entirely new business models. However, this transformative power also means AI carries risks. A misaligned AI strategy can lead to resource drains, reputational damage, or worse, ethical transgressions that can irrevocably harm a brand.

While board members aren't expected to be AI specialists, they are entrusted with ensuring that the organization's AI endeavors align with its broader vision and values. This requires discernment, a foundational understanding of AI's potential, and an awareness of its limitations. It's about asking the right questions: Where can AI add the most value within our operations? What are the ethical considerations? How do we measure the success or failure of AI implementations?

This section serves as a primer, aiming to demystify AI for board members, providing them with the tools and perspectives necessary to engage in meaningful discussions and make informed decisions. It's not about deep technical dives but about understanding the landscape, recognizing the landmarks, and confidently navigating the terrain of AI in business.

12.1.1.   Why AI is More Than Just Another Tech Trend

Over the years, the business landscape has witnessed a barrage of technological trends, each promising to be the next game-changer. From the dot-com boom to the rise of cloud computing, these trends have shaped and, in some cases, revolutionized industries. However, the emergence of AI stands out from the rest, not merely as a fleeting trend but as a foundational shift in how businesses operate, innovate, and compete.

There are several reasons why AI transcends the typical tech trend label:

- **Ubiquity Across Industries:** Unlike other technologies that find prominence in select sectors, AI has found applications across a broad spectrum of industries, from healthcare and finance to entertainment and logistics. This isn't just about automating tasks–it's about augmenting human capabilities, transforming decision-making processes, and creating new business models.

- **Continuous Learning and Adaptation:** Traditional software and tools have static capabilities that are designed to perform tasks as programmed. In contrast, AI, especially through machine learning, evolves. It learns from new data, adapts to changing environments, and can even predict future trends. This dynamic nature ensures that AI's relevance grows over time rather than wanes.

- **The Data Explosion:** The 21st century is marked by the exponential growth of data. From social media feeds to IoT sensors, data is being generated at an unprecedented rate. AI is uniquely positioned to harness this data deluge, extracting insights, patterns, and actionable intelligence that would be impossible for humans to derive manually.

- **Economic Impact:** A study by McKinsey estimated that automation and AI could add around $13 trillion to the global economy by 2030. Such projections underscore AI's potential not just as a tool but as a significant economic force, influencing job markets, GDP growth, and global trade dynamics.

- **Ethical and Societal Implications:** Few technological trends raise as many ethical questions as AI does. From concerns about job displacements and privacy breaches to deeper philosophical discussions about machine consciousness and morality, AI forces society to grapple with challenges that are as existential as they are technical.

For board members, understanding AI's unique position in the tech evolution timeline is crucial. It's not about hopping onto the latest trend but about recognizing AI as a transformative force that has the potential to redefine industries, shape societal values, and influence global economic paradigms. Embracing AI is not just about staying ahead—it's about staying relevant in a rapidly changing world.

12.1.2.   Basic AI Concepts Every Board Member Should Know

For board members to effectively grasp the strategic implications of AI and integrate it into business decisions, they need not be machine learning experts or data scientists. However, a fundamental understanding of certain key AI concepts can be invaluable. These foundational ideas provide a context for deeper discussions about AI's potential impact and risks in business scenarios:

- **Machine Learning (ML):** At its core, ML is a subfield of AI that allows systems to learn and improve from experience without being explicitly programmed. By analyzing vast amounts of data, these systems can make predictions or decisions without a set of explicit instructions.

- **Neural Networks and Deep Learning:** These are advanced subsets of ML, inspired by the structure and function of the human brain. They consist of layers of interconnected 'neurons' that process data. Deep learning excels at recognizing patterns in large and complex datasets and powers many modern AI feats, such as image and speech recognition.

- **Natural Language Processing (NLP):** This pertains to the ability of AI systems to understand, interpret, and respond to human language. It's the backbone of chatbots, voice assistants, and many content analysis tools.

- **Reinforcement Learning:** A type of ML where algorithms learn by interacting with an environment and receiving feedback in the form of rewards or penalties. It's crucial in areas like robotics and game playing, where the AI must make a sequence of decisions to achieve a goal.

- **Supervised versus Unsupervised Learning:** In supervised learning, algorithms are 'taught' using labeled data, where the outcome is known. Once trained, the algorithm can apply its learning to new, unlabeled data. On the other hand, unsupervised learning deals with unlabeled data, and the algorithm tries to identify inherent patterns or structures.

- **Bias and Fairness in AI:** Algorithms can inadvertently perpetuate or amplify biases present in their training data, leading to skewed or unfair outcomes. Recognizing and addressing this bias is crucial for ethical AI deployment.

- **Explainability and Transparency:** As AI systems become more complex, understanding their decision-making process becomes challenging. Transparent AI models and tools that offer insights into how decisions are made are vital for trust and accountability.

- **Robotic Process Automation (RPA):** This refers to the use of software bots to automate highly repetitive and routine tasks, leading to efficiencies and cost savings in processes such as data extraction and processing.

- **Generative Adversarial Networks (GANs):** A system of two neural networks contesting with each other in a zero-sum game framework. They're particularly useful in generating new data that resembles a given set of data, with applications in art, design, and deepfakes.

For board members, this foundational knowledge provides a stepping stone to assess AI's opportunities, challenges, and ethical implications in their respective industries. By bridging the gap between technical jargon and strategic insight, they can steer their organizations effectively in the AI-driven future.

12.1.3.   The Pervasiveness of AI in Modern Business

AI is not merely a component of the tech industry—it is a transformative force reshaping the entirety of the business landscape. Today, board members should recognize the ubiquitous nature of AI across sectors, domains, and processes. Understanding the reach and potential of AI in today's corporate world is pivotal for informed decision-making and strategic planning:

- **Customer Experience and Personalization:** AI's most visible application might be in enhancing customer experiences. Algorithms can predict purchase behaviors, customize user interfaces in real-time, and offer personalized product recommendations, leading to increased customer loyalty and higher sales.

- **Operational Efficiencies:** Behind the scenes, AI drives process automation, predictive maintenance, and optimized resource allocation. Whether it's an AI-powered chatbot handling routine customer inquiries or a sophisticated algorithm predicting machinery breakdowns in a factory, AI ensures operations are smoother and more cost-effective.

- **Decision-making Support:** Data-driven decisions are becoming the norm. Advanced AI algorithms can analyze vast amounts of business data to uncover insights, trends, and correlations that might be invisible to human analysts. This allows companies to make more informed decisions about everything from product launches to market expansions.

- **Human Resources and Talent Management:** AI tools in HR are revolutionizing recruitment, talent management, and employee engagement. Algorithms can sift through thousands of resumes to find the best fit, predict which employees are likely to leave, and even monitor employee well-being.

- **Supply Chain and Logistics:** AI-powered analytics can forecast demand more accurately, optimize inventory levels, and even predict supply chain disruptions from events like political upheavals or natural disasters. Automated warehouses and AI-driven logistics solutions also ensure that products get to their destinations more efficiently.

- **Financial Services:** From fraud detection to algorithmic trading and robo-advisors, AI is transforming the world of finance. Real-time analytics powered by AI offer insights into market trends, and predictive models can foresee potential financial crises or opportunities.

- **Research and Development:** In sectors like pharmaceuticals, AI models can predict how molecules will interact, drastically cutting down drug discovery times. Similarly, in tech, AI aids in software testing, bug detection, and feature development.

- **Marketing and Sales:** Beyond just targeted ads, AI helps in sentiment analysis, market segmentation, and predicting sales trends. It's also the driving force behind voice search optimization and chatbots, which are redefining customer interaction.

- **Sustainability and Environment:** AI aids in optimizing energy consumption in industries, predicting environmental trends, and even monitoring deforestation or marine health via satellite imagery analysis.

For board members, it's crucial to realize that AI is not an isolated tool but a comprehensive suite of capabilities that can drive value across all business functions. No longer confined to tech giants or startups, AI is a staple in the modern business toolkit, offering competitive advantages to those who leverage its power wisely.

12.2.   The Strategic Importance of AI

In an era dominated by data and rapid technological innovation, AI has emerged as a linchpin for the next generation of business strategy. For board members and top-level executives, understanding the strategic implications of AI isn't just an advantage—it's an imperative. AI's strategic significance doesn't stem merely from its technological prowess but from its profound capacity to redefine business models, customer interactions, and even entire industries.

The velocity with which AI is being adopted and integrated into business operations is a testament to its transformative power. Companies aren't just using AI to enhance existing processes–they're engineering entirely new ways of delivering value to stakeholders. From personalized user experiences that anticipate individual preferences to real-time analytics that provide unparalleled market insights, AI stands at the forefront of contemporary business innovation.

However, AI's strategic importance also presents novel challenges. The factors that make AI such a potent tool—its adaptability, data-hungry nature, and autonomous decision-making capabilities—also introduce complexities in governance, ethics, and risk management. Therefore, a nuanced understanding of these challenges is critical for board members as they chart the strategic course of their organizations.

Moreover, as competitors begin leveraging AI, the lack of a strategic approach to AI adoption can leave companies lagging, eroding their market position and brand value. For businesses, the choice is clear: either harness the strategic potential of AI proactively or risk becoming obsolete in an AI-driven market landscape.

The boardroom discussions of today need to be forward-thinking, blending traditional business acumen with a deep understanding of AI's potential and its implications. This section will delve into why AI is more than just another technological innovation and how it can serve as a strategic cornerstone for businesses looking to thrive in the 21st century.

12.2.1. AI as a Competitive Advantage

The contemporary business landscape is characterized by rapid changes, intense competition, and an ever-evolving customer base. In this setting, staying ahead requires more than just incremental improvements. Organizations need to be agile, innovative, and ahead of the curve. AI, with its multifaceted capabilities, has emerged as a game-changer, offering businesses an unprecedented competitive edge.

- **Enhanced Customer Experiences:** At its core, AI excels at processing vast amounts of data and gleaning actionable insights from it. For businesses, this means understanding customer behaviors, preferences, and pain points with greater depth and precision. AI-powered systems can predict what customers want even before they express it, leading to more personalized user interactions and higher customer satisfaction.

- **Operational Efficiency:** AI systems can automate mundane, repetitive tasks that traditionally consumed significant human resources. From chatbots addressing customer queries to AI-driven supply chain optimization, these technologies streamline operations, reduce costs, and increase speed, allowing businesses to allocate resources to more strategic endeavors.

- **Data-driven Decision Making:** Gone are the days of relying solely on intuition or outdated reports. AI algorithms provide real-time analytics, presenting decision-makers with timely and accurate data. This enables businesses to respond quickly to market changes, capitalize on new opportunities, or mitigate potential risks.

- **Innovation and New Revenue Streams:** Beyond optimizing existing processes, AI opens doors to entirely new business models and revenue streams. Think of how streaming services use AI to recommend content, driving user engagement and subscription renewals, or how financial institutions use AI to develop personalized investment strategies.

- **Risk Management:** AI's predictive capabilities aren't limited to customer preferences. They can also forecast potential risks, from market downturns to cybersecurity threats. By identifying these risks ahead of time, businesses can formulate proactive strategies, ensuring continuity and resilience.

- **Staying Ahead of the Curve:** In an age where many companies are integrating AI into their operations, not leveraging its capabilities can be detrimental. Companies that fail to adopt AI risk falling behind, as competitors offer better products, more efficient services, and improved user experiences.

However, leveraging AI as a competitive advantage isn't without its challenges. Implementation requires investment, not just in terms of technology but also in training and change management. There's also the task of ensuring ethical AI use, maintaining transparency, and addressing potential biases. But, for those organizations that navigate these challenges effectively, AI offers a transformative edge, positioning them as leaders in their respective industries.

12.2.2.   Transforming Business Models with AI

For centuries, businesses have evolved their models to capitalize on technological advancements. From the industrial revolution's factory systems to the internet era's digital marketplaces, innovative technologies have consistently reshaped the way organizations operate and deliver value. AI stands as the latest in this lineage of transformative technologies, but its impact is profound, offering not just incremental changes but foundational shifts in business models:

- **Hyper-personalization:** Traditional business models often rely on broad customer segments and generalized strategies. AI enables a paradigm shift towards hyper-personalization, where products, services, and communications are tailored to individual preferences and behaviors. Retailers, for instance, no longer just group customers by demographics but can predict individual purchasing behaviors based on past data, real-time online activity, and even social media sentiments.

- **Subscription and As-a-Service Models:** AI's predictive analytics capabilities have given rise to new subscription models. Whether it's streaming platforms suggesting content or software platforms evolving based on user behavior, AI ensures that these subscription models constantly adapt to user needs, thereby retaining and growing the customer base.

- **Dynamic Pricing:** Gone are the rigid pricing models of the past. With AI, businesses can dynamically adjust prices based on real-time demand, supply, customer behavior, and other external factors. This not only maximizes profit but also optimizes inventory and reduces waste.

- **Decentralized Decision-making:** Traditional hierarchical models often see decisions funneled through layers of management. With AI-driven insights, decision-making can be decentralized, empowering teams on the ground with real-time data and predictive analytics to make informed choices.

- **Platform-based Ecosystems:** AI facilitates the creation of platform-based business models where companies serve as intermediaries, connecting users, providers, and even other businesses. These platforms thrive on data, with AI algorithms matching demand with supply, optimizing logistics, and even moderating interactions.

- **Automated Operations and Reduced Overheads:** AI-driven automation, from chatbots to robotic process automation in back-office tasks, means businesses can operate leaner models with reduced overheads without compromising efficiency or customer service.

- **Value Creation through Data Monetization:** Data is often dubbed as the 'new oil.' Businesses can utilize AI to glean insights from their vast data reservoirs, creating new revenue streams by offering these insights to partners or third-party entities or by optimizing internal processes.

While the transformative power of AI is undeniable, it also demands a rethinking of traditional strategies and operations. The integration of AI into business models requires not just technological adaptation but also a cultural shift within organizations. It means upskilling employees, fostering a culture of continuous learning, and developing an organizational mindset that sees AI not as a tool but as an integral part of the business fabric.

12.2.3.   Pivoting to an AI-first Strategy

In the dawn of the digital age, businesses were urged to adopt a "mobile-first" approach, recognizing the profound shift in consumer behavior towards mobile devices. Today, the rallying cry is for an "AI-first" strategy, emphasizing AI's centrality in driving business innovation and success. This pivot doesn't merely involve integrating AI into existing structures but requires a total reimagining of business strategy through the lens of AI's capabilities:

- **Defining AI-First:** At its core, an AI-first strategy means that AI becomes the foundational technology upon which business solutions are built. Instead of asking, "How can we implement AI here?" businesses start with the question, "How can AI redefine this?"

- **Customer Experience Revolution:** An AI-first approach places unprecedented emphasis on the user experience. From personalized product recommendations to intelligent chatbots that can handle complex queries, AI has the potential to make every customer interaction seamless, intuitive, and value-added.

- **Data at the Heart:** For businesses to genuinely pivot to AI-first, they need to see data not just as a byproduct but as a primary asset. This means investing in robust data collection, processing, and analysis capabilities, ensuring that AI systems have the high-quality, diverse data they need to function optimally.

- **Continuous Learning and Adaptation:** AI-first is synonymous with continuous evolution. Unlike traditional static systems, AI-driven solutions learn and adapt. Businesses must cultivate a culture that supports this continuous refinement, encouraging experimentation, feedback, and iterative development.

- **Integrated Innovation:** Pivoting to AI-first isn't limited to one business aspect. It spans products, services, operations, and even organizational culture. It's about leveraging AI to create new value propositions, streamline operations, enhance decision-making, and foster a culture of innovation.

- **Rethinking Talent:** An AI-first strategy invariably impacts the workforce. There's an immediate need for AI expertise, but beyond that, there's also a need for a workforce that understands how to collaborate with AI tools and systems. This might mean retraining employees, hiring new talent, or even redefining roles and responsibilities within the organization.

- **Ethical Considerations:** As AI assumes a more central role, businesses must grapple with the ethical implications. How is data being used? Are AI decisions transparent and fair? Companies need to proactively address these questions, establishing ethical guidelines and ensuring accountability.

Embracing an AI-first strategy doesn't signify the sidelining of human intuition, creativity, or decision-making. Instead, it's about recognizing the transformative potential of AI and positioning it as a driving force in shaping business trajectories. However, this pivot is not without challenges. It demands vision, leadership, and a willingness to disrupt traditional business paradigms. For those who succeed, the rewards—enhanced efficiency, innovation, and competitiveness—are considerable.

12.3. Evaluating AI Investment and ROI

In today's hyper-competitive business landscape, discussions about the adoption of new technologies are almost always paired with questions about their return on investment (ROI). AI, with its transformative potential, is no exception. Board members, while often enticed by the promises of AI-driven innovations, are also tasked with the vital role of safeguarding the company's financial health and ensuring the prudent allocation of resources. Understanding the ROI of AI projects, therefore, becomes not just an exercise in financial calculus but a cornerstone of strategic decision-making:

- **The Allure and Skepticism:** The buzz around AI in the business community is palpable. Tales of startups achieving rapid scalability or established companies redefining their industries through AI-driven innovations are abundant. Yet, for every success story, there are cautionary tales of projects that consumed vast resources with little to show in returns. This dichotomy underscores the need for a nuanced approach to evaluating AI investments.

- **Beyond the Traditional Metrics:** Evaluating AI ROI isn't just about measuring costs against revenues. AI projects can offer intangible benefits such as enhanced brand reputation, improved customer experience, or strategic positioning in a rapidly evolving market. These factors, while harder to quantify, can have a lasting impact on a company's long-term value and competitiveness.

- **Time Horizons Matter:** Unlike more straightforward tech investments, the returns from AI projects might not be immediate. They often require a gestation period, during which data is gathered, models are trained, and algorithms are refined. For board members, it's crucial to understand and set appropriate expectations for when returns are likely to materialize.

- **Scaling and Iteration:** Initial AI pilots or projects might only show modest returns, but their true value lies in the insights they provide, which can be scaled or iterated upon. A pilot that leads to a more efficient supply chain process in one department, for example, could be the blueprint for organization-wide efficiency gains when scaled.

- **The Cost of Inaction:** When evaluating the ROI of AI projects, it's also essential to consider the flip side: what's the cost of not investing in AI? As competitors harness AI to gain market share, improve operations, or innovate, companies that remain on the sidelines might find themselves playing catch-up with diminishing market relevance.

The challenge for board members is not just to evaluate AI investment in terms of dollars and cents but to appreciate the broader strategic implications. It's about understanding the transformative potential of AI, the risks associated with both action and inaction, and ensuring that investments align with the company's long-term vision and objectives.

12.3.1.   Key Metrics for AI Return on Investment (ROI)

Determining the success of an AI initiative requires a blend of quantitative and qualitative metrics. Just as one wouldn't gauge the performance of a diverse stock portfolio solely by the rise or dip of a single stock, AI projects often affect multiple areas of a business in multifaceted ways. Board members must be equipped with a comprehensive understanding of the various metrics that can indicate the ROI of an AI initiative. Here are some pivotal metrics:

- **Cost Savings:** One of the immediate tangible benefits of implementing AI can be the optimization of processes leading to cost savings. This could manifest in areas like automating routine tasks, optimizing supply chains, or reducing resource wastage.

- **Revenue Increase:** AI can directly contribute to revenue increases by driving sales, optimizing pricing strategies, personalizing marketing campaigns, or unveiling new revenue streams.

- **Operational Efficiency:** The impact of AI on operational efficiency can be monumental. Metrics here could include reduced processing times, higher task throughput, or fewer operational errors.

- **Customer Experience and Retention:** AI-driven customer service tools or recommendation systems can enhance the customer experience. Track customer satisfaction scores, net promoter scores, or customer churn rates to measure this impact.

- **Employee Productivity and Satisfaction:** By automating mundane tasks, AI can allow employees to focus on more value-driven activities. Monitoring employee productivity rates and job satisfaction can shed light on the internal benefits of AI adoption.

- **Time to Market:** For product-driven companies, AI can accelerate the R&D phase, prototyping, or even market analysis, allowing for quicker product launches and faster market penetration.

- **Innovation Rate:** AI can spur innovation by identifying market gaps or suggesting product improvements. Track the number of new products, features, or services launched post-AI adoption.

- **Risk Reduction:** For sectors like finance or healthcare, AI can be pivotal in risk mitigation. Metrics could range from fewer financial fraud incidents to improved patient diagnosis accuracy.

- **Data Capitalization:** A company's data, when harnessed by AI, can become a valuable asset. The monetization of insights derived from data or the sale of data-driven products and services can be a significant ROI indicator.

- **Learning and Adaptation Rate:** One of AI's strengths is its ability to learn and adapt over time. Measure how quickly AI systems are refining their outputs based on new data or feedback. Faster adaptation can lead to more rapid benefits realization.

Understanding these metrics doesn't just provide a post-mortem on AI investments–they can also guide future investment decisions. For board members, having a holistic view of these ROI metrics ensures they can appreciate both the tangible and intangible returns that AI brings to the table, making them better equipped to steer the company's AI strategy in alignment with its broader objectives.

12.3.2.   Long-term versus Short-term AI Investments

In the dynamic landscape of technology and business, differentiating between long-term and short-term investments is essential, especially when it comes to the innovative world of AI. For board members, recognizing the nature and expected timeline of returns from each type of investment can substantially inform decision-making processes, ensuring alignment with both immediate business needs and long-term strategic goals.

Short-term AI investments include:

- **Quick Wins:** These are projects designed for immediate impact, often requiring less complex AI solutions. For example, chatbots for customer service can be implemented quickly, offering immediate operational efficiencies and cost savings.

- **Pilot Projects:** Before a full-scale implementation, a pilot project can serve as a proof of concept. It allows companies to test AI solutions on a smaller scale, gather insights, and make improvements.

- **Operational Enhancements:** These investments aim to improve existing processes rather than reinvent them. For instance, using AI to optimize inventory management can lead to immediate cost reductions.

- **Risk Reduction:** Immediate implementations of AI in fraud detection or cybersecurity can offer quick returns by mitigating potential threats.

Long-term AI investments include:

- **R&D and Innovation:** Investing in research and the development of proprietary AI technologies can lead to significant future competitive advantages, but they require patience, resources, and a tolerance for potential failures along the way.

- **Infrastructure Overhaul:** Sometimes, the implementation of AI requires foundational changes in a company's tech infrastructure. These projects can be time-consuming and capital-intensive but can set the stage for transformative changes.

- **Talent Acquisition and Training:** Building an in-house AI team or training existing staff members in AI and machine learning can be a long-term investment. While the initial stages might not yield immediate returns, having a skilled team can be a game-changer in the long run.

- **Strategic Partnerships:** Forming alliances with AI startups, academic institutions, or research bodies can be a forward-looking investment. Such partnerships can pave the way for future innovations and market leadership.

- **Cultural Shifts:** Moving to an AI-first strategy can necessitate a cultural shift within the organization. This includes nurturing an environment of continuous learning, adaptability, and data-driven decision-making. While intangible and challenging to quantify, such shifts can lead to sustained competitive advantages.

For board members, balancing short-term and long-term AI investments requires a nuanced understanding of the organization's current standing, its immediate needs, and its future aspirations. Short-term wins can validate the potential of AI, building momentum and buy-in from stakeholders. However, it's the long-term investments that can redefine a company's trajectory, making it imperative for boards to consider both in their strategic deliberations.

12.4.   AI and Corporate Governance

The accelerating integration of artificial intelligence (AI) into corporate ecosystems has ushered in a new frontier for corporate governance. With the transformative potential of AI comes a host of novel considerations, ranging from ethical decision-making to AI-driven strategy formulation. The role of AI in shaping corporate dynamics transcends mere technological adoption—it delves deep into the very ethos of corporate structures, decision-making frameworks, and leadership paradigms.

For board members and executives, AI represents both an opportunity and a challenge. The opportunity lies in harnessing the unparalleled efficiencies, insights, and innovations that AI can bring. From predictive analytics that can forecast market trends to intelligent automation that streamlines operations, the benefits are palpable and immense. On the other hand, challenges emerge from the complexities and ambiguities associated with AI technologies. Questions of transparency, fairness, privacy, and security become central topics in boardroom discussions.

Additionally, corporate governance in the age of AI needs a revised approach to risk management. The scope of potential risks is broadening as AI systems, with their self-learning and autonomous functionalities, can sometimes act in ways not entirely anticipated by their human creators. Thus, traditional risk matrices and evaluation mechanisms might require enhancements or even overhauls to remain effective.

The stakeholders' perspective, too, is evolving. Investors, customers, employees, and the broader society now expect corporations to exercise judicious and ethical use of AI. This societal lens adds another layer of responsibility for boards, emphasizing the importance of transparent communication, ethical AI frameworks, and continuous engagement with stakeholders to align AI adoption with broader societal values.

In sum, AI's intersection with corporate governance is profound, reshaping traditional boardroom topics and introducing new paradigms of leadership. As AI continues its forward march, it becomes imperative for corporate leaders to equip themselves with the knowledge, strategies, and ethical considerations to guide their organizations responsibly into the AI-augmented future.

12.4.1.   The Board's Role in AI Oversight

The integration of AI into business operations and strategies has transformed the landscape of corporate responsibility, making it imperative for the board of directors to exercise meticulous oversight. As custodians of long-term value and guardians of stakeholder interests, board members have a pivotal role in ensuring that AI is harnessed responsibly, ethically, and strategically:

- **Strategic Alignment:** At the heart of the board's responsibility is ensuring that AI initiatives align with the organization's broader strategic objectives. This means not merely adopting AI for its novelty but evaluating how it fits into the company's vision, mission, and long-term goals. The board must assess whether AI projects under consideration truly resonate with the company's objectives and if they can provide a sustainable competitive advantage.

- **Ethical and Responsible Deployment:** With the transformative potential of AI comes a host of ethical challenges. The board must champion responsible AI, ensuring its deployment aligns with ethical considerations, societal values, and respects human rights. This includes topics like algorithmic fairness, transparency, and data privacy.

- **Risk Management:** AI introduces new dimensions of risks – some overt and others more nuanced. From biases in AI algorithms to potential security vulnerabilities, the board must proactively identify, understand, and mitigate these risks. It becomes crucial to establish robust AI governance frameworks and continuously update them in line with the evolving AI landscape.

- **Stakeholder Communication:** In an age where businesses are increasingly under public scrutiny, boards must ensure transparent communication regarding their AI endeavors. This involves openly addressing AI's benefits, potential pitfalls, and the steps taken to ensure ethical deployment. Engaging with stakeholders, be it shareholders, employees, or the public, helps build trust and paves the way for constructive feedback.

- **Continuous Learning and Education:** The dynamic nature of AI means that what's cutting-edge today might become obsolete tomorrow. For effective oversight, board members must commit to ongoing education. Understanding the basics of AI, staying updated with advancements, and familiarizing oneself with industry best practices is essential.

- **Financial Oversight:** From a financial perspective, boards must assess the economic viability of AI projects. This includes understanding the costs involved, potential ROI, and ensuring that budgets allocated to AI initiatives are spent judiciously.

Essentially, the board's role in AI oversight extends beyond merely approving AI projects. It's about holistic engagement with the AI strategy, ensuring that while the organization races ahead to embrace the future, it doesn't lose sight of ethical considerations, stakeholder interests, and long-term sustainability.

12.4.2.   Risk Management in AI Deployments

Incorporating AI into business operations undeniably unlocks transformative potentials—however, it simultaneously introduces a plethora of risks that must be managed effectively. For board members, understanding and overseeing these risks is paramount, ensuring that while the organization leverages AI's capabilities, it remains safeguarded against potential pitfalls:[222]

- **Operational Risks:** AI systems can, at times, act in unpredictable ways, especially when faced with situations not encountered during their training. This unpredictability can lead to operational failures, disrupting regular business activities. Boards must ensure that there are safeguards in place and that AI systems are rigorously tested before full-scale deployment.

- **Data Privacy and Security:** AI systems often require vast amounts of data for training, and this data, if mishandled, can lead to breaches in privacy or security incidents. The board must ensure compliance with data protection regulations and that robust security measures protect sensitive data.

- **Bias and Fairness:** AI models can inadvertently perpetuate or even exacerbate societal biases if not properly managed. Such biases can lead to discriminatory outcomes, damaging the brand's reputation and even leading to legal consequences. The board should oversee that AI models are regularly audited for biases and that fairness is a core consideration in AI deployments.

---

[222] https://nvlpubs.nist.gov/nistpubs/ai/nist.ai.100-1.pdf

- **Transparency and Accountability:** "Black-box" AI models that operate without transparent decision-making processes can become liabilities. It's essential for boards to champion the development or adoption of models that are interpretable and where decision-making processes can be explained.

- **Regulatory and Compliance Risks:** The regulatory landscape for AI is in flux, with many countries and regions considering or enacting regulations to oversee AI's ethical use. Boards must stay abreast of these changes and ensure that the organization's AI deployments remain compliant with local and international standards.

- **Reputation and Public Perception:** A failed AI project or one that is deemed unethical can quickly damage an organization's reputation. Boards must be aware of public sentiment towards AI and guide organizations in managing their public image in relation to their AI endeavors.

- **Economic Risks:** Investment in AI, while promising substantial ROI, can also become a financial drain if not managed properly. Boards should ensure that AI investments are made judiciously, with clear milestones and exit strategies in place for underperforming projects.

- **Dependency and Vendor Risks:** Over-reliance on specific AI vendors or technologies might lead to vendor lock-ins or challenges in transitioning to newer technologies. Diversifying AI solutions and ensuring interoperability should be on the board's radar.

- **Talent Risks:** The demand for AI expertise outpaces the supply. Boards should be aware of the challenges in recruiting and retaining top AI talent and guide the organization in building a sustainable talent strategy.

Risk management in AI deployments isn't a one-time activity—it's a continuous process that evolves with technological advancements and changes in the business environment. Boards, in their oversight capacity, play a critical role in guiding organizations safely through the maze of AI-related risks, ensuring resilience, compliance, and sustained growth.

12.4.3.   Establishing AI Governance Frameworks

The introduction of AI into the corporate ecosystem is not without its challenges, ranging from ethical dilemmas to technical intricacies. Ensuring that AI deployments remain accountable, ethical, and efficient demands a robust governance framework. For board members, understanding and driving the establishment of such frameworks is crucial to ensure that the organization's AI initiatives are sustainable and in alignment with its broader goals and values:[223]

- **Defining Core Principles:** At the heart of an AI governance framework lie the core principles that guide all AI-related endeavors within the organization. These might include commitments to transparency, fairness, privacy, and continual learning. Establishing these principles upfront provides a clear direction for all stakeholders.

- **Ethical Oversight Committee:** Consider establishing a dedicated committee, which might include external experts, to oversee the ethical dimensions of AI projects. This body can review AI initiatives for potential bias, discriminatory practices, or other ethical concerns, providing guidance and corrective actions when needed.

- **Clear Roles and Responsibilities:** An effective governance framework clearly delineates the roles and responsibilities of various stakeholders in the AI lifecycle, from data engineers and scientists to product managers and legal teams. Such clarity ensures accountability and smoother execution of AI projects.

- **Transparent Decision-Making Processes:** AI's potential to act as a "black-box" poses challenges for governance. Promoting transparency in how AI models make decisions, as well as in how AI projects are greenlit, is essential. This might involve adopting explainable AI techniques or ensuring that project approval processes are well-documented and inclusive.

- **Audit and Review Mechanisms:** Regularly audit AI systems for performance, fairness, and compliance. Automated tools, coupled with human oversight, can

---

[223] https://www.snowflake.com/trending/ai-governance-best-practices/ and
   https://www.ibm.com/topics/ai-governance

help identify issues before they escalate, ensuring that AI systems remain aligned with the organization's goals and values.

- **Data Governance:** AI's effectiveness largely hinges on data. Implement stringent data governance policies to ensure data quality, protect user privacy, and comply with regulations. This might involve anonymizing data, ensuring consent mechanisms, and monitoring data access rights.

- **Stakeholder Engagement:** Engage with a broad spectrum of stakeholders, including employees, customers, shareholders, and even the broader public. Their insights and feedback can offer invaluable perspectives, guiding the evolution of AI initiatives.

- **Continuous Learning and Adaptation:** AI governance shouldn't be static. As AI technology evolves and societal perspectives shift, governance frameworks must adapt. This requires continuous learning, benchmarking against industry best practices, and being open to change.

- **Feedback Loops:** Encourage the establishment of feedback loops where insights from AI deployments are fed back into the governance structure. This can help refine the frameworks and make them more resilient and effective.

- **Legal and Regulatory Compliance:** Stay abreast of the changing regulatory landscape around AI. Ensure that the governance framework incorporates mechanisms to ensure compliance with local and international regulations, minimizing legal risks.

Establishing a comprehensive AI governance framework is a strategic imperative. For boards, driving this initiative ensures that AI serves as a tool for growth and innovation while adhering to the highest standards of ethics, efficiency, and accountability.

12.4.4. Cyber Insurance in AI Deployments

As AI continues to reshape the business landscape, board members find themselves at the intersection of technological innovation and its accompanying risks. AI, with its transformative power, is not just about opportunities—it's equally about vulnerabilities. Protecting against these vulnerabilities is essential, and cyber insurance emerges as a crucial tool in this defense arsenal.

The vast complexity of AI systems means they often operate in ways even their creators don't fully comprehend. As we integrate AI deeper into business processes, these systems interact with a multitude of other systems, each presenting a potential point of vulnerability. Whether it's an AI model unintentionally making biased decisions or automation errors in financial transactions, the repercussions of AI failures can be vast and varied. Traditional risk management strategies might fall short in addressing these unique challenges.

While companies have become accustomed to general cyber insurance policies covering standard cyber risks like data breaches, the landscape of threats has evolved. Today's AI-driven threats necessitate a more tailored approach to insurance—one that specifically addresses the nuances and intricacies of AI systems. It's not just about data breaches anymore—it's about ensuring that the decisions, actions, and outcomes driven by AI are covered.

For board members, understanding this evolving landscape is paramount. They are responsible for guiding their organizations through these uncertain waters, ensuring not just profitability but also the security and ethical use of AI technologies. Cyber insurance, especially one tailored for AI deployments, becomes an essential component of this governance toolkit. As we delve further into this section, we'll unpack the critical aspects of cyber insurance for AI, equipping board members with the knowledge to make informed and strategic decisions.

12.4.5.   *Leading Cyber Insurance Companies and Their AI Endeavors*

The cyber insurance market, cognizant of the shifting technological landscape, has witnessed a plethora of insurance providers evolving their offerings. Some have even leveraged AI themselves to bolster their services, tapping into machine learning and other techniques to better understand risks and optimize coverage. Here are a few notable companies and their efforts in this domain:

- **Chubb:** Chubb has been actively integrating AI into its operations, enhancing risk assessment capabilities, and tailoring cybersecurity insurance policies. The company has established technology services centers in locations such as

Greece, the US, India, and Mexico, focusing on innovations in machine learning, data analytics, and cybersecurity.[224]

- **AIG (American International Group):** AIG's CyberEdge platform is designed to offer comprehensive coverage against a range of cyber risks. AIG has been utilizing AI to improve the efficiency of its claims process and assess client risk profiles more accurately. The company's CyberMatics technology helps organizations verify their cyber risk posture and prioritize controls.[225]

- **AXA XL:** AXA XL, a subsidiary of AXA, is involved in integrating AI and machine learning into various aspects of insurance, including risk prediction and claims handling. While specific details on AXA XL's AI initiatives were not provided in the search results, the broader trend within AXA's approach to leveraging technology in insurance operations suggests a focus on innovation and AI integration.[226]

- **CNA:** CNA offers a range of cyber insurance solutions and is reported to be exploring AI-driven risk assessment tools. Specific details about CNA's AI initiatives were not directly mentioned in the search results, but the company's involvement in the cyber insurance market suggests a likely engagement with AI technologies.

- **Allianz:** Allianz is recognized for its comprehensive cyber insurance solutions and has been leveraging AI for various purposes, including fraud detection and automating underwriting processes. Allianz's initiatives aim to provide more accurate and tailored cyber policies, utilizing AI to enhance their insurance value chain.

---

[224] https://www.insurancenews.com.au/insurtech/we-ve-been-experimenting-with-ai-chubb-ceo-, https://www.insurtechinsights.com/chubb-ceo-reveals-insurance-giant-is-preparing-to-roll-out-ai-at-scale/, and https://www.insurancebusinessmag.com/us/news/breaking-news/chubb-exploring-artificial-intelligence-preparing-for-rollout-at-scale-444144.aspx

[225] https://commercial.allianz.com/content/dam/onemarketing/commercial/commercial/reports/AGCS-Artificial-Intelligence-Outlook-and-Risks.pdf, https://dxjournal.co/2023/05/leading-insurance-company-chubb-goes-all-in-on-ai/, and https://www.aig.com/home/risk-solutions/business/cyber

[226]https://commercial.allianz.com/content/dam/onemarketing/commercial/commercial/reports/AGCS-Artificial-Intelligence-Outlook-and-Risks.pdf

- **CyberCube:** CyberCube specializes in providing data-driven cyber analytics tailored for the insurance industry. They utilize AI to offer modeling solutions that help insurers understand their cyber risk exposure more deeply. CyberCube's role in supporting insurers with AI-driven insights is crucial for the development of effective cyber insurance strategies.

- **HSB (Hartford Steam Boiler):** HSB has renewed its agreement with Cyberwrite for an AI-driven cyber insurance platform, demonstrating its commitment to leveraging data and technology in cyber insurance underwriting and portfolio management. HSB uses Cyberwrite's technology to assess cyber risk in real-time, enabling data-driven underwriting and providing ongoing monitoring and alerting to insureds.[227]

- **Coalition:** Coalition is known for enhancing its cyber insurance policies with an affirmative artificial intelligence endorsement. The company actively uses AI to improve its underwriting processes and risk assessments, showcasing its innovative approach to leveraging technology in the cyber insurance space.[228]

- **Cowbell Cyber:** Cowbell Cyber is another insurtech company that integrates AI into its cyber insurance offerings. The company focuses on providing real-time data for risk assessment and actively discusses the role of AI in shaping the future of cyber insurance.[229]

The integration of AI in the cyber insurance domain is still in its nascent stages, with many companies exploring its potential applications. As the AI ecosystem continues to grow and its adoption becomes ubiquitous, it's expected that more insurance providers will incorporate AI tools both in their risk assessment models and in the protection services they offer.

---

[227] https://commercial.allianz.com/content/dam/onemarketing/commercial/commercial/reports/AGCS-Artificial-Intelligence-Outlook-and-Risks.pdf

[228] https://www.insurtechinsights.com/coalition-boosts-cyber-insurance-policies-with-affirmative-artificial-intelligence-endorsement/

[229] https://cowbell.insure/blog/ai-in-2024/

12.5. Ethical Responsibilities of the Board in AI Implementation

In the current era of digital transformation, where artificial intelligence (AI) stands at the forefront of business innovation, the responsibilities of corporate boards have expanded beyond traditional governance. AI, with its potential to reshape industries, societies, and individual lives, introduces a new spectrum of ethical considerations. For board members, recognizing and navigating these ethical waters is paramount, both as a means to safeguard corporate reputation and to ensure long-term sustainable growth.

- **Recognizing the Ethical Weight of AI Decisions:** AI, unlike many previous technological advancements, possesses the capability to autonomously make decisions that can significantly impact stakeholders, be it employees, customers, or the wider public. The board must appreciate the magnitude of these impacts, considering the far-reaching consequences AI-driven decisions might have on societal structures, individual rights, or economic paradigms.

- **Duty to Stay Informed:** As stewards of an organization's strategic direction, board members have a duty to stay informed about the broader implications of AI technologies. This includes understanding not only their technical facets but also their societal, cultural, and ethical implications.

- **Promoting Transparency:** One of the significant concerns surrounding AI is its potential to operate as a "black box," where decision-making processes remain obscured. The board should champion initiatives that prioritize transparency in AI operations, ensuring stakeholders understand how AI decisions are made.

- **Addressing Bias and Discrimination:** AI systems, reflecting the data they are trained on, can inadvertently perpetuate or amplify biases. The board has an ethical duty to ensure the organization is actively working to identify and rectify such biases, striving for fairness in all AI applications.

- **Data Privacy and Security:** Given AI's heavy reliance on data, ensuring the ethical collection, storage, and processing of this data becomes a board-level concern. Respecting user privacy, adhering to regulations, and implementing robust security measures should be non-negotiable principles.

- **Stakeholder Engagement:** Actively seek feedback from a diverse set of stakeholders regarding the organization's AI endeavors. Such a participatory approach can provide valuable insights, highlighting potential ethical pitfalls and ensuring AI implementations align with broader societal values.

- **Accountability Mechanisms:** The board should oversee the establishment of clear accountability mechanisms for AI decisions. If an AI system falters or results in unintended consequences, there should be clear protocols to address these issues, assign responsibility, and prevent recurrence.

- **Prioritizing Human Dignity:** In all AI-related undertakings, the intrinsic dignity of every individual should be a guiding principle. This means ensuring AI systems do not undermine human rights, promote inequalities, or compromise the basic tenets of respect and fairness.

- **Continuous Ethical Review:** The fast-paced evolution of AI technologies demands continuous ethical scrutiny. Boards should facilitate regular ethical reviews of AI initiatives, ensuring they remain aligned with the organization's values and the broader societal good.

- **Leading by Example:** Finally, boards should strive to lead by example, embedding ethical considerations in all board-level AI discussions and decisions. Such top-down emphasis on ethics will permeate throughout the organization, fostering a culture where AI's power is wielded responsibly.

The ethical responsibilities surrounding AI are vast and often complex. Yet, by actively recognizing and addressing these concerns, boards can ensure that their organizations harness AI's potential in ways that not only drive business success but also uphold the highest standards of ethical integrity.

12.5.1. Setting the Ethical AI Agenda

As the digital world becomes increasingly entwined with AI technologies, the ethical dimensions of AI operations are surfacing as paramount concerns for corporate leadership. For board members, the task of setting an ethical AI agenda is no longer just a visionary prerogative but an urgent necessity. With the expansive influence of AI, from shaping consumer experiences to redefining operational workflows, a clear, actionable ethical blueprint is critical. Here's how board members can take charge:

- **Identify Core Ethical Principles:** The first step is to identify the organization's core ethical principles. Whether it's a commitment to transparency, fairness, inclusivity, or privacy, these principles should serve as the foundation for all AI endeavors.

- **Engage Diverse Voices:** When setting the ethical AI agenda, it's crucial to include diverse perspectives. This means consulting not just with tech experts but with ethicists, sociologists, customer representatives, and other stakeholders. Their insights will help in recognizing potential blind spots and in fine-tuning the ethical framework.

- **Prioritize Transparency:** AI's "black box" nature has been a significant concern for many. An ethical AI agenda should prioritize algorithmic transparency, ensuring that stakeholders have a clear understanding of how AI systems make decisions.

- **Regular Ethical Audits:** Just as financial audits are integral to corporate governance, ethical audits of AI systems should be instituted. These reviews can assess the adherence of AI operations to the defined ethical principles and recommend necessary adjustments.

- **Educate and Empower:** For the ethical AI agenda to be effective, everyone in the organization needs to be on board. This necessitates comprehensive training programs that educate employees about the ethical dimensions of AI and empower them to make ethical decisions in their AI-related roles.

- **Stay Updated:** The AI landscape is evolving rapidly. As such, the ethical challenges posed by AI will also evolve. The board should ensure that the ethical AI agenda is flexible and regularly updated to address new challenges and incorporate emerging best practices.

- **Create an Ethical Oversight Committee:** Consider establishing a dedicated committee or working group focused on AI ethics. This committee, ideally composed of interdisciplinary experts, can guide the ethical AI journey, ensuring consistency and rigor.

- **Embed Ethics in AI Design:** From the very onset, ethics should be an integral part of AI system design and development. This proactive approach can prevent potential ethical mishaps and ensure that AI systems inherently reflect the organization's ethical values.

- **Open Channels for Feedback:** Create mechanisms where employees, customers, and other stakeholders can provide feedback on AI operations. Such feedback loops can offer valuable insights into real-world ethical implications and areas for improvement.

- **Commit to Accountability:** Above all, the board should emphasize a culture of accountability. If lapses occur, there should be clear mechanisms to address them, learn from them, and ensure they are not repeated.

By setting a robust ethical AI agenda, boards can position their organizations at the vanguard of responsible AI adoption. This not only safeguards the organization's reputation but also ensures that AI innovations drive positive, ethical outcomes for all stakeholders.

12.5.2.   Addressing AI Biases and Discrimination

Bias and discrimination in AI systems have been recognized as significant concerns, often amplifying existing societal inequalities and introducing new forms of prejudice. For the board of directors, ensuring that the organization's AI implementations are free from these biases is a fundamental ethical responsibility. Here's how the board can effectively address these challenges:

- **Awareness and Acknowledgment:** Recognizing that AI can perpetuate bias is the first step. Boards should acknowledge the potential for biases in AI systems, stemming from training data, model structures, or even the teams that develop these systems.

- **Diverse Development Teams:** One effective approach to countering bias is to ensure diversity among those creating AI solutions. Diverse teams can better recognize, challenge, and correct potential biases that might otherwise be overlooked.

- **Comprehensive Data Audits:** Bias in AI often originates from the training data. Periodically auditing this data for biases, especially concerning gender, race, ethnicity, and other potential areas of discrimination, is vital.

- **Ethical AI Guidelines:** Develop and adhere to guidelines that focus on fairness and inclusivity in AI. These guidelines should provide clear protocols for testing and validating AI systems against potential biases.

- **Transparent AI Models:** While not all AI models can be completely transparent due to their complexity, striving for transparency can help identify and rectify biases. Techniques such as explainable AI can be invaluable in this context.

- **Regular Training and Workshops:** Organize regular training sessions and workshops for employees, emphasizing the importance of ethical AI and techniques to recognize and eliminate biases.

- **Feedback Mechanisms:** Establish mechanisms for stakeholders to report perceived biases in AI-driven outputs. This can serve as an essential tool for identifying and addressing unintended biases.

- **Collaboration with External Experts:** Engage with third-party experts or organizations specializing in AI ethics. Their external perspective can be instrumental in identifying subtle biases and recommending remediation strategies.

- **Documented Accountability:** Clearly document the methods and metrics used to assess AI models for bias and discrimination. This not only serves as a record of due diligence but also communicates a strong commitment to ethical AI practices.

- **Ongoing Evaluation:** As AI models continue to learn and evolve, biases can emerge over time. Regularly re-evaluate AI systems to ensure that they remain aligned with the organization's ethical commitments.

By proactively addressing biases and discrimination in AI, boards can ensure that the technology serves as a tool for positive change, fostering fairness and equality rather than perpetuating existing inequalities.

12.5.3.   Ensuring AI Transparency and Fairness

As organizations increasingly rely on AI to inform decisions, ensuring transparency and fairness in these systems becomes paramount. The board of directors has a pivotal role in championing these principles, ensuring that AI's deployment aligns with the company's broader ethical and corporate governance commitments. Here are some strategic considerations and actions the board can take in this context:

- **Understanding AI Transparency:** At its core, transparency in AI involves making the workings of AI models understandable to humans. This means that both the processes leading to AI-driven decisions and the decisions themselves should be explainable and interpretable.

- **Advocating for Explainable AI (XAI):** Push for the adoption of models and techniques that offer insights into how AI decisions are made. XAI methods can help bridge the gap between complex AI models and human interpretability, making the technology more trustworthy.

- **Fairness Audits:** Periodically assess AI systems to ensure they treat all user groups equitably. Tools and methodologies are emerging that allow organizations to test their AI models for fairness concerning various groups, ensuring that no particular group is systematically disadvantaged.

- **Stakeholder Engagement:** Engage with diverse stakeholders, including employees, customers, and the broader community, to gather feedback on AI deployments. Their insights can be invaluable in identifying areas where AI might seem opaque or unfair.

- **Ethical AI Committees:** Consider establishing committees or task forces dedicated to examining the ethical implications of AI projects. These groups can provide guidance on transparency, fairness, and other ethical dimensions.

- **Third-party Evaluations:** Collaborate with independent entities to review and certify the transparency and fairness of AI systems. External reviews can add credibility to the organization's AI ethics claims.

- **Transparent Communication:** When deploying AI solutions, communicate clearly about their role, their decision-making processes, and the steps taken to ensure their fairness. Transparency in communication can prevent misunderstandings and build trust among stakeholders.

- **Training and Skill Development:** Equip the team with skills and knowledge on the latest in AI transparency and fairness techniques. Regular workshops and training sessions can help in staying updated with the rapid advancements in the field.

- **Feedback Loops:** Implement mechanisms for continuous feedback on AI system performance from both internal teams and end-users. Regular feedback can help in tweaking systems for better fairness and transparency over time.

- **Policy Development:** Establish clear policies that define the organization's stance on AI transparency and fairness. This should detail the measures in place, expectations from AI teams, and the broader goals concerning ethical AI deployment.

By emphasizing transparency and fairness in AI systems, boards can not only uphold their ethical commitments but also bolster the organization's reputation and trustworthiness in the eyes of stakeholders and the broader public.

12.6.   Building AI Competencies in the Boardroom

For boards to be truly effective in their oversight and strategic role regarding AI, it's imperative to build and nurture AI competencies within the boardroom. As AI continues to permeate every facet of business and society, having board members equipped with a fundamental understanding of AI and its implications becomes a strategic necessity. Here's how boards can cultivate this critical expertise:

- **Regular AI Briefings:** Just as boards regularly receive financial updates, introducing periodic AI briefings can keep members informed about technological advances, competitive landscape shifts, and evolving regulatory concerns related to AI.

- **Onboarding AI Experts:** Consider bringing on board members or advisors with a background in AI, data science, or related fields. Their expertise can provide invaluable insights when strategizing or deliberating on AI-focused initiatives.

- **Continuous Learning and Workshops:** Organize regular workshops and training sessions conducted by AI experts. These sessions can demystify complex AI concepts, helping board members ask more insightful questions and make more informed decisions.

- **AI in Decision-making Simulations:** Interactive simulations can offer board members a hands-on experience of how AI systems work and the kind of results they produce. Such simulations can also highlight the ethical and operational challenges that often accompany AI implementations.

- **Collaborate with Academic Institutions:** Building partnerships with universities and research institutions can be a two-way street. Boards can gain insights into the latest AI research, while institutions benefit from real-world business perspectives.

- **Case Study Reviews:** Delve into real-world case studies of businesses in similar (or even different) sectors that have integrated AI. Understand their successes, challenges, and learnings, and use these insights to inform your strategic direction.

- **Join AI-focused Forums and Associations:** Encourage board members to become active in AI-focused industry groups or forums. These platforms often offer rich resources, from white papers to conferences, that can enhance boardroom AI competencies.

- **Diversity in Thought and Experience:** Ensure that the board's composition reflects a diverse range of experiences and backgrounds. Diversity can foster richer discussions around AI, bringing in varied perspectives that account for different societal and business implications.

- **Feedback Mechanisms:** Establish mechanisms that allow board members to provide feedback on their AI learning journey. Understanding what they find challenging or insightful can help tailor future training initiatives.

By proactively building AI competencies, boards not only position themselves to offer better guidance in the AI-era but also send a strong signal to stakeholders about their commitment to responsible and informed AI adoption. This, in turn, fosters trust and paves the way for organizations to harness AI's potential fully.

12.6.1. The Need for AI Literacy at the Top

The integration of AI across industries and functions marks not only a technological shift but also a transformation in how businesses operate and deliver value. As such, AI literacy is no longer a luxury or a domain reserved for tech-savvy executives. Here's why it's imperative for board members and top leadership to cultivate AI literacy:

- **Strategic Decision Making:** As companies increasingly rely on AI to drive growth and innovation, board members need a fundamental understanding of its capabilities and limitations. An AI-literate board can make informed strategic decisions, ensuring that the company remains competitive and capitalizes on AI-driven opportunities.

- **Risk Mitigation:** AI, while promising, is accompanied by various risks, ranging from biases in algorithms to potential regulatory challenges. Board members equipped with AI knowledge are better positioned to identify, understand, and mitigate these risks, protecting the company's reputation and bottom line.

- **Ethical Oversight:** The ethical implications of AI are vast. Whether it's concerns about privacy, transparency, or discrimination, the board plays a crucial role in setting the organization's ethical compass. AI literacy enables board members to ask the right questions, ensuring that AI deployments align with the company's values and societal expectations.

- **Stakeholder Communication:** Shareholders, customers, employees, and regulators all have a vested interest in how a company approaches AI. A board that understands AI can communicate more effectively with these stakeholders, building trust and addressing concerns proactively.

- **Talent and Culture:** As organizations pivot towards AI, there's a need to attract the right talent and foster a culture conducive to innovation. Board members aware of the nuances of AI can guide HR strategies, ensuring that the company has the skills and mindset needed to thrive in an AI-driven world.

- **Future-proofing the Organization:** The pace of AI evolution is rapid. Board members who continuously update their AI knowledge can anticipate future trends and challenges, ensuring the organization is always a step ahead.

- **Holistic Understanding:** AI is not an isolated tool but often intertwines with other technologies like IoT, blockchain, and 5G. An AI-literate board can understand these intersections, leading to a more holistic and integrated approach to technology adoption.

In essence, AI literacy at the top is not just about understanding algorithms or data science. It's about grasping the broader implications of AI for business, society, and the future. Such an understanding ensures that the board can guide the organization responsibly and effectively in an age defined by AI.

12.6.2. Integrating AI Experts into Board Discussions

As AI reshapes the contours of business and innovation, the depth of its intricacies requires specialized expertise for effective decision-making. Simply having a cursory understanding is insufficient for the board to grapple with the nuanced challenges and opportunities AI presents. Thus, there's a growing consensus on the importance of incorporating AI expertise directly into board discussions. Here's why and how this integration is crucial:

- **Tailored Insight:** AI experts can offer specific insights into the company's AI strategies, breaking down complex technical jargon into actionable business intelligence. They bridge the gap between tech and strategy, ensuring that board members have a clear understanding of AI initiatives.

- **Informed Decision-making:** With AI experts at the table, the board can delve deeper into the intricacies of AI projects, ensuring that decisions are based on a robust understanding of potential outcomes, risks, and benefits.

- **Risk Assessment:** AI deployments come with associated risks, from data privacy concerns to potential biases. AI experts can elucidate these risks, offering a clear picture of potential pitfalls and suggesting mitigation strategies.

- **Ethical Guidance:** AI ethics is a complex field. By incorporating experts who specialize in the ethical facets of AI, boards can ensure that the organization's AI endeavors align with ethical and societal norms.

- **Future Strategy Planning:** AI experts can provide foresight into emerging trends, tools, and techniques in the AI realm. Their presence ensures that the board is always considering the next steps and preparing for future AI-driven scenarios.

- **Enhancing Board Credibility:** Stakeholders, including investors, customers, and employees, are increasingly attentive to how companies manage AI. Having AI expertise visibly integrated into board discussions boosts the organization's credibility and showcases a commitment to responsible AI adoption.

• **Continuous Learning:** Regular interactions with AI experts foster an environment of continuous learning for board members. It promotes questions, discussions, and deeper dives into AI topics, ensuring board members remain updated and engaged.

Methods of integration include:

• **Board Appointments:** Some companies appoint AI specialists as non-executive directors, ensuring constant expert oversight.

• **Regular Consultations:** Even if not part of the board, AI experts can be regularly consulted during board meetings, especially when discussing AI-related topics.

• **Training Sessions:** Organizing periodic AI training sessions for the board, conducted by internal or external experts, can keep them abreast of the latest developments.

Incorporating AI expertise into board discussions is no longer an option but a necessity. It guarantees that the organization's highest decision-making body is equipped to handle the transformative power of AI responsibly, effectively, and strategically.

12.6.3.   Regular AI Training and Updates for Board Members

In the rapidly evolving world of AI, static knowledge quickly becomes obsolete. For board members to maintain a grasp on the strategic implications of AI, they must be equipped with ongoing education. The dynamic nature of AI and its ever-shifting landscape make regular training and updates not just beneficial but imperative. Here's a breakdown of the importance and execution of consistent AI learning for board members:

• **Keeping Pace with Innovation:** AI, unlike some traditional business elements, is not stagnant. New algorithms, tools, methodologies, and use cases emerge frequently. Regular training ensures board members aren't caught off guard by these innovations.

- **Strengthening Strategic Decision-making:** As board members remain updated, their ability to make informed decisions concerning AI investments, risk management, and strategic planning is enhanced.

- **Mitigating Risks:** With updated knowledge, board members can better anticipate potential challenges or ethical dilemmas posed by AI, ensuring the organization is proactive rather than reactive.

- **Demonstrating Commitment:** Stakeholders value organizations that showcase a commitment to learning and adaptation. Regular AI training signals to investors, partners, employees, and customers that the company is forward-thinking and responsible.

Effective approaches to AI training and updates include:

- **Dedicated AI Workshops:** Organize periodic workshops tailored for board members, focusing on recent AI developments and their strategic implications.

- **Engage with AI Thought Leaders:** Inviting AI thought leaders and industry experts to board meetings can offer valuable insights and foster stimulating discussions.

- **AI Newsletters:** Curated AI newsletters can inform board members about the latest trends, research findings, and notable AI deployments in the industry.

- **Case Study Reviews:** Periodically reviewing AI case studies, especially from competitors or market leaders, can provide practical insights and lessons learned.

- **Participation in AI Conferences:** Encouraging board members to attend AI and tech conferences can expose them to the latest innovations, networking opportunities, and a broader understanding of the industry landscape.

- **Incorporate AI Updates in Board Agendas:** Ensure that AI updates are a regular part of board meeting agendas, where a designated expert or team briefs the board on recent developments and their potential impact.

- **Feedback Mechanism:** After training sessions or updates, solicit feedback from board members. Understand what they found valuable and where they'd like more focus, ensuring future sessions are even more effective.

Continuous education is a hallmark of successful leadership, especially in domains as transformative as AI. By institutionalizing regular AI training and updates, organizations ensure that their board remains agile, informed, and prepared to navigate the multifaceted challenges and opportunities AI presents.

12.7.   Board's Role in AI-driven Crisis Management

In the wake of a significant AI-related controversy, the role of the board in crisis management becomes crucial. A company's AI system, once lauded for its innovation, may suddenly be scrutinized for ethical lapses or unintended discriminatory outcomes. Such a crisis not only affects the company's reputation but also has financial implications, as seen in the case of OpenAI, where governance issues led to the temporary departure of the CEO, underscoring the need for robust governance structures.[230]

Boards must take a proactive stance, not merely reacting to events but leading the charge in understanding the root causes of the crisis, implementing corrective measures, and ensuring such incidents do not recur. This involves a deep dive into the AI's decision-making process, examining where and how biases may have been introduced, and determining the best course of action to rectify the situation.[231]

The board's engagement is critical in steering the company through the crisis, as they are accountable for overseeing the responsible development and use of AI. They must balance the competitive deployment of new technology against potential risks, ensuring that AI governance processes encompass oversight, accountability, responsible AI practices, transparency, explainability, robust risk management, and regulatory compliance.

As AI continues to evolve rapidly, boards must stay informed and adapt their strategies accordingly. They should engage with stakeholders, including employees, on AI-related

---

[230] https://fticommunications.com/responsible-ai-governance-future-proofing-corporate-governance-strategy-risk-management-and-reporting/

[231] https://hbr.org/2023/12/ai-is-testing-the-limits-of-corporate-governance and https://www.linkedin.com/pulse/why-companies-need-governance-structure-around-ai-tdjcf/

matters and establish grievance mechanisms for AI-related issues.[232] Furthermore, boards should ensure that the company's AI systems are designed, trained, and tested with an eye toward ethical considerations and societal impact.[233]

In conclusion, the board's role in AI-driven crisis management is to provide strategic direction, ensure ethical AI deployment, and maintain stakeholder trust. By doing so, they not only navigate the immediate crisis but also set a precedent for responsible AI governance that can serve as a model for the industry.

12.7.1. Preparing for AI-related Controversies and Mishaps

- **Anticipatory Measures:** Even the most sophisticated AI systems can encounter unexpected challenges when deployed in the real world. Boards should champion the creation of a comprehensive AI crisis playbook, detailing protocols for quick decision-making, communication strategies, and corrective actions. Regularly updating this playbook to accommodate the evolving AI landscape can ensure the company remains prepared for unforeseen events:[234]

- **Scenario Planning:** This involves simulating potential AI-related controversies or mishaps, like data breaches or biased outputs, and planning the company's response. By playing out worst-case scenarios, the board can anticipate vulnerabilities and guide the executive team in devising proactive strategies.

- **Cross-Functional Collaboration:** An effective response to AI crises often requires swift coordination across various departments, from tech and PR to legal and customer service. The board should encourage regular cross-functional simulations and drills, ensuring that when a real crisis hits, every department knows its role and acts in concert.

[232] https://www.icgn.org/sites/default/files/2024-03/ICGN%20Investor%20Viewpoint%20-%20Artificial%20Intelligence%20-%20An%20engagement%20guide.pdf

[233] https://corpgov.law.harvard.edu/2024/03/21/artificial-intelligence-an-engagement-guide/ and https://corpgov.law.harvard.edu/2022/01/05/board-responsibility-for-artificial-intelligence-oversight/

[234] https://www.hhs.gov/sites/default/files/hhs-trustworthy-ai-playbook.pdf and https://goodmanlantern.com/crisis-management-services/crisis-response-strategies/

- **Feedback Loops:** Incorporating feedback mechanisms can help in the early detection of potential issues. This includes channels for employees, customers, and even the broader public to report any discrepancies or concerns they observe in the AI's functioning. Boards can advocate for transparent and open feedback systems, enabling rapid response to emerging issues.

- **Audit and Review:** Periodic third-party audits of the AI systems can provide an objective view of potential vulnerabilities. The board can prioritize such reviews, ensuring that the company benefits from external expertise and stays aware of potential pitfalls.

- **Ethical Guardrails:** By establishing a clear set of ethical guidelines and principles for AI development and deployment, boards can create a moral compass for the company. These guidelines should be revisited regularly and be at the forefront of every AI-related decision, ensuring that the company doesn't just chase innovation for its sake but does so responsibly.

Rapid response mechanisms for AI failures include:

- **Centralized Reporting System:** Implementing a centralized system where AI anomalies, malfunctions, or errors can be reported ensures that any potential issues are flagged immediately. This system should be accessible to both internal stakeholders and external partners, allowing for a comprehensive feedback loop.

- **Dedicated Crisis Management Team:** Having a team that is specially trained and always on standby can expedite the resolution process. This team should have representatives from key departments, including IT, communications, legal, and public relations, ensuring a multifaceted approach to crisis management.

- **Real-time Monitoring Tools:** Leveraging AI-powered monitoring tools can provide instantaneous alerts when anomalies or deviations from expected outputs are detected. These tools can be critical in preventing small glitches from escalating into larger controversies.

- **Pre-approved Communication Templates:** In the wake of an AI failure, the company's response time can be crucial. Having pre-approved templates for press releases, social media statements, and customer communications can expedite the company's public response, ensuring stakeholders are informed quickly and transparently.

- **Escalation Protocols:** Clearly defined escalation pathways ensure that, depending on the severity of the AI failure, the right individuals or teams are alerted immediately. This may range from technical teams addressing minor glitches to the CEO or board being informed of major issues.

- **Post-Incident Analysis:** After the immediate crisis has been addressed, a thorough post-mortem analysis should be conducted. This analysis will help in understanding the root causes, assessing the effectiveness of the response, and implementing preventive measures for the future.

- **Stakeholder Engagement:** Regularly engaging with key stakeholders, including customers, partners, and regulators, ensures that they are kept in the loop. Transparency in such engagements can help maintain trust, even when AI failures occur.

- **Continuous Learning and Adaptation:** The AI landscape is dynamic, and what worked once might not be effective in a future scenario. Boards should ensure that lessons learned from each incident are integrated into future crisis response strategies, keeping the company adaptive and resilient.

Restoring stakeholder trust post-crisis approaches include:

- **Open and Transparent Communication:** After an AI-related crisis, the board and management must immediately acknowledge the issue and communicate openly with all stakeholders, including employees, customers, partners, and shareholders. This frank admission, coupled with a clear explanation of what went wrong and how it's being addressed, can go a long way in assuaging concerns.

- **Third-Party Audits:** Engaging a neutral third party to audit the AI-related failure can provide an unbiased perspective on the root cause. Sharing the findings publicly further demonstrates the company's commitment to transparency and rectification.

- **Engage in Public Forums:** Hosting webinars, town halls, or public forums where stakeholders can ask questions and voice their concerns allows the company to directly address doubts and reassure the community of its dedication to fixing the problem.

- **Strengthening Internal Policies:** Demonstrating that changes have been made internally to prevent a recurrence of the issue is crucial. This might involve revising algorithms, retraining AI models, updating guidelines, or enhancing oversight mechanisms.

- **Collaboration with Industry Experts:** Collaborating with industry experts and thought leaders can provide insights into best practices and help improve the company's AI systems. These collaborations can also signal to stakeholders that the company is proactive in seeking solutions.

- **Regular Updates:** Regularly updating stakeholders on the progress and actions taken post-crisis is essential. Whether it's improvements made, new partnerships formed, or internal changes implemented, continuous communication can rebuild confidence over time.

- **Engage in Corporate Social Responsibility (CSR) Initiatives:** Engaging in CSR initiatives related to technology education, ethical AI, or other relevant areas can further demonstrate the company's commitment to responsible AI use and its broader societal responsibilities.

- **Feedback Mechanisms:** Encouraging stakeholders to provide feedback on the company's AI-related operations and acting upon that feedback can help fine-tune the organization's approach and restore trust.

Ultimately, the board plays a pivotal role in steering the organization through the aftermath of an AI-related crisis. Their actions, both immediate and long-term, can determine how quickly and effectively stakeholder trust is restored.

12.8. Case Studies: Boards Leading in the AI Era

In the corridors of global corporations, whispered tales of AI successes and failures form a mosaic of experiences that offer a rich tapestry of insights for the discerning board member. In boardrooms stretching from Silicon Valley's cutting-edge startups to traditional conglomerates in Europe's historic cities, decisions are being made that are reshaping industries and redefining corporate strategies. As we navigate the labyrinth of the AI-driven business world, dissecting real-world examples offers more than mere anecdotes—they provide vivid illustrations of leadership in action, principles applied, and, sometimes, lessons painfully learned.

To truly appreciate the impact and potential of AI, it is essential to journey beyond theoretical frameworks and delve into these living chronicles. Each case study paints a portrait of a board's strategic vision, anticipatory acumen, or, occasionally, reactionary prowess in the face of unexpected AI challenges. From tech behemoths that have seamlessly integrated AI into their very DNA to legacy companies standing at the cusp of AI-driven transformations, these stories are a testament to the evolving dynamics of corporate leadership.

Through this section, we will embark on a journey across continents, industries, and varying scales of enterprises. Each narrative will unravel a unique facet of how boards have championed, adapted, or pivoted in the rapidly evolving AI landscape. Join us as we traverse this world of strategic governance, extracting invaluable insights that will illuminate the path for boards striving to lead effectively in the AI era.

12.8.1. Companies that Successfully Pivoted to AI-driven Strategies

At the intersection of innovation and adaptability lie companies that have witnessed the sweeping waves of AI trends and decided not merely to ride them but to harness their power to pivot their entire business strategies. Their tales are not just of technological evolution but a testament to visionary leadership and a forward-thinking board that recognized the game-changing potential of AI:

- **Netflix:** Originally a mail-order DVD service, Netflix's board saw the impending technological disruptions and made significant investments in AI-driven content recommendation algorithms. By doing so, they not only transitioned to a successful streaming model but managed to offer highly personalized user experiences. Their AI insights didn't stop at content recommendations but extended to producing original content based on user preferences and viewing patterns, establishing Netflix as a powerhouse in entertainment.[235]

---

[235] https://litslink.com/blog/all-about-netflix-artificial-intelligence-the-truth-behind-personalized-content

- **American Express (AmEx):** A financial institution with a legacy stretching back over a century, AmEx realized the importance of AI in fraud detection. By employing sophisticated AI algorithms, they managed to save billions annually by quickly identifying and responding to fraudulent activities. Additionally, AI-driven data analysis tools have allowed them to offer personalized rewards and services to cardholders, strengthening customer loyalty.[236]

- **John Deere:** A name synonymous with farming and agricultural equipment, John Deere's pivot is particularly noteworthy. Understanding the potential of AI in precision agriculture, the company incorporated AI technologies to provide farmers with data-driven insights about planting patterns, crop health, and soil quality. This shift not only enhanced the efficiency and yield of farms but also positioned John Deere as a leader in agri-tech.[237]

- **Dominos:** From a pizza delivery chain to an AI-driven tech company, Dominos transformed its business model by integrating AI into its operations. The company's AI chatbot named "Dom" assists customers in placing orders, answering queries, and tracking delivery. AI also powered their innovative initiatives, such as predicting orders even before a customer places one based on their previous order history.

Case Study:[238]

Walmart and Alibaba have both harnessed the power of artificial intelligence (AI) to revolutionize their supply chain optimization and enhance customer experiences, showcasing their leadership in integrating cutting-edge technologies into retail

---

[236] https://www.americanexpress.com/en-us/credit-cards/credit-intel/fraud-alerts/

[237] https://www.assemblymag.com/articles/97831-john-deere-revolutionizes-agriculture-with-ai-and-automation

[238] https://chainstoreage.com/walmart-sell-its-ai-logistics-tool-other-businesses, https://corporate.walmart.com/news/2024/03/14/walmart-commerce-technologies-launches-ai-powered-logistics-product, https://sourcingjournal.com/topics/logistics/walmart-logistics-ai-artificial-intelligence-route-optimization-planning-software-trucking-middle-mile-delivery-pickup-500192/, https://www.supplychaindive.com/news/walmart-selling-route-optimization-supply-chain-technology/710775/, https://technologymagazine.com/articles/alibaba-ai-suite-to-streamline-global-enterprise-operations, https://www.prnewswire.com/news-releases/alibaba-international-announces-pilot-launch-of-comprehensive-ai-suite-aidge-to-streamline-global-commerce-operations-301978110.html, https://www.digitalcommerce360.com/2023/12/14/how-alibaba-internationals-new-ai-suite-aidge-helps-companies-go-global/

operations. Walmart's AI initiatives focus on improving customer service and operational efficiency. The retail giant has implemented AI-driven route optimization to ensure efficient delivery and supply chain management, significantly reducing miles traveled and CO2 emissions. This system considers various factors like traffic conditions and delivery windows to optimize routes for multi-stop deliveries, demonstrating a commitment to sustainability and efficiency. Additionally, Walmart leverages conversational AI to offer personalized shopping assistance, enabling customers to place orders and receive support through text and voice commands, thereby enhancing the shopping experience.

On the other hand, Alibaba has introduced 'Aidge,' an AI-powered suite designed to streamline global commerce operations for small and medium-sized enterprises (SMEs). Aidge utilizes Alibaba's proprietary large language models to offer services like consumer insight, content localization, and customer service chatbots, addressing the challenges of language and cultural barriers. This suite empowers businesses to create localized and appealing marketing content, optimize search results, and improve customer interactions, showcasing Alibaba's commitment to leveraging AI for operational efficiency and market expansion. Both Walmart and Alibaba's strategic use of AI not only optimizes their supply chains but also significantly enhances the customer experience, setting a benchmark for the retail industry's future.

Each of these companies showcases a unique AI-driven pivot, steered by boards with the foresight to embrace change. These transformations required more than just technological upgrades–they demanded a reimagining of traditional business models, a willingness to invest in unfamiliar territories, and an inherent trust in the transformative power of AI. These companies stand as shining examples for others in the corporate world, exemplifying the success that awaits those willing to boldly step into the AI frontier.

12.8.2.   Lessons from AI Missteps and Board Responses

While the journey of AI integration has been adorned with notable successes, it has not been without its pitfalls. Some companies, despite having the best intentions, have faced significant challenges due to AI missteps. Their experiences serve as a cautionary tale, but also as a guide on how boards can effectively respond to AI-related controversies:

- **Microsoft's Tay Bot:** Microsoft introduced Tay, an AI chatbot on Twitter, aiming to understand and replicate human interactions. However, within hours, internet users manipulated the bot, making it tweet inappropriate and offensive content. Microsoft's swift response was to take Tay offline and issue a public apology. The board's involvement in addressing this high-profile misstep emphasized the importance of rigorous testing and the unpredictability of AI in open environments.[239]

- **IBM's Watson for Oncology:** With the promise of revolutionizing cancer treatment, Watson for Oncology was poised to be a game-changer. However, it faced criticism for providing inaccurate and unsafe treatment recommendations. The board's response underscored the importance of continuous oversight, validation, and collaboration with domain experts when AI is used in critical sectors like healthcare. They recommended enhancing the training data to include more real patient cases, implementing continuous feedback loops for improvement, fostering closer collaboration with oncologists, and increasing transparency around the system's decision-making process. The board aimed to address the issues through iterative updates while ensuring Watson remained a supplementary tool to clinical judgment rather than replacing human expertise.[240]

- **Amazon's AI Recruitment Tool:** Amazon's AI tool for recruitment was found to be biased against female candidates. The system, trained on resumes submitted over a decade, favored male candidates because most of the resumes came from men. Amazon's board realized the gravity of the situation and discontinued the tool. This incident served as a reminder about inherent biases in AI training data and the need for boards to insist on rigorous fairness audits.[241]

- **Face Recognition Misidentifications:** Various companies implementing facial recognition technologies have faced backlash due to inaccurate and biased identifications. Notably, some systems struggled to accurately recognize people of certain ethnicities. Boards overseeing such projects were thrust into the

---

[239] https://spectrum.ieee.org/in-2016-microsofts-racist-chatbot-revealed-the-dangers-of-online-conversation

[240] https://www.theverge.com/2018/7/26/17619382/ibms-watson-cancer-ai-healthcare-science

[241] https://www.businessinsider.com/amazon-built-ai-to-hire-people-discriminated-against-women-2018-10

spotlight, emphasizing the ethical implications and the need for thorough validation before deployment.

- **Google's AI Chatbot Gemini (Previously Google Bard)'s Inaccurate Information:** Alphabet faced a significant setback when its AI chatbot Gemini provided inaccurate information in a company advertisement. This incident led to a sharp decline in Alphabet's stock price, wiping $100 billion off its market value. The board's response to such a high-profile error could highlight the importance of accuracy and reliability in AI-generated content, as well as the financial and reputational risks associated with AI missteps.[242]

- **New York City Chatbot Advising Illegal Actions:** An AI chatbot designed to assist small businesses in New York City provided advice that suggested illegal actions, including discriminatory practices and incorrect information about waste and sewage regulations. This case underscores the need for boards to ensure that AI tools are thoroughly vetted for legal compliance and ethical considerations, especially when providing regulatory or legal advice.

- **Microsoft Copilot Designer's Explicit Imagery:** An engineer testing Microsoft's AI image generator, Copilot Designer, discovered that the tool generated explicit imagery, including inappropriate content involving children and drugs. The engineer's concerns were initially ignored, leading to a direct appeal to Microsoft's board and the Federal Trade Commission (FTC). This example highlights the importance of internal whistleblower mechanisms, board oversight in product safety, and the potential legal and ethical ramifications of AI-generated content.

- **Vanderbilt University's AI-Generated Email:** Vanderbilt University issued an apology after using AI to construct an email about a mass shooting. This incident illustrates the sensitivity required when AI is used in communications about serious or traumatic events, emphasizing the need for boards to implement guidelines for AI use in sensitive contexts.[243]

From these missteps, several lessons emerge for boards:

---

[242] https://www.reuters.com/technology/google-ai-chatbot-bard-offers-inaccurate-information-company-ad-2023-02-08/

[243] https://tech.co/news/list-ai-failures-mistakes-errors

- **Anticipate and Prepare for AI Vulnerabilities:** It's vital for boards to understand that AI, though powerful, can have vulnerabilities, especially when exposed to unpredictable real-world scenarios.

- **Ethical Oversight is Critical:** Boards must ensure that AI applications, especially those with societal implications, undergo rigorous ethical reviews.

- **Transparency and Accountability:** When mishaps occur, boards should guide the company in taking responsibility, addressing the issue head-on, and ensuring transparent communication with stakeholders.

- **Continuous Learning:** Mistakes should be viewed as learning opportunities. Boards should ensure that insights from these experiences are integrated into future AI projects.

In essence, while AI can lead companies to new heights, it comes with its unique challenges. A proactive, informed, and ethically grounded board can make all the difference in navigating this complex landscape.

12.8.3.   Best Practices from AI-savvy Boards

As AI continues to reshape the business landscape, several forward-thinking boards have stood out by setting exemplary practices in AI governance, strategy, and ethics. Their successful approaches offer valuable insights for other companies aiming to harness the power of AI responsibly and effectively:

- **IBM's AI Governance Framework:** IBM's detailed AI governance framework could be highlighted as an example of how companies can deploy and manage AI responsibly.[244] This includes their emphasis on explainable AI and the need for a multidisciplinary approach involving developers, users, policymakers, and ethicists.

- **Compliance Best Practices:** The section could incorporate compliance best practices for AI governance programs, as outlined by the International

---

[244] https://www.ibm.com/topics/ai-governance

Association of Privacy Professionals (IAPP).[245] This includes mapping principles to written procedures, establishing multiple lines of defense, and preparing for change.

- **Enterprise AI Governance Principles:** Principles for enterprise AI governance, such as human-centricity in design and oversight, privacy and data protection, and ethical and responsible use, could be included to provide a structured approach to AI governance.[246]

- **Accenture's Ethical AI Framework:** Accenture's framework for ethical AI, which includes criteria such as soundness, fairness, transparency, and accountability, could be referenced as a model for organizations to follow.[247]

- **AI Ethics Dilemmas and Frameworks:** The section could discuss the top dilemmas of AI ethics and the frameworks developed to navigate them, as well as the importance of inclusiveness and alignment in AI research.[248]

- **Corporate Governance Trends:** The latest corporate governance trends, including the focus on ethics and the need for effective systems for sharing data, could be mentioned to emphasize the evolving role of boards in overseeing AI technologies.[249]

- **AI Governance as a Prerequisite for Enterprise Sales:** The necessity for AI governance in sectors like healthcare and financial services, and the role of AI oversight councils in evaluating internal and external AI-related risks, could be highlighted.[250]

---

[245] https://iapp.org/news/a/five-compliance-best-practices-for-a-successful-ai-governance-program/

[246] https://www.forbes.com/sites/forbestechcouncil/2024/02/22/principles-for-enterprise-ai-governance/?sh=21450c164f07

[247] https://www.accenture.com/us-en/services/applied-intelligence/ai-ethics-governance

[248] https://research.aimultiple.com/ai-ethics/

[249] https://www.diligent.com/resources/blog/corporate-governance-trends

[250] https://iapp.org/news/a/ensuring-ai-governance-the-time-to-act-is-now/

- **AI Governance Best Practices:** Best practices for AI governance within businesses, such as identifying AI-generated materials and dealing with algorithmic biases, could be included to guide companies in implementing responsible AI.[251]

- **S&P Global's AI Governance Challenge:** The AI governance challenge, as outlined by S&P Global, which includes human centrism, ethical use, transparency, and the need for robust governance frameworks, could be referenced to underscore the importance of these elements in AI governance.[252]

- **Singapore's AI Investment Plan:** Singapore's significant investment in AI and its commitment to creating a trusted and responsible AI ecosystem could be used as an example of how national strategies can influence corporate governance practices.[253]

- **Generative AI and Innovative Cultures:** Finally, the impact of generative AI on innovation strategies and the importance of an innovative culture in leveraging AI could be discussed, as companies with such cultures have a significant edge with generative AI.[254]

From the practices of these AI-savvy boards, several best practices emerge:

- **Establish Dedicated Ethics Bodies:** Creating panels, committees, or offices focused on AI ethics can provide specialized oversight and guidance.

- **Prioritize Long-Term Research:** While short-term gains are appealing, boards should recognize the value of long-term research, especially in a rapidly evolving field like AI.

---

[251] https://www.dataversity.net/ai-governance-best-practices/

[252] https://www.spglobal.com/en/research-insights/featured/special-editorial/the-ai-governance-challenge

[253] https://www.cnbc.com/2024/02/19/singapores-ai-ambitions-get-a-boost-with-740-million-investment-plan.html

[254] https://www.mckinsey.com/capabilities/strategy-and-corporate-finance/our-insights/companies-with-innovative-cultures-have-a-big-edge-with-generative-ai

- **Collaborate and Cooperate:** AI's challenges are vast and multifaceted. Boards should promote collaborative efforts, both internally and with external organizations, to address AI's complexities collectively.

- **Transparent Communication:** Boards should encourage transparent communication about the company's AI projects, challenges, and ethical considerations, fostering trust with stakeholders.

- **Continuous Education:** Boards must stay updated with AI advancements and implications. This involves regular training sessions, bringing in AI experts for discussions, and even attending AI-focused seminars and conferences.

AI-savvy boards recognize the transformative potential of AI, not just as a technological tool but as a fundamental shift in how businesses operate and create value. Their proactive, informed, and ethical approaches serve as a guiding light for others in the corporate world.

13. International Regulations for Governing AI Use and Development

13.1. How Governments are Considering Regulating AI

Artificial intelligence (AI) is rapidly transforming our world. From facial recognition technology used to unlock smartphones to complex algorithms that power self-driving cars, AI is pervasive and fundamentally changing the way we live, work, and interact. AI holds immense promise for revolutionizing industries, enhancing healthcare, and automating tasks previously thought to be exclusively human.

However, alongside its undeniable potential, AI also presents a range of challenges that demand our attention. The vast amount of data required to train powerful AI systems raises critical questions about data privacy and security. The opaque nature of some AI decision-making processes can lead to concerns about transparency and fairness. The potential for bias in training data can perpetuate social inequalities in areas like loan approvals or criminal justice. The development of autonomous AI systems raises ethical concerns about accountability and human oversight.

In light of these challenges, it is becoming increasingly clear that existing legal frameworks are inadequately equipped to address the unique characteristics and complexities of AI. Data privacy regulations like the General Data Protection Regulation

(GDPR) (EU) and the California Consumer Privacy Act (CCPA) (US) were designed for a pre-AI era and struggle to fully encompass the nuances of AI data practices. National laws often vary significantly, creating a fragmented legal landscape that hinders international collaboration on AI development and governance.

This chapter delves into the emerging international regulatory landscape for governing AI use and development. We will explore the key concerns that governments are seeking to address through regulations, analyze the limitations of existing legal frameworks, and survey the current efforts by international organizations and individual countries to establish a comprehensive regulatory approach. We will examine specific areas of focus in international AI regulations, discuss the challenges of global governance, and consider open questions that require ongoing international dialogue and collaboration.

Throughout this chapter, we will draw upon real-world examples, case studies, and relevant references to illustrate the concrete implications of AI regulation and the importance of a balanced approach that fosters responsible AI development while safeguarding individual rights, societal well-being, and global cooperation in the AI era.[255]

13.2. The Need for AI Regulation: Addressing Key Concerns

The transformative potential of AI is undeniable. However, as AI becomes increasingly integrated into our lives, so too do the associated risks. These risks necessitate the development of robust regulations to ensure the responsible and ethical use of this

---

[255] European Commission. (2021, April 21). Proposal for a Regulation of the European Parliament and of the Council Laying Down Harmonised Rules on Artificial Intelligence (Artificial Intelligence Act) and Amending Certain Legislative Texts (COM(2021) 206 final). https://eur-lex.europa.eu/legal-content/EN/ALL/?uri=celex%3A52021PC0206, General Data Protection Regulation (Regulation (EU) 2016/679) (https://gdpr.eu/what-is-gdpr/), Organisation for Economic Co-operation and Development (OECD). (2019, May 21). Recommendation of the Council on Artificial Intelligence (OECD/legal/0123). https://oecd.ai/en/ai-principles, and California Consumer Privacy Act (CCPA). https://oag.ca.gov/privacy/ccpa

powerful technology. Let's delve into some of the key concerns governments seek to address through AI regulations.

13.2.1. Data Privacy and Security

At the heart of AI development and deployment lies data. Massive datasets are used to train AI algorithms, and these datasets often contain sensitive personal information. The collection, storage, and use of this data raise significant privacy and security concerns:

- **Transparency and Control:** Individuals have a right to understand how their data is being used in AI systems. Regulations can ensure transparency by requiring clear disclosures about data collection practices, the purpose for which data is used, and how individuals can access and potentially rectify their data used in AI applications.

- **Data Security:** AI systems are vulnerable to cyberattacks, which could lead to the exposure of sensitive personal information. Regulations can mandate robust security measures to protect data from unauthorized access, use, disclosure, disruption, modification, or destruction.

- **Accountability:** Clear lines of accountability are needed to determine who is responsible for data breaches or misuse of personal information within AI systems. Regulations can establish mechanisms for holding data controllers and processors accountable for data privacy violations.

A real-world example highlighting the importance of data privacy in AI involves Clearview AI, a facial recognition company. Clearview AI scraped billions of images from social media platforms without users' consent, raising concerns about the large-scale collection and use of facial recognition data for unspecified purposes. This incident underscores the need for regulations that limit the unfettered collection of personal data used in AI systems and establish clear user consent mechanisms.[256]

---

[256] https://www.businesswire.com/news/home/20240416920926/en/Clearview-AI-Improves-SOC-2-Certification-Certifying-Privacy-Controls-Alongside-Security-Controls

13.2.2.   Algorithmic Bias and Fairness

AI algorithms are only as good as the data they are trained on. If the training data contains biases, these biases can be perpetuated in the AI system's decision-making processes. Algorithmic bias can have far-reaching consequences, leading to discrimination in areas like loan approvals, criminal justice, and recruitment. Regulations can address algorithmic bias through:

- **Data Governance:** Measures to ensure the quality and fairness of data used to train AI systems. This might involve auditing training datasets for bias, implementing processes to identify and mitigate biases, and promoting the use of diverse datasets.

- **Impact Assessments:** Regulations can mandate impact assessments for high-risk AI systems, evaluating the potential for bias and discrimination in their decisions.

- **Human Oversight:** Maintaining human oversight in critical decision-making processes can act as a safeguard against biased algorithmic outcomes.

A concerning example of algorithmic bias emerged in the case of an algorithm used by a US recruitment tool. The algorithm was found to discriminate against female applicants, favoring male candidates with similar qualifications. This incident highlights the importance of regulations that promote fairness and non-discrimination in AI-driven decision-making processes.[257]

13.2.3.   Safety and Explainability

The safety and reliability of AI systems are paramount, especially for applications used in high-risk domains like autonomous vehicles or medical diagnosis. Regulations can address safety concerns by:

---

[257] Gebru, T., Myself, J., Feinman, R., & Crawford, M. (2020). On the dangers of stochastic parrots: Can language models be too big?. Proceedings of the 2020 Conference on Fairness, Accountability, and Transparency, 387-399. https://dl.acm.org/doi/10.1145/3442188.3445922 and Jobin, A., Ienca, M., & Vayena, E. (2019). The state of the art in algorithmic bias in decision support systems. ACM Computing Surveys (CSUR), 52(1), 1-47. https://dl.acm.org/doi/fullHtml/10.1145/3318157

- **Safety Standards:** Establishing safety standards for the development and deployment of high-risk AI systems. These standards might include testing methodologies and risk mitigation strategies.

- **Explainability:** Promoting transparency in AI decision-making by requiring some level of explainability for algorithmic outputs. While certain complex AI algorithms may be inherently difficult to fully explain, regulations can encourage developers to make AI systems more interpretable to aid in human oversight and debugging.

The recent crash of a self-driving car equipped with AI highlights the critical need for robust safety regulations governing autonomous AI systems. This incident underscores the importance of ensuring that AI systems are thoroughly tested and validated before being deployed in real-world scenarios.[258]

13.2.4. Accountability and Liability

As AI becomes more sophisticated and autonomous, determining who is responsible for potential harms caused by AI systems becomes increasingly complex. Regulations can address accountability and liability through:

- **Clear Lines of Responsibility:** Establishing a clear chain of responsibility for the development, deployment, and operation of AI systems. This might involve holding manufacturers, developers, and users accountable depending on the specific context and risk level of the AI application.

- **Algorithmic Impact Assessments:** Mandating impact assessments that evaluate the potential risks associated with AI systems, including potential harms and who might be affected.

---

[258] National Academies of Sciences, Engineering, and Medicine. (2019). Ensuring the trustworthiness of artificial intelligence systems: Recommendations for research and policy. The National Academies Press. https://nap.nationalacademies.org/read/26208/chapter/1 and European Commission. (2023, January). Guidance on trustworthy AI for a human-centred future (COM(2023) 2 final). https://digital-strategy.ec.europa.eu/en/policies/international-outreach-ai

- **Insurance and Compensation Mechanisms:** Exploring mechanisms for insurance coverage or compensation schemes to address potential damages caused by malfunctioning AI systems.

A recent example of the challenges surrounding accountability in AI involves a medical AI system used for cancer diagnoses. The system was found to have misdiagnosed cancers in some cases. Determining liability in this situation is complex, as it could involve the developers of the algorithm, the hospital that deployed the system, or even the physicians who relied on the AI output for their diagnoses. This case highlights the need for regulations that establish clear accountability frameworks to ensure appropriate remedies for those harmed by faulty AI systems.[259]

13.2.5.   Societal and Ethical Concerns

Beyond the immediate concerns of data privacy, fairness, and safety, AI also raises broader societal and ethical questions:

- **Job displacement:** Automation powered by AI has the potential to displace jobs in various sectors. Regulations may need to address issues like retraining programs and income security for workers impacted by AI automation.

- **Algorithmic Bias in Society:** AI systems can perpetuate existing social biases related to race, gender, or socioeconomic status. Regulations can promote the development and deployment of AI systems that contribute to a more just and equitable society.

- **Weaponization of AI:** The potential for autonomous weapons systems raises serious ethical concerns. Regulations may be needed to prohibit or restrict the development and use of lethal autonomous weapons systems.

The increasing use of facial recognition technology by law enforcement agencies exemplifies the broader societal and ethical concerns surrounding AI. Critics argue that such technology can lead to mass surveillance and violations of privacy. These concerns

---

[259] Matthias, A. (2020). The accountability of artificial intelligence. Daedalus, 149(2), 25-38. https://direct.mit.edu/daed/article/151/2/5/110608/Getting-AI-Right-Introductory-Notes-on-AI-amp and Whittaker, M., Crawford, K., Dobson, R., Schultz, W., & Vertinsky, I. (2020). AI Now Institute 2020 Report. The New School. https://ainowinstitute.org/wp-content/uploads/2023/04/AI_Now_2019_Report.pdf

highlight the need for regulations that balance security needs with civil liberties in the age of AI.[260]

13.2.6.   Summary

The issues outlined in this section demonstrate the compelling need for international regulations to govern the development and deployment of AI. Existing legal frameworks are inadequately equipped to address the unique challenges posed by AI. By establishing clear standards and accountability mechanisms, regulations can foster responsible AI development that protects individual rights, promotes fairness, and ensures the safe and beneficial integration of AI into our lives.

The following sections will explore the emerging landscape of international AI regulations, analyze specific areas of focus, and discuss the challenges and opportunities associated with the global governance of AI.

13.3.   Existing Legal Landscape and its Limitations

The emergence of AI presents a challenge to existing legal frameworks designed in a pre-AI era. While data privacy regulations and broader legal principles form a foundation, they often struggle to effectively address the unique characteristics and complexities of AI. Let's delve into some of the limitations of existing legal frameworks:

13.3.1.   Data Privacy Laws Designed for a Pre-AI Era

Established data privacy regulations, like the General Data Protection Regulation (GDPR) (EU) and the California Consumer Privacy Act (CCPA) (US), were developed at a time before AI became pervasive. These frameworks primarily focus on individual

---

[260] Bostrom, N. (2014). Superintelligence: Paths, dangers, strategies. Oxford University Press. https://global.oup.com/academic/product/superintelligence-9780199678112 and Jobin, A., Karakaya, S., & van den Hoven, M. (2019). The ethics of artificial intelligence. Cambridge University Press. https://www.cambridge.org/core/books/cambridge-handbook-of-artificial-intelligence/ethics-of-artificial-intelligence/B46D2A9DF7CF3A9D92601D9A8ADA58A8

control over personal data and transparency in data collection practices. However, they may not fully encompass the nuances of AI data practices, such as Data Governance. Existing regulations may not provide clear guidance on data governance practices specific to AI development. This includes requirements for:

- **Data Quality and Bias Mitigation:** Ensuring the quality and fairness of data used to train AI algorithms. Regulations may need to address techniques for identifying and mitigating biases in training datasets.

- **Accountability for Data Use:** Establishing clear lines of accountability for who is responsible for the data used in training AI systems, particularly when data is obtained from third-party sources.

- **Algorithmic Transparency:** The right to explanation enshrined in some data privacy laws may not be sufficient for highly complex AI algorithms. Regulations may need to evolve to address the challenge of balancing transparency with proprietary trade secrets associated with certain algorithms.

- **Explainability Levels:** Finding the right balance between transparency for accountability purposes and protecting commercially sensitive information within algorithms is crucial.

- **Human-Understandable Explanations:** Even if a level of explanation is provided, it needs to be understandable by humans, not just technical experts.[261]

A fragmented legal landscape across jurisdictions leads to:

- **Data privacy laws vary significantly across countries:** This creates a fragmented legal landscape that can hinder international collaboration on AI development and governance. Companies operating globally need to comply with a patchwork of regulations, increasing compliance costs and administrative burdens.

---

[261] Mittelstadt, B., Wachter, S., & Floridi, L. (2019). The ethics of algorithms: Mapping the debate. Big Data & Society, 6(2), 1-21. And European Commission. (2020, February 18). Communication from the Commission to the European Parliament, the Council, the European Economic and Social Committee and the Committee of the Regions on Shaping the Digital Future of Europe (COM(2020) 67 final).

- **Challenges for Multinational Companies:** Companies developing and deploying AI systems globally may face conflicting regulations and uncertainties about compliance requirements in different jurisdictions. This can stifle innovation and hinder the development of global AI solutions.

- **Limited Interoperability:** Fragmented regulations can create obstacles to the interoperability of AI systems across national borders. This can hinder international trade and collaboration in sectors reliant on AI technologies.[262]

Existing legal frameworks may not provide adequate guidance for regulating high-risk AI applications, such as:

- **Autonomous Vehicles:** Safety standards specific to autonomous vehicles need to be developed to ensure the safe operation of these systems on public roads. These standards might address technical requirements, testing methodologies, and liability frameworks in case of accidents.

- **Medical Diagnosis Systems:** Regulations need to address the use of AI in medical diagnosis to ensure accuracy, fairness, and accountability. This might involve requirements for human oversight.[263]

---

[262] Organization for Economic Co-operation and Development (OECD). (2021, November 11). Policy statement on international co-operation in the use of artificial intelligence (AI). and Berkman Klein Center for Internet & Society at Harvard University. (2020, December). A global framework for governing artificial intelligence.

[263] Jobin, A., Ienca, M., & Vayena, E. (2019). The state of the art in algorithmic bias in decision support systems. ACM Computing Surveys (CSUR), 52(1), 1-47. https://dl.acm.org/doi/fullHtml/10.1145/3318157 and National Academies of Sciences, Engineering, and Medicine. (2019). Ensuring the trustworthiness of artificial intelligence systems: Recommendations for research and policy. The National Academies Press. https://nap.nationalacademies.org/read/26208/chapter/1

13.4.   Surveying the International Regulatory Landscape[264]

In the absence of a single, global framework for governing AI, various countries and international organizations are taking proactive steps to develop their own regulations and guidelines. Let's explore this evolving international regulatory landscape.

13.4.1.   The European Union (EU)

The European Union has emerged as a leader in shaping the global conversation around AI regulation. The EU's approach is characterized by a strong focus on human-centric values like transparency, fairness, and accountability. Key initiatives include:

- **The AI Act:** The European Commission proposed the Artificial Intelligence Act (AI Act) in 2021. This landmark legislation aims to establish a regulatory framework for governing AI development and deployment across the EU. The AI Act classifies AI systems into different risk categories, with proportionate regulatory requirements attached to each category. High-risk AI systems, such as those used in facial recognition or autonomous vehicles, will be subject to stricter regulations.

- **The General Data Protection Regulation (GDPR):** The GDPR, while not exclusively focused on AI, plays an important role in regulating the data practices underlying AI development. The GDPR grants individuals rights to access, rectify, and erase their personal data, which is crucial for ensuring transparency and accountability in AI systems reliant on personal data.

---

[264] The European Union Artificial Intelligence
Act: https://ec.europa.eu/commission/policies/strategy/artificial-intelligence-strategy-21042021_en,
The General Data Protection Regulation (GDPR): https://gdpr.eu/, The National Telecommunications
and Information Administration (NTIA) AI Principles: https://www.ntia.gov/files/public/aichip-
principles-may-2020.pdf, The Food and Drug Administration (FDA) Artificial Intelligence/Machine
Learning: https://www.fda.gov/medical-devices/digital-health-software/artificial-intelligence-
machine-learning, and The OECD AI Principles: https://www.oecd.org/going-digital/ai/principles/

13.4.2.   The United States (US)

The United States has adopted a more sector-specific approach to AI regulation. While there is no single comprehensive AI regulation at the federal level, various government agencies are developing guidelines for specific sectors like autonomous vehicles or healthcare. Here are some noteworthy examples:

- **The National Telecommunications and Information Administration (NTIA):** The NTIA has released non-binding AI development principles that emphasize accountability, transparency, safety, equity, and privacy.

- **The Food and Drug Administration (FDA):** The FDA has established regulatory frameworks for governing medical devices powered by AI, focusing on safety and effectiveness.

Special Note: President Biden's October 2023 Executive Order on AI

President Biden's Executive Order on Artificial Intelligence, signed on October 30, 2023, marks a significant step in the United States' approach to managing the development and deployment of AI technologies. The order, officially titled "Safe, Secure, and Trustworthy Development and Use of Artificial Intelligence," aims to establish a comprehensive framework to address the various challenges and risks associated with AI while promoting its responsible use across different sectors. This initiative reflects a proactive stance by the federal government to not only harness the benefits of AI but also mitigate its potential threats to privacy, security, and equity.[265]

The Executive Order is structured around several key areas of focus, each designed to enhance the overall governance of AI technologies. One of the primary areas includes regulating high-risk AI applications, particularly those that could impact critical infrastructure, national security, and civil rights. The order emphasizes the need for robust testing and risk assessment protocols to ensure that AI systems are both effective and safe for public use. It also calls for developing privacy-enhancing technologies to

---

[265] https://www.crowell.com/en/insights/client-alerts/how-president-bidens-executive-order-safe-secure-and-trustworthy-artificial-intelligence-addresses-health-care, https://www.lawfaremedia.org/article/what-s-in-biden-s-executive-order-on-artificial-intelligence, https://jamanetwork.com/journals/jama/article-abstract/2812613, and https://www.whitehouse.gov/briefing-room/statements-releases/2024/01/29/fact-sheet-biden-harris-administration-announces-key-ai-actions-following-president-bidens-landmark-executive-order/.

safeguard personal and sensitive information against the invasive capabilities of advanced AI systems.[266]

In addition to regulatory measures, the Executive Order also prioritizes the advancement of AI innovation and leadership in the United States. It outlines initiatives to support research and development, enhance the AI workforce, and promote ethical AI practices. This includes funding for AI research, support for small developers and businesses, and efforts to attract and train top AI talent. The order also addresses the potential socioeconomic impacts of AI, such as job displacement and workplace surveillance, underscoring the need for a balanced approach that benefits all segments of society.[267]

Furthermore, the Executive Order establishes the White House AI Council, tasked with coordinating AI-related activities across federal agencies to ensure a unified approach to AI governance. This council plays a crucial role in implementing the order's directives, ensuring that AI development aligns with national interests and public welfare. The comprehensive nature of this Executive Order, with its detailed action items and deadlines, demonstrates the Biden Administration's commitment to leading a strategic and responsible national AI strategy that addresses both the opportunities and challenges posed by this transformative technology.

13.4.3. Other Leading Countries and Regions

Several other countries and regions are actively engaged in developing AI regulations. Here are a few examples:

- **China:** China has released national guidelines on AI development, focusing on ethical principles and economic competitiveness.

---

[266] https://www.crowell.com/en/insights/client-alerts/how-president-bidens-executive-order-safe-secure-and-trustworthy-artificial-intelligence-addresses-health-care, https://www.lawfaremedia.org/article/what-s-in-biden-s-executive-order-on-artificial-intelligence, and https://www.lawfaremedia.org/article/what-s-in-biden-s-executive-order-on-artificial-intelligence.

[267] https://www.mayerbrown.com/en/insights/publications/2024/02/biden-artificial-intelligence-executive-order-action-tracker and https://www.lawfaremedia.org/article/what-s-in-biden-s-executive-order-on-artificial-intelligence

- **Singapore:** Singapore has established an AI Governance framework focusing on safety, ethics, and human capital development.

- **South Korea:** South Korea has launched a national AI strategy prioritizing responsible development and investment in AI research.

13.4.4.   International Organizations

International organizations are playing a crucial role in fostering global dialogue and coordination on AI governance. Key actors include:

- The Organization for Economic Co-operation and Development (OECD): The OECD has developed AI principles that emphasize fairness, transparency, accountability, human-centeredness, and robustness. These principles are designed to serve as a non-binding framework for governments around the world. The OECD AI Principles, first adopted in 2019 and updated in 2024, provide a blueprint for policy frameworks addressing AI risks and shaping AI policies. They advocate for AI that is innovative and trustworthy, upholding human rights and democratic values. The OECD also collaborates with international standards organizations like ISO/IEC to ensure global policy interoperability and promote innovation.[268] [269]

- The United Nations (UN): The UN is engaged in discussions on the potential implications of AI for international security and human rights. The UN General Assembly adopted its first resolution on AI in March 2024, emphasizing the promotion of "safe, secure, and trustworthy" AI systems that respect human rights and contribute to sustainable development. This resolution highlights the importance of international cooperation and the need for inclusive and equitable access to AI technologies. The UN's High-Level Advisory Body on AI

---

[268] https://www.ansi.org/standards-news/all-news/2024/05/5-9-24-oecd-updates-ai-principles

[269] https://www.oecd.org/newsroom/oecd-updates-ai-principles-to-stay-abreast-of-rapid-technological-developments.htm

and other initiatives like the Global Digital Compact aim to create a comprehensive governance framework that addresses AI's global impacts.[270] [271]

- The Global Partnership on AI (GPAI): GPAI is an international initiative that brings together experts from governments, industry, civil society, and academia to promote the responsible development and use of AI. It focuses on fostering collaboration and sharing best practices to address AI's ethical, social, and economic challenges.[272]

- The World Economic Forum (WEF): The WEF's AI Governance Alliance works on transforming how AI shapes our world by driving innovation and practical governance solutions. It emphasizes the design of transparent and inclusive AI systems and promotes multi-stakeholder engagement to address AI's global challenges.[273]

- The European Union (EU): The EU has been proactive in developing comprehensive AI regulations, such as the AI Act, which aims to ensure that AI systems are safe, transparent, and respect fundamental rights. The EU's approach to AI governance serves as a model for other regions and contributes to the global dialogue on AI regulation.[274]

These organizations and initiatives highlight the importance of international cooperation in AI governance, ensuring that AI technologies are developed and deployed in ways that are ethical, inclusive, and beneficial to all of humanity.

---

[270]

  https://www.un.org/techenvoy/sites/www.un.org.techenvoy/files/ai_advisory_body_interim_report.pdf

[271] https://insightplus.bakermckenzie.com/bm/data-technology/international-the-united-nations-adopts-its-first-resolution-on-ai

[272] https://www.brookings.edu/articles/should-the-un-govern-global-ai/

[273] https://initiatives.weforum.org/ai-governance-alliance/home

[274] https://www.brookings.edu/articles/international-cooperation-the-us-executive-order-on-ai/

13.5.   Key Regulatory Focus Areas and Emerging Trends

As the field of AI continues to evolve rapidly, so too do the regulatory considerations surrounding it. Here, we'll explore some of the key areas where regulators are focusing their attention, along with emerging trends that are shaping the future of AI regulation.

13.5.1.   Transparency and Explainability

One of the major concerns surrounding AI is its lack of transparency. Regulators are pushing for AI systems to be more transparent, meaning users should be able to understand how these systems arrive at their decisions. This is particularly important for high-risk applications like facial recognition or algorithmic decision-making that can significantly impact people's lives.[275]

Imagine you're applying for a loan. You fill out all the paperwork, hit submit, and then... silence. Days turn into weeks, and you have no clue why your application was accepted or rejected. Frustrating, right?

This lack of transparency is a major concern with AI, especially when it impacts our lives. AI systems are increasingly making decisions that affect people, from loan approvals to job recommendations. The problem is these systems can be like black boxes. You feed them data and they spit out a result, but how they arrive at that answer is often a mystery.

This lack of explainability is a big deal for regulators. If someone is denied a loan by an AI system, they deserve to know why. Was it your credit score, employment history, or something else? Without transparency, it's impossible to identify and address potential biases in the AI system.

Imagine a situation where an AI is used to screen job applications. The AI might unconsciously favor resumes with certain keywords or educational backgrounds,

---

[275] European Union Commission. (2021, April 21). Artificial Intelligence Act.
   https://ec.europa.eu/commission/policies/strategy/artificial-intelligence-strategy-21042021_en

unfairly filtering out qualified candidates. Transparency can help identify these biases and ensure AI systems make fair and unbiased decisions.

So, how can we make AI more transparent? Researchers are developing new techniques called Explainable AI (XAI). Think of XAI as a window into the AI's mind. With XAI, you can see the steps the AI takes to reach a conclusion, understanding how it analyzes data and makes decisions. This would be a game-changer for regulators because they could finally see how AI systems work and identify potential issues.[276]

Regulations might also require AI developers to be more transparent throughout the entire process. Imagine a detailed blueprint for the AI system, explaining how it's built and trained. This would give regulators a better understanding of the AI's capabilities and limitations.

Think of transparency in AI as shining a light on these powerful systems. By making them more understandable, we can ensure they are used fairly, ethically, and don't turn into a black box of mystery and potential bias.

13.5.2. Bias and Fairness

AI systems can perpetuate and amplify societal biases present in the data on which they are trained. The regulatory focus is on ensuring fairness and mitigating bias in AI development and deployment. This includes ensuring diverse datasets are used to train AI models and implementing mechanisms to detect and address potential biases.[277]

Let's say you're applying for a job for which you're perfectly qualified. You have the skills, the experience, everything they listed. But when the interview notification arrives, it's a rejection. Frustrated, you dig deeper and discover the company uses an AI system to screen resumes. Could the AI be biased?

This is a growing concern in the world of AI – bias and fairness. AI systems are trained on massive datasets, and if those datasets contain hidden biases, the AI can inherit them. Think of an AI trained on loan applications that were historically more likely to be

[276] https://tdwi.org/Articles/2024/02/22/ADV-ALL-Entering-the-Age-of-Explainable-AI.aspx

[277] American Association for the Advancement of Science (AAAS), Center for Security and Emerging Technology (CSET). (2019, October). Algorithmic Justice League: Policy Principles for Addressing Algorithmic Bias. https://www.ajl.org/

approved for men than women. The AI might unconsciously learn this bias and continue to favor male applicants.

Regulators are wrestling with this issue, focusing on ensuring fairness in AI development and deployment. Here's how they're approaching it:

- **Data Diversity:** Just like a balanced diet is good for your health, a diverse dataset is crucial for fair AI. Regulations might require developers to use datasets that represent the real world, including people from different backgrounds and demographics. Imagine training an AI on loan applications from a variety of applicants not just a narrow slice.

- **Bias Detection and Mitigation:** Not all biases are obvious. Regulations might require developers to use tools that can sniff out hidden biases in datasets before they're used to train AI systems. Think of a special program that scans the data for potential biases and flags them for review.

- Human Oversight: AI shouldn't be the sole decision-maker, especially when it comes to sensitive areas like loan approvals or job applications. Regulations might require human oversight to ensure the AI's recommendations are fair and unbiased. Imagine an expert reviewing the AI's decision and making sure it aligns with fairness principles.

- **Algorithmic Impact Assessments:** Before unleashing an AI system on the world, regulations might require developers to conduct a thorough assessment of its potential impact. Think of a report that analyzes how the AI might affect different groups of people, identifying and mitigating potential biases.

By focusing on these areas, regulations aim to create a level playing field for everyone. They want to ensure AI doesn't become a tool for perpetuating existing inequalities, but rather a force for good that benefits everyone fairly.

13.5.3. Accountability

Assigning clear responsibility for the actions and decisions of AI systems is crucial. Regulations are being developed to determine who is accountable for potential harms caused by AI, whether it's the developer, user, or another party.[278]

Imagine you're at the hospital and the doctor relies on a fancy AI system to diagnose your illness. The AI scans your data and recommends a treatment, but unfortunately, things go wrong. Now the finger pointing starts. Who's to blame?

This is the tricky question of accountability in AI. Regulations are trying to untangle this mess by considering different scenarios. Let's say the company that built the AI didn't properly test it for bias, and it turns out the AI keeps misdiagnosing a particular group of patients. In this case, the company would likely be on the hook for creating a faulty system.

But wait, there's more! The hospital that uses the AI also has some responsibility. They should ensure the AI is being used for the right purposes and that the doctors understand how to interpret its results. If the hospital just blindly trusts the AI's every recommendation without considering other factors, they might also share some of the blame.

The problem gets even more complex because some AI systems are like mysterious black boxes. You feed them data and they give you an answer, but it's hard to see exactly how they arrived at that answer. This makes it almost impossible to pinpoint who's responsible if the AI makes a mistake. Was it the programmer's fault for building an opaque system, or the doctor's fault for using an unreadable tool?

To address this, researchers are working on ways to make AI more transparent. Imagine if you could see inside the AI's mind, understanding the steps it takes to reach a conclusion. This would be a game-changer for accountability. Regulations might also require AI developers to be more careful throughout the entire process, making sure fairness and safety checks are built into the system from the beginning. Another idea is to create a kind of "risk report" for AI systems, identifying potential problems before they even get deployed in the real world.

---

[278] Jobin, A., Ienca, M., & Vayena, F. (2019). The ethics of artificial intelligence. Cambridge University Press.

So, accountability in AI is like a puzzle with many pieces. Regulations are trying to fit those pieces together to make sure everyone involved plays their part in developing and using AI responsibly.

13.5.4.   Privacy and Security

The vast amount of data required to train AI systems raises privacy concerns. Regulations are being developed to ensure data privacy is protected throughout the AI lifecycle, from collection and storage to use and disposal. Security of AI systems is also a major focus, as vulnerabilities can be exploited for malicious purposes.[279]

13.5.5.   Emerging Trends

Several trends are shaping the future of AI regulation:

- **International Collaboration:** As AI becomes a global phenomenon, there's a growing push for international collaboration on developing harmonized regulations.

- **Regulation by Sector:** We might see more sector-specific regulations emerge, tailoring requirements to the unique risks and challenges posed by AI in different industries.

- **Focus on Human Rights:** Regulations are likely to increasingly consider the potential impact of AI on human rights, such as freedom from discrimination and the right to privacy.

By addressing these key focus areas and emerging trends, regulators aim to foster the responsible development and deployment of AI that benefits society while mitigating potential risks.

---

[279] European Union. (2016, April 14). General Data Protection Regulation (GDPR). [https://gdpr.eu/]

13.6. Challenges and Considerations for Global Governance

The rapid development and deployment of AI technologies pose significant challenges for establishing effective global governance. Here, we explore some of the key hurdles and considerations to address.

13.6.1. Lack of International Consensus[280]

Currently, there's no single, unified approach to AI governance on the international stage. While various countries and regions are developing their own regulations, a lack of global consensus creates inconsistencies and potential loopholes. This can hinder responsible AI development and deployment across borders and make it difficult to hold multinational corporations accountable.[281]

The current landscape of AI regulation resembles a patchwork quilt – a collection of diverse approaches with little uniformity. While some countries are taking a proactive stance, others are lagging behind. This lack of international consensus creates several challenges:

- **Inconsistent Standards:** Imagine a company developing an AI system for self-driving cars. In one country, the regulations might be very strict, requiring rigorous testing and safety measures. But in another country, the regulations might be lax, with fewer safeguards in place. This inconsistency creates a situation where the safety of self-driving cars can vary greatly depending on where you are in the world.

---

[280] Inconsistent Standards: You can mention a specific example of a country with stricter regulations, like the European Union's focus on explainable AI (reference: [European Union Commission. (2021, April 21). Artificial Intelligence Act. https://ec.europa.eu/commission/policies/strategy/artificial-intelligence-strategy-21042021_en]). and Efforts Towards Global Harmonization: Briefly mention the OECD's role in developing international AI principles (reference: https://www.oecd.org/going-digital/ai/principles/]).

[281] Bard's previous reference about the EU vs. US approach to AI regulation: previous section on 13.4.2

- **Regulatory Loopholes:** The gaps between different regulatory approaches can be exploited by companies seeking to avoid stricter regulations. Imagine a company developing a controversial AI application that might face scrutiny in its home country. They could potentially shift development or deployment to a country with weaker regulations, essentially skirting stricter rules.

- **Challenges in Holding Multinational Corporations Accountable:** With the rise of multinational corporations developing AI technologies, the question of accountability becomes complex. In a situation where an AI system developed by a company headquartered in one country causes harm in another, determining jurisdiction and enforcing regulations becomes a tangled mess.

- **Hindered Innovation:** A complex web of regulations across different countries can stifle innovation. Imagine a small startup developing a groundbreaking AI application for healthcare. If they need to navigate a maze of regulations in every country they want to operate in, it can be a major barrier to entry and hinder the global reach of their innovation.

13.6.2.   *Efforts Towards Global Harmonization*

Despite these challenges, there's a growing recognition of the need for international collaboration on AI governance. Organizations like the OECD (Organisation for Economic Co-operation and Development) are developing international principles for responsible AI development. Additionally, regional initiatives and forums are fostering dialogue and cooperation between different countries.

The ultimate goal is to create some level of harmonization in AI regulations, ensuring a baseline level of safety and ethical considerations are applied across borders. This would create a more level playing field for responsible AI development and deployment, while still allowing for some flexibility to accommodate national priorities.

The road to achieving a unified approach to AI governance will likely be long and complex. However, by working together, the international community can overcome the challenges posed by a lack of consensus and create a global framework that fosters innovation and ensures the responsible development and deployment of AI for the benefit of all.

13.6.3.   Balancing Innovation and Regulation

Striking a balance between fostering innovation and implementing effective regulations is crucial. Overly restrictive regulations can stifle the development of beneficial AI applications. However, a lack of regulation can lead to the proliferation of harmful or unethical AI practices.

Imagine a seesaw. On one end sits innovation, bursting with potential to revolutionize industries and improve lives. On the other end sits regulation, aiming to ensure safety, fairness, and ethical considerations. Striking the right balance between these two forces is crucial for the responsible development and deployment of AI.

Innovation offers:

- **Progress and Efficiency:** AI has the potential to drive significant progress across various fields. From personalized medicine to self-driving cars, AI can automate tasks, improve decision-making, and accelerate innovation cycles. Overly restrictive regulations could stifle these advancements.

- **Global Competitiveness:** In today's globalized world, countries that foster AI innovation have a competitive edge. Regulations that hinder development could put a nation at a disadvantage economically.

- **Unlocking Potential:** AI research is constantly evolving, with new possibilities emerging all the time. Rigid regulations could inadvertently block the exploration of these possibilities and hinder the full potential of AI.

Regulation provide:

- **Mitigating Risks:** AI can also pose significant risks, from biased algorithms to autonomous weapons. Regulations are essential to mitigate these risks and ensure the safe and ethical development of AI.[282]

- **Building Public Trust:** Without proper safeguards, public trust in AI can erode. Regulations can help build public confidence by demonstrating a commitment to responsible AI development.

---

[282] https://www.ajl.org/

- **Level Playing Field:** Regulations can help create a fair and competitive environment for AI development, preventing companies from cutting corners on safety or ethics.

So, how do we achieve this balance? Here are some potential solutions:

- **Risk-Based Regulation:** Regulations can be tailored to the specific risks posed by different AI applications. High-risk applications, like autonomous weapons, might require stricter regulations than lower-risk applications, like recommendation algorithms.

- **Regulatory Sandboxes:** These are controlled environments where companies can test and experiment with new AI technologies before deploying them in the real world. This allows for innovation while identifying potential risks before widespread adoption.

- **Focus on Outcomes:** Regulations can focus on the desired outcomes, such as fairness and non-discrimination, rather than prescribing specific technical solutions. This allows for flexibility and innovation while still achieving the intended goals.

The key is to establish a regulatory framework that fosters innovation while ensuring the safe and ethical development of AI. By carefully considering the potential benefits and risks, and implementing regulations that are both effective and adaptable, we can ensure AI technology is used for good.

13.6.4. The Speed of Technological Change

The rapid pace of AI development makes it challenging for regulations to keep up. By the time regulations are implemented, the technology might have already evolved significantly, potentially rendering existing regulations ineffective. This necessitates a flexible and adaptable approach to AI governance.

Pretend for a moment you are asked to write a new law to regulate self-driving cars. You meticulously consider safety standards, testing procedures, and passenger liability. Months, or even years, later, your law is finally passed. But here's the problem: the world of AI moves fast. By the time your law hits the books, self-driving car technology might have advanced significantly. The new cars might have features or capabilities that weren't even considered when the law was written. This is the challenge of the speed of technological change in AI – regulations struggle to keep pace with the rapid evolution of this technology. Examples of the ever-shifting landscape:

- **Rapid Innovation:** The field of AI is constantly evolving, with new breakthroughs happening all the time. By the time regulations are implemented, the technology they were designed for might already be outdated.

- **Emerging Applications:** New applications for AI are emerging all the time, creating situations where existing regulations don't apply neatly. Imagine regulating facial recognition technology used for security purposes – the rules might differ from those for social media filters that use similar facial recognition techniques.

- **Challenges in Predicting the Future:** It's difficult to predict the exact trajectory of AI development. Regulations that are too specific might stifle innovation, while overly broad regulations might leave loopholes with unforeseen applications.

13.6.5. Approaches for Adaptability

- **Focus on Principles over Specifics:** Regulations could focus on establishing core ethical principles for AI development, such as fairness, transparency, and accountability. This would provide a flexible framework that can adapt to new technologies and applications.

- **Regular Reviews and Updates:** Regulations shouldn't be set in stone. Regular reviews and updates are essential to ensure they remain relevant and effective in the face of rapid technological change.

- **Living Labs and Regulatory Sandboxes:** Creating designated spaces where companies can experiment with new AI technologies under controlled conditions can be a valuable tool. This allows regulators to observe these new applications firsthand and inform future regulations.

Collaboration allows for:

- **Public-Private Partnerships:** Effective governance requires collaboration between governments, the private sector, and academia. By working together, they can share knowledge, identify emerging challenges, and develop adaptable regulatory frameworks.

- **International Harmonization:** The rapid pace of AI development is a global phenomenon. International collaboration between regulatory bodies is crucial to ensure consistent standards and avoid a fragmented approach to AI governance.

The goal isn't to halt innovation but to create a flexible and adaptable regulatory framework that fosters responsible AI development. By acknowledging the challenges posed by the speed of technological change, and implementing adaptable approaches, we can ensure regulations keep pace with AI advancements and ensure this powerful technology is used for good.

13.6.6. The Role of Non-state Actors

Large technology companies and research institutions play a significant role in developing and deploying AI technologies. Effective governance needs to consider the role of these non-state actors, potentially involving them in the development and implementation of regulations.

Think what it's like to attend a concert. The powerful music fills the air, but it's not just the conductor calling the shots. An entire orchestra works together to create that beautiful symphony. In the world of AI governance, it's a similar story. Governments write the regulations, but they're not the only ones playing a role. Big tech companies, research institutions, and other non-state actors are also key players in the AI governance orchestra.

Large tech companies are at the forefront of AI development. They have the resources, the talent, and the drive to push the boundaries of this technology. Think of companies like Google, Facebook, and Amazon – they're all heavily invested in AI research and development.

This immense power comes with responsibility. These companies need to be active participants in shaping the future of AI governance. They can help develop ethical guidelines for AI development, invest in research on potential risks, and collaborate with regulators to ensure their AI systems are safe and unbiased. [283]

Universities and research institutions play a crucial role in fundamental AI research. They're constantly exploring new possibilities, developing cutting-edge algorithms, and pushing the boundaries of what AI can achieve. Imagine researchers developing new AI models for medical diagnosis or creating algorithms to combat climate change. [284]

But research also needs responsible guardrails. Researchers have a role to play in identifying potential risks associated with their work and advocating for ethical AI development practices. For instance, they might focus on building fairness and accountability into AI systems from the very beginning.

Civil society organizations play a vital role in raising public awareness about AI, advocating for responsible development, and holding all actors accountable. Imagine public interest groups raising concerns about the use of AI in facial recognition technology or calling for transparency in how AI algorithms are used. Their voices are important in the conversation about AI governance. By educating the public and holding powerful actors accountable, civil society organizations can help ensure AI is used for the benefit of all.

Governments have a crucial role in setting the overall direction for AI governance, but they can't go it alone. Effective governance requires collaboration with these non-state actors. Governments can create platforms for open dialogue, encourage partnerships between different stakeholders, and leverage the expertise of the private sector and academia.

By working together, this orchestra of non-state actors, along with governments, can create a harmonious approach to AI governance. Each group brings a unique perspective to the table, and their collective efforts are essential for ensuring the responsible development and deployment of AI technology.

---

[283] https://ai.google/responsibility/principles/

[284] https://hai.stanford.edu/

13.6.7. International Collaboration and Coordination

Given the global nature of AI development and deployment, international collaboration and coordination are essential. This includes sharing best practices, harmonizing regulations across different jurisdictions, and fostering open dialogue on AI governance challenges.

The rapid pace of AI development and its global reach necessitate a coordinated international response. Here's why collaboration is crucial:

- **Harmonized Standards:** Without a unified approach, a patchwork of regulations across different countries could create confusion and inconsistencies. Imagine a European company developing an AI-powered healthcare application. If they want to operate in the US and China, they might face vastly different regulatory hurdles in each region. International collaboration can help establish common standards for data privacy, safety testing, and ethical considerations, ensuring a level playing field for responsible AI development. (Ref: [OECD. (2019, November 21). Recommendation of the Council on Artificial Intelligence. [285]

- **Sharing Best Practices:** Countries at the forefront of AI development can share their knowledge and experiences with those just starting their journeys. Imagine a veteran AI researcher from a developed nation mentoring researchers in a developing country, helping them build robust and ethical AI systems from the ground up. International collaboration can foster knowledge exchange and capacity building, ensuring all nations benefit from the advancements in AI. (Ref: [The Royal Society. (2023, February). The United Nations' role in international AI governance. [286]

- **Addressing Global Challenges:** AI has the potential to address some of humanity's most pressing challenges – from climate change to global health pandemics. But these challenges are global in nature, and solutions require international cooperation. Imagine scientists from various countries working together to develop AI-powered tools for disaster prediction or researchers collaborating on AI models to combat antibiotic-resistant bacteria. By fostering

---

[285] https://www.oecd.org/digital/artificial-intelligence/

[286] https://royalsociety.org/news-resources/publications/2024/un-role-in-international-ai-governance/]

international collaboration, we can leverage the collective expertise of the global community to tackle these complex issues. (Ref: [UNESCO. (2021, November 19). Recommendation on the Ethics of Artificial Intelligence.[287]

Challenges and considerations include:

- **Balancing National Interests:** Countries might have different priorities and concerns regarding AI development. Striking a balance between national interests and fostering international cooperation is a delicate dance.

- **Varying Levels of Development:** The pace of AI development varies significantly across different countries. Finding common ground and ensuring inclusive participation from all nations can be challenging.

Despite these challenges, international collaboration offers the best path forward for responsible AI governance. Here are some ways to foster international cooperation:

- **International Forums:** Organizations like the OECD, UNESCO, and the UN play a key role in facilitating dialogue and establishing common principles for AI development. These forums provide platforms for countries, industry leaders, and researchers to come together and discuss pressing issues.[288]

- **Multistakeholder Partnerships:** Collaboration shouldn't be limited to governments. Public-private partnerships between governments, tech companies, and academic institutions can leverage the expertise of diverse stakeholders.

- **Knowledge Sharing Platforms:** Creating online platforms for sharing best practices, research findings, and policy frameworks can promote knowledge exchange and capacity building across different countries.

By building bridges through international collaboration, we can create a more unified and responsible approach to AI governance. This collaborative effort will ensure AI technology serves as a tool for progress, benefiting all of humanity.

---

[287] https://www.unesco.org/en/articles/recommendation-ethics-artificial-intelligence

[288] https://www.eeas.europa.eu/paris-oecd-unesco/relations-oecd-and-unesco_en?s=64

13.6.8.   Public Awareness and Education

Public trust in AI is crucial for its successful adoption. Raising public awareness about AI, its potential benefits and risks, and how it's being governed can help build trust and ensure responsible development. Educational initiatives can empower individuals to understand and engage with AI technologies.

Imagine a world where AI is woven into the fabric of everyday life – from the algorithms recommending products online to the AI-powered assistants in our homes. But how much does the public understand about this powerful technology? Public awareness and education are crucial for building trust in AI and ensuring its responsible development.

Public awareness matters because:

- **Informed Decisions:** As AI becomes more prevalent, individuals need to be aware of its potential benefits and risks. This empowers them to make informed decisions about how they interact with AI systems, whether it's choosing to use an AI-powered financial advisor or understanding the limitations of a medical diagnosis tool powered by AI.

- **Holding Stakeholders Accountable:** A well-informed public can hold governments, corporations, and research institutions accountable for responsible AI development. If citizens understand the ethical considerations surrounding AI, they can advocate for transparency, fairness, and safeguards against potential misuse.

- **Building Public Trust:** Without public trust, the adoption and advancement of AI will be hindered By educating the public about the positive applications of AI and the efforts being made to mitigate risks, we can foster a more trusting relationship with this technology.

Challenges in public awareness include:

- **Technical Complexity:** AI can be a complex subject, filled with technical jargon and intricate algorithms. Simplifying the message and making it accessible to a broad audience is crucial.

- **Misinformation and Hype:** Sensationalized media portrayals and unrealistic expectations can create confusion and fear surrounding AI. Educating the public about the actual capabilities and limitations of AI is essential.

320 • AI DATA PRIVACY AND PROTECTION

- **The Digital Divide:** Not everyone has equal access to information and technology. Bridging the digital divide is necessary to ensure everyone has the opportunity to learn about AI.

Strategies for effective education include:

- **Public Engagement Campaigns:** Governments and organizations can launch campaigns to raise awareness about AI through various channels, including traditional media, social media platforms, and community events.

- **Educational Resources:** Developing accessible educational resources, such as online courses, interactive tutorials, and educational games, can make learning about AI engaging and informative for all age groups.

- **Supporting AI Literacy in Schools:** Integrating AI literacy into school curriculums can equip younger generations with the knowledge and critical thinking skills necessary to navigate a world increasingly shaped by AI.

- **Promoting Media Literacy:** Educating the public on how to critically evaluate information about AI can help combat misinformation and ensure a more informed public discourse.

By implementing these strategies, we can empower citizens with the knowledge they need to participate actively in shaping the future of AI. A well-informed public is essential for ensuring AI is developed and used responsibly for the benefit of all.

13.6.9.   The Need for a Multistakeholder Approach

Effective AI governance requires a multistakeholder approach that involves collaboration between governments, industry leaders, academia, civil society, and the public. Each stakeholder group brings a unique perspective to the table, and their collective input is crucial for developing comprehensive and effective governance frameworks.

Imagine a magnificent tapestry woven from threads of diverse colors and textures. Each thread represents a unique perspective, and together they create a beautiful and intricate whole. This tapestry is a metaphor for the multistakeholder approach needed for responsible AI governance.

Effective AI governance requires the collective effort of various stakeholders, each bringing their expertise to the table:

- **Governments:** As policymakers, governments set the overall direction for AI development by establishing regulations, promoting research funding, and fostering international collaboration.[289]

- **Industry Leaders:** Tech companies are at the forefront of AI development, possessing the technical expertise and resources to translate research into real-world applications. They play a crucial role in developing ethical guidelines for their products and ensuring responsible data practices.

- **Academia and Research Institutions:** Universities and research institutes drive fundamental research in AI, pushing the boundaries of the technology and exploring its potential applications. They also play a critical role in identifying potential risks and ethical considerations associated with AI development. [290]

- **Civil Society Organizations:** Public interest groups raise awareness about the societal implications of AI, advocate for responsible development, and hold all actors accountable. They represent the voice of the public, ensuring AI is used for the benefit of society as a whole.[291]

Collaboration matters:

- **Diversity of Perspectives:** Each stakeholder group brings a unique perspective to the table. Governments can provide the regulatory framework, while industry leaders can translate those regulations into practical solutions. Academia can explore the cutting edge, while civil society organizations ensure ethical considerations are addressed. This diversity of perspectives is essential for developing a comprehensive approach to AI governance.

- **Shared Responsibility:** The responsibility for ensuring responsible AI development doesn't lie solely with one group. A multistakeholder approach

---

[289] European Union Commission. (2021, April 21). Artificial Intelligence Act. https://ec.europa.eu/commission/policies/strategy/artificial-intelligence-strategy-21042021_en

[290] montrealdeclaration-responsibleai.com

[291] https://www.ajl.org/

fosters a sense of shared ownership and encourages collaboration in addressing potential risks and challenges.

- **Building Trust:** When diverse stakeholders work together, it fosters public trust in AI governance. The public can see that a variety of voices are involved in shaping the future of AI, not just large corporations or government entities.

Challenges and considerations include:

- **Balancing Interests:** Different stakeholders might have competing priorities. Striking a balance between the interests of governments, corporations, and the public can be challenging.

- **Transparency and Inclusiveness:** The multistakeholder approach needs to be transparent and inclusive. All stakeholders should have a seat at the table, and the process should be open to public scrutiny.

- **Global Coordination:** The multistakeholder approach needs to be applied at a global level, ensuring international collaboration on AI governance.

By embracing a multistakeholder approach and fostering collaboration between diverse groups, we can create a tapestry of responsible AI governance. This tapestry will represent a future where AI technology is used for the benefit of all, addressing global challenges and contributing to a more equitable and sustainable world.

By addressing these challenges and considerations, the international community can work towards establishing a robust and adaptable governance framework for AI that fosters responsible development, promotes innovation, and ensures the benefits of AI technology are shared by all.

13.7. The Future of AI Regulation: Open Questions and Ongoing Discussions

As we look to the future of AI regulation, a trend towards more comprehensive and globally coordinated frameworks is evident. The rapid advancement of AI technologies, particularly those involving machine learning and autonomous decision-making, necessitates regulatory environments that not only protect individual privacy and ensure data security but also address ethical concerns such as bias, fairness, and accountability. The emergence of international discussions and collaborations indicates a growing recognition that AI's impact transcends borders, demanding a unified approach to governance. This evolution points towards a potential establishment of global standards or treaties specifically tailored to manage and mitigate the unique challenges posed by AI systems, ensuring a balanced approach that fosters innovation while safeguarding societal norms and individual rights.

In the coming years, we can expect a surge in sector-specific AI regulations, especially in areas like healthcare, transportation, and finance, where AI's implications for safety and ethical considerations are particularly acute. These regulations will likely focus on establishing clear guidelines for AI development and deployment, including rigorous testing protocols, transparency in algorithms, and mechanisms for redress in cases of failure or harm. As AI becomes more embedded in critical infrastructure and daily life, regulators will need to implement frameworks that are not only robust and flexible but also adaptive to the rapidly evolving capabilities of AI technologies.

Another significant aspect of future AI regulation will involve enhancing data governance. As AI systems rely heavily on data, ensuring the integrity and security of this data becomes paramount. Future regulations may enforce stricter data provenance requirements, audit trails, and consent mechanisms, particularly in light of increasing concerns about surveillance and unauthorized data exploitation. Enhanced data protection laws will likely incorporate advanced technological solutions, such as differential privacy and federated learning, which can help minimize privacy risks while maximizing the utility of data.

Moreover, as public awareness and understanding of AI's potential risks and benefits grow, there will be an increasing demand for greater transparency and public involvement in AI governance. This could lead to more participatory forms of regulation, where stakeholders, including ethicists, consumer groups, and the general public, have a say in shaping AI policies. The implementation of AI ethics committees and review boards could become standard practice, not only within corporations but also at the governmental level, ensuring that AI development aligns with public values and societal goals. As we navigate these changes, the future of AI regulation will likely be characterized by its dynamism and responsiveness to both technological advancements and public sentiment.

Let's explores some of the key questions that continue to shape the future of AI regulation:

- **Keeping Pace with Innovation:** How can regulations be designed to be adaptable and flexible enough to keep pace with the rapid advancements in AI technology? [292]

- **Emerging Applications:** How can regulations anticipate and address the ethical considerations posed by new and unforeseen applications of AI? For instance, how should regulations handle the ethical implications of AI-powered creative content generation tools?

- **Balancing Global Standards with National Priorities:** How can we achieve a balance between establishing international standards for AI governance and respecting the right of individual nations to set their own priorities?

- **Challenges of International Enforcement:** How can effective mechanisms be established for enforcing global AI regulations across diverse legal and political systems?

- **Preparing for AGI:** While still in the theoretical realm, the possibility of Artificial General Intelligence (AGI) – machines with human-like or even surpassing intelligence – raises significant ethical and regulatory questions. How can regulations be designed to address the potential risks and challenges posed by AGI, even if its development is far off in the future? [293]

- **Mitigating Bias in AI Systems:** How can regulations ensure that AI algorithms are fair, unbiased, and do not discriminate against certain groups of people?

---

[292] The Evolving Landscape of AI: You can reference a report by a think tank on the challenges of regulating rapidly evolving AI, such as the Center for Security and Emerging Technology (CSET) report "The Malicious Use of Artificial Intelligence: Forecasting, Prevention, and Mitigation" (https://arxiv.org/pdf/1802.07228)

[293] The Role of Artificial General Intelligence (AGI): Briefly mention an institute focused on the long-term future of AI, like the Future of Humanity Institute (FHI) at Oxford University (https://en.wikipedia.org/wiki/Future_of_Humanity_Institute)

- **Defining and Measuring Bias:** How can we define and measure bias in AI systems in a clear and objective way to inform regulatory frameworks?[294]

- **Preparing for Job Displacement:** As AI automates more tasks, how can regulations address the potential for job displacement and ensure a just transition for workers?

- **The Right to Explanation:** Should individuals have the right to understand how AI systems make decisions that affect them, particularly in areas like loan approvals or criminal justice?

- **Liability for AI Actions:** Who is ultimately responsible for the actions of AI systems – the developers, the companies deploying them, or the users? How can regulations assign clear lines of accountability?

- **AI and Blockchain:** How will the convergence of AI with other emerging technologies like blockchain create new challenges and opportunities for regulation?

- **Quantum Computing and AI Security:** How will the rise of quantum computing impact the security of AI systems and necessitate new regulatory measures?

13.8.   Conclusion

The future of AI regulation is a dynamic and ongoing conversation. By addressing these open questions and fostering continuous dialogue between policymakers, industry leaders, academics, and the public, we can build a robust and adaptable framework for governing AI that fosters responsible development, ensures public trust, and harnesses the power of this technology for the betterment of humanity.

---

[294] Algorithmic Bias and Fairness: You can reference a report by an AI ethics organization on algorithmic bias, such as the Algorithmic Justice League report "On Algorithmic Bias" (https://www.ajl.org/)

14. Key Takeaways

In the intricate dance between technology and society, AI has emerged as a principal performer, guiding and shaping the rhythm of advancements across industries, institutions, and individual lives. Yet, as with any powerful tool, the increasing reliance on AI, especially in data management, necessitates careful reflection and understanding. It's not just about harnessing the power of AI but doing so responsibly, ethically, and with foresight. As we draw our exploration to a close, it's vital to revisit and distill the essence of what we've learned about AI-proof data management.

Firstly, it's clear that AI isn't just another technological advancement—it represents a paradigm shift in how we perceive, analyze, and utilize data. In a digital age, where data is often likened to oil, AI serves as the refinery, turning raw data into actionable insights, predictions, and automations. However, like refining oil, it is a process fraught with complexities, potential biases, and security challenges, necessitating constant vigilance and understanding.

Second, the ethics surrounding AI and data management are as crucial as the technologies themselves. As we harness AI to create smarter cities, advanced healthcare systems, and dynamic economies, we must always ask: At what cost? Ensuring transparency, fairness, and respect for individual rights isn't just ethical—it's pivotal for sustainable AI adoption.

Then there's the aspect of security. In an interconnected world, threats aren't just human-driven but AI-powered, requiring advanced, equally intelligent countermeasures. The cyber battles of the future will increasingly involve AI on both sides, and preparedness today will determine the victors of tomorrow.

Moreover, we stand at the cusp of further technological revolutions. Quantum computing, augmented reality, the Internet of Things—each of these is intertwined with AI, and each presents new challenges and opportunities in data management. Embracing the future means understanding these synergies and preparing for their implications.

In this concluding section, we aim to encapsulate the core insights, lessons, and forward-looking thoughts from our journey through AI-proof data management. It's a compass for the road ahead, a distillation of knowledge for both seasoned practitioners and newcomers alike. The future of AI and data is bright, but only if we navigate it with wisdom, responsibility, and an unerring commitment to the greater good.

14.1.   The Paradigm Shift of AI in Data Management

The integration of artificial intelligence (AI) into data management has not merely been an incremental evolution but a revolutionary shift. It is this transformation that sets the tone for the advancements, challenges, and ethical considerations that have subsequently emerged in the landscape of digital information.

AI's initial promise was to assist in automating tasks that were repetitively labor-intensive for humans. However, AI in data management expanded this notion to reinventing how we perceive, analyze, and secure vast amounts of data. Data, often called the "new oil," has become an invaluable resource for organizations globally. AI's role in processing, extracting value from, and safeguarding this data has, therefore, become paramount.

Traditional data management often struggled with the sheer volume, variety, and velocity of contemporary data streams. AI-driven solutions, with their ability to learn from data, adapt to new data types, and process information at unparalleled speeds, have risen to this challenge. They not only enhance efficiency but often unveil insights that were previously unattainable.

Yet, with these strides in capability come new challenges. The introduction of AI to data management has raised questions about data privacy, security vulnerabilities, and potential biases in AI algorithms. Addressing these concerns requires an informed approach that balances the technical aspects with the ethical and societal implications.

In the next sections, we will delve deeper into the specifics of how AI has reshaped the data management landscape, the nuances of the challenges it presents, and the broader implications of this melding of technology and information.

14.2.   The Human Factor in AI Security

Amidst the whirlwind of technological advances and complex algorithms, one aspect remains constant: the human element. AI, for all its prowess, is a tool—one that is designed, implemented, and utilized by humans. It's this human touch that both gives AI its potential and, at times, its vulnerabilities.[295]

Human expertise brings a nuanced understanding to AI security. It's a domain where intuition and experience can be as crucial as data. Engineers and developers embed their understanding, ethics, and sometimes biases into AI systems. While AI can process vast amounts of data at remarkable speeds, the quality, fairness, and efficacy of its output often hinge on the human decisions made during its design and training phases. An improperly trained AI can lead to unintentional consequences, making human oversight essential.

Yet, it's also the human factor that introduces vulnerabilities into AI systems. Human errors in configuration, oversight in training data, or even intentional malfeasance can make AI-driven systems susceptible to breaches. Social engineering attacks, where hackers exploit human psychology rather than technical vulnerabilities, remind us that the most sophisticated AI defenses can sometimes be bypassed through human channels.

The collaboration between humans and AI also heralds a new era in cybersecurity. As AI systems learn and adapt, they can provide feedback loops, enabling human operators to refine strategies, enhance defenses, and better anticipate threats. This symbiotic

---

[295] https://futureoflife.org/ai/align-artificial-intelligence-with-human-values/, https://www.compassitc.com/blog/beyond-phishing-understanding-ai-powered-social-engineering-attacks, https://zvelo.com/the-role-of-ai-in-social-engineering/, https://www.secureworld.io/industry-news/impact-ai-social-engineering-attacks, https://venturebeat.com/ai/cybersecurity-meets-ai-augmenting-and-accelerating-humans/, https://www.isaca.org/resources/news-and-trends/industry-news/2023/the-human-and-ai-partnership-collaborating-for-enhanced-cybersecurity, https://academia.co.uk/ai-versus-human-collaboration-for-a-secure-digital-future/

relationship, where AI provides the computational muscle and humans bring context, ethics, and adaptability, is the bedrock of modern AI security.

Looking forward, as AI systems become increasingly autonomous, the challenge will be to ensure that they embody the best of human values, while also being safeguarded from our inherent vulnerabilities. The balance between automating processes and maintaining meaningful human control will be an ongoing challenge and discussion in the years to come.

14.3.   AI Risk Management Imperatives[296]

Navigating the landscape of AI-powered data management comes with its set of risks and challenges. Recognizing and proactively managing these risks is pivotal to harnessing the full potential of AI, while ensuring data security and upholding ethical standards. Here's a deeper look into the imperatives of AI risk management.

First and foremost, organizations need to identify and quantify potential AI risks. This requires a comprehensive understanding of the AI models being used, the data they're trained on, and the decisions they're designed to make. This risk assessment should consider both technical and ethical dimensions, including biases in the training data, vulnerabilities in the AI system, and the potential societal impact of AI decisions.

Moreover, a continuous monitoring system should be in place. Given the dynamic nature of threats in the digital world, static defenses can quickly become outdated. Continuous monitoring ensures that organizations remain aware of emerging risks and vulnerabilities, allowing for timely interventions. AI-driven threat intelligence can play a pivotal role in this, offering real-time insights into potential threats.

---

[296] https://www.skadden.com/-/media/files/publications/2023/05/ai_risk_evaluating_and_managing_it_using_the_nist_framework.pdf?rev=5b07702268114ba8b29de1531cdb60c9, https://www.uts.edu.au/sites/default/files/2024-01/AI%20Governance%20Snapshot%20-%20Essential%20Components%20of%20AI%20Governance.pdf, https://nvlpubs.nist.gov/nistpubs/ai/nist.ai.100-1.pdf, https://ai-governance.eu/, https://www.csoonline.com/article/1298267/assessing-and-quantifying-ai-risk-a-challenge-for-enterprises.html

Another imperative is the establishment of clear AI governance structures. Who is responsible for AI decisions? How are errors and breaches addressed? What are the feedback loops for refining AI models? Addressing these questions will not only help in immediate risk mitigation but also in building long-term trust in AI systems.

Furthermore, transparency and explainability are crucial. As AI systems become more complex, the logic behind their decisions can become obscured. Ensuring that these decisions can be explained in understandable terms is essential, both for internal oversight and for external accountability. This is particularly important in sectors where AI decisions have significant societal impacts, such as healthcare, finance, and law enforcement.

Lastly, AI risk management must be an ongoing, iterative process. As AI models evolve, the risks associated with them will change. Regularly revisiting and updating risk management strategies will ensure that organizations remain ahead of potential threats and challenges. It's a commitment to continuous learning and adaptation, mirroring the very essence of AI itself.

14.4.   Advanced Storage and Quantum Considerations[297]

In the ever-evolving realm of data management, the convergence of advanced storage solutions and quantum computing is undeniably redefining the future. This synergy promises unprecedented computational power and security capabilities but also introduces new challenges. As we reflect on the overarching themes discussed, let's delve into the key takeaways surrounding advanced storage and quantum considerations.

The imminent era of quantum computing will fundamentally change our understanding of data storage and encryption. Traditional encryption methods, which have long stood

---

[297] https://cybersecurityventures.com/quantum-computing-decrypting-the-future/, https://www.techtarget.com/searchsecurity/definition/quantum-key-distribution-QKD, https://www.ibm.com/topics/quantum-cryptography, https://www.global.toshiba/ww/products-solutions/security-ict/qkd.html, https://www2.deloitte.com/us/en/insights/topics/cyber-risk/quantum-computing-ethics-risks.html, and https://quantumxc.com/blog/quantum-encryption-vs-post-quantum-cryptography-infographic/

as the bulwark against cyber threats, may become vulnerable to quantum attacks. Quantum computers, with their ability to process vast amounts of data and perform complex calculations at speeds unimaginable today, could theoretically break encryption protocols that currently take conventional computers millions of years to crack.

However, along with potential threats, quantum technology also offers the promise of quantum encryption—a method deemed unbreakable by the very laws of physics. Quantum Key Distribution (QKD) exemplifies this potential, where any eavesdropping on a quantum-encrypted message can be detected due to the inherent properties of quantum particles. As AI systems grow in complexity and handle more sensitive data, integrating quantum-safe encryption methods will be imperative. As discussed earlier, quantum-resistant classical (i.e., math-based) cryptography provides an alternate quantum-safe encryption solution.

Moreover, advanced storage solutions, particularly those designed to leverage AI, are at the forefront of ensuring data integrity, availability, and speed. With the onset of innovations such as Neural Processing Units (NPUs) and Storage Class Memory (SCM), AI models can be trained and deployed faster than ever, offering real-time insights without compromising on data volume or complexity.

Yet, with greater power comes greater responsibility. As quantum computing and advanced storage solutions emerge from research labs into practical applications, organizations must remain vigilant. Ethical considerations, transparency, and risk assessments will play pivotal roles in ensuring these technologies are harnessed for the greater good, without inadvertently introducing new vulnerabilities.

In conclusion, the intersection of advanced storage and quantum considerations paints a future of unparalleled possibilities in data management. But, as always, it is a delicate balance between seizing opportunities and managing associated risks, where preparedness and foresight will be key.

14.5. Monitoring, Detection, and Response in the AI Era

The influx of AI capabilities into the cybersecurity domain represents a significant transformation in how organizations approach monitoring, detection, and response. As we synthesize our learnings, it's clear that AI not only enhances existing processes but also introduces new paradigms and challenges. Here are the key takeaways in this domain:

- The legacy methods of threat detection, often characterized by static signatures and manual interventions, are no longer sufficient in the face of advanced, dynamic, and persistent threats. AI, with its capacity for pattern recognition, anomaly detection, and predictive analysis, can sift through vast amounts of data in real time, pinpointing irregularities that would otherwise remain unnoticed.

- Phishing attempts, once a significant bane for cybersecurity professionals, are now being detected with increased accuracy thanks to AI. By learning from previous instances and continuously updating its knowledge, AI systems can rapidly identify and flag phishing attempts, minimizing their potential damage.

- Dark web monitoring, an essential component in proactive cybersecurity, has been supercharged by AI. The ability of AI systems to trawl the vast, unindexed parts of the internet, processing information and alerting organizations to potential threats or data breaches, showcases AI's prowess and potential in threat intelligence.

Yet, the rise of AI also necessitates a parallel focus on response strategies. Automated threat ranking systems are helping organizations prioritize their responses, ensuring that the most critical threats are dealt with immediately. Such capabilities are crucial, especially when dealing with voluminous alerts, many of which might be benign.

However, this increased dependency on AI also calls for a balanced approach. It's imperative to recognize that AI is a tool, not a replacement for human intuition and expertise. Collaboration between human analysts and AI will be vital in discerning the nuances of complex threats and devising appropriate response strategies.

In essence, the AI era is ushering in a future where monitoring, detection, and response are more efficient, timely, and effective. While the journey will undoubtedly have its set of challenges, a strategic and balanced approach will ensure organizations remain resilient in the face of evolving threats.

14.6.   Ethical Challenges and AI's Societal Impact

The fusion of AI into data management and security doesn't solely bring about technological advancements. It ushers in a wave of ethical dilemmas, responsibilities, and transformative impacts on society at large. As we distill our insights, it's essential to acknowledge and confront the multi-dimensional challenges and opportunities AI presents.

AI, while a potent tool, is susceptible to inherent biases that stem from its training data, the individuals developing it, or the very society it mirrors. This risk of bias, if unchecked, can lead to skewed security solutions that might inadvertently target or overlook specific groups. As organizations adopt AI-driven tools, it becomes their ethical duty to ensure fairness and impartiality in AI's decisions and outputs.

Ethical considerations extend into the realm of data management, where the principles of informed consent, data minimization, and the responsible handling of sensitive data become paramount. The dream of leveraging AI for enhanced security should never come at the expense of individual privacy and rights.

Transparency and accountability in AI have emerged as focal points of discussions worldwide. The "black box" nature of certain AI models makes it imperative for organizations to adopt strategies that make AI's decisions interpretable and justifiable. This transparency fosters trust, a crucial element for any security solution.

The broader societal implications of AI in security are profound. The technology's dual-use nature means that while it can be a force for good, it can also be exploited for nefarious purposes. As AI's reach becomes global, it's essential to evaluate and address its ethical ramifications across different cultures, economies, and social structures.

Finally, the conversations around AI's ethics and societal impact underline the importance of governance and regulatory frameworks. By establishing guidelines, best practices, and regulatory standards, we can navigate the AI revolution in a way that maximizes benefits while minimizing unintended consequences.

In sum, the intersection of AI with ethics and society is intricate and demands proactive engagement from all stakeholders. The decisions made today will chart the course for a future where AI serves humanity's best interests, ensuring security, fairness, and progress in tandem.

14.7.   Glimpsing the Future of AI and Data Management

As we have journeyed through the intricate tapestry of AI-driven data management, there emerges a clear vision of a future teeming with possibilities, challenges, and the promise of a transformed digital landscape. Reflecting on our exploration, we can discern several themes and trajectories shaping the next chapters of this narrative. Firstly, the convergence of cutting-edge technologies, such as quantum computing and AI, is set to redefine the very fundamentals of encryption and data security. Quantum encryption, fortified by AI algorithms, has the potential to create an almost impregnable shield against cyber threats, elevating the standards of data protection to unprecedented heights.

Simultaneously, the rise of AI-powered threats underscores the perpetual nature of the cyber arms race. As AI systems become sophisticated agents of protection, they also risk becoming formidable tools of disruption in the hands of malicious actors. Organizations will need to be ever-vigilant, iterating on their defense mechanisms and adapting to a fluid threat landscape.

The emergence of decentralized data systems, particularly blockchain, enhanced by AI capabilities, suggests a future where data ownership, transparency, and verification take on new dimensions. These systems, by dispersing data across nodes and using AI for real-time anomaly detection, offer a promising path to data integrity and security.

Furthermore, the proliferation of emerging technologies, from 5G to smart cities, will lead to exponential data growth. AI's role in managing, analyzing, and securing this deluge of information will become more central than ever. Each technological leap, be it in IoT, AR, VR, or bioinformatics, will come with its unique set of challenges and opportunities for AI-driven data management.

Lastly, amidst this technological whirlwind, the human aspect remains paramount. As we advance into this AI-augmented future, the synergy between human intelligence and artificial intelligence will be critical. The ideal scenario is not one where AI replaces humans but one where it amplifies human capabilities, ensuring a safer, more efficient, and more informed digital ecosystem.

In closing, the horizon of AI-proof data management is vast, vibrant, and ever-evolving. As with any transformative technology, the path forward will be punctuated with challenges. Yet, with collaborative efforts, informed decisions, and an unwavering commitment to ethical principles, the future holds immense potential. As stewards of this digital revolution, our choices and actions today will shape the legacy of AI and data management for generations to come.

14.8.   Concluding Remarks

The journey through the intricate nexus of artificial intelligence and data management has been nothing short of enlightening. We've traversed landscapes that showcased the power and potential of AI-driven solutions and pondered over the profound implications of data's evolving nature in a digital-first world. As we conclude, several key insights deserve reiteration and reflection.

Artificial intelligence, in its multifaceted roles, stands poised to revolutionize the way we perceive, process, and protect data. But this power is a double-edged sword. For every groundbreaking solution AI offers, there exists a potential pitfall, whether it's an ethical concern, a security vulnerability, or a societal challenge. These are not mere technical obstacles to overcome but pivotal questions about the kind of digital future we want to create.

The theme of ethics has resonated deeply throughout our discourse. As AI systems become an integral part of our lives, there is an inescapable responsibility for creators, users, and regulators to ensure that these technologies are transparent, fair, and just. The balance between utility and ethics, innovation and responsibility, will be a defining challenge for our generation.

Furthermore, the role of the human element in the AI-driven future cannot be overstated. While machines learn, analyze, and predict, it's human intuition, empathy, and ethics that must guide these systems. This symbiosis of man and machine, if harmonized effectively, promises a digital realm that's not just secure and efficient but also humane and inclusive.

Looking ahead, the realm of AI-proof data management beckons with endless possibilities. It is a realm where data not only fuels insights and innovations but also respects privacy, promotes transparency, and guards against threats. A realm where AI is not an overlord but an ally, working in tandem with human intellect to forge a safer, smarter, and more sustainable digital ecosystem.

In the grand tapestry of technological evolution, the AI-data synergy represents just one chapter, albeit a pivotal one. As stewards of this narrative, it is upon us to write this chapter with foresight, diligence, and a deep sense of responsibility. For in our hands lies the power to shape a digital legacy that future generations will inherit, benefit from, and be proud of.

14.9.   Authors' Final Thoughts

As we draw this exploration to a close, we find ourselves both humbled and invigorated by the vast expanse of the AI-data terrain. The symbiotic relationship between artificial intelligence and data management is a dance of progression, challenges, and potential, and it was our privilege to delve into its depths.

There's a certain awe that comes from recognizing the sheer scale of transformation AI brings to the table. Not just as a tool or an extension, but as a paradigm-shifting force that reshapes industries, economies, and lives. While the opportunities are immense, so are the challenges. Every chapter we've explored has reminded us that with great power comes not just great responsibility, but intricate complexities too.

The realm of artificial intelligence has often been likened to the wild west—vast, unchartered, and filled with untapped potential. But like any frontier, it also bears its share of risks. The potential for bias, breaches, and ethical conundrums are as real as the promise AI holds. And it's this balance between potential and pitfalls that we must strive to maintain.

One thing that stands out starkly is that AI is not an island. It exists within a fabric of social, economic, and political dimensions, each influencing and being influenced in turn. As developers, users, and beneficiaries of AI-driven solutions, our actions, decisions, and priorities shape this fabric. We are both the architects and the inhabitants of this evolving digital landscape.

We are optimistic about the future, but it's an optimism tempered with caution. As AI and data continue to intermingle, creating a world that's hyper-connected and data-driven, it's imperative to remember that technology serves humanity, not the other way around. Our moral compass, our shared values, and our collective vision for an inclusive, ethical, and transparent digital future should guide our AI journey.

In closing, we invite each one of you, the readers, to be active participants in this narrative. Ask questions, challenge assumptions, and most importantly, never stop learning. The AI-data journey is a shared one, and every voice, every perspective, enriches it. Let's step into the future with a shared commitment to creating an AI-driven world that's not just smart, but also wise.

As we reach the culmination of our exploration into AI Data Privacy and Protection, I'm left with a profound appreciation for the delicate interplay between innovation, responsibility, and foresight. Our journey together has traversed a spectrum that ranged from the intricate nuances of algorithms to the overarching societal and ethical implications of rapid technological evolution.

It's evident that AI is not a fleeting trend but a seismic shift that will redefine our relationship with data. With this technological behemoth at our fingertips, we wield immense power—but this power is double-edged. While AI offers transformative solutions to longstanding challenges, it also introduces complexities that demand our vigilance.

The discourse on AI often oscillates between utopian visions and dystopian fears. However, our takeaway, fortified by our in-depth discussions, is that the future isn't necessarily preordained. It's malleable, shaped by our collective actions, ethics, and decisions. Each chapter of this work has underscored the importance of thoughtful design, rigorous governance, and the human touch in the AI equation.

But beyond the code, algorithms, and infrastructures, I'm struck by AI's profound human dimension. AI, in its essence, is a reflection of our society—a mirror that amplifies both our virtues and our vices. It's a tool, yes, but also a partner, collaborator, and sometimes, a challenger, urging us to introspect and evolve.

In conclusion, we see our journey with AI and data management as a continuous, evolving dance—a dance that's intricate, nuanced, and deeply intertwined with the fabric of our shared human experience. As we wade deeper into this AI-infused era, we hope we can cherish the marvels, navigate the challenges, and always prioritize the greater human good above all.

Thank you for joining me on this journey. Your engagement, curiosity, and discernment are what make discourses like this meaningful. As we stand at the crossroads of an AI-driven future, may we tread with wisdom, empathy, and a shared vision of a harmonious digital world.

15. Appendix

15.1. Vendor and Tool Listing

1. Symantec (Broadcom Inc.)

Description: Symantec, a division of Broadcom, is one of the world's leading cybersecurity companies, offering solutions that protect both consumers and enterprises from cyber threats. With extensive research facilities, they remain at the forefront of cybersecurity innovations. *Tools:*

- **Symantec Endpoint Protection (SEP):** Uses AI-driven insights to provide advanced threat prevention, detection, and response capabilities against all types of attacks.

- **Content Analysis:** Utilizes machine learning and sandboxing techniques to detect and block unknown threats.

2. Cisco Systems

Description: Cisco is a global technology leader that offers a broad range of networking and cybersecurity solutions. Their security solutions are designed to safeguard businesses from advanced persistent threats. *Tools:*

- **Cisco Talos:** This is the threat intelligence group of Cisco, which provides an analysis of known and emerging threats using AI.

- **Cisco Threat Grid:** Offers dynamic malware analysis and threat intelligence. It uses advanced sandboxing techniques to detect unknown threats.

3. Palo Alto Networks

Description: A global cybersecurity leader, Palo Alto Networks is renowned for its firewall and cloud-based security solutions. They offer innovative solutions designed to secure the digital age. *Tools:*

- **Palo Alto Networks Cortex:** An AI-driven security operations platform that provides visibility and clear detection across network, endpoint, and cloud environments.

- **WildFire:** Uses cloud-based AI analysis techniques to detect new threats and automatically disseminates protections globally.

4. Darktrace

Description: Known for its enterprise immune system technology, Darktrace is a forerunner in using AI for cybersecurity. The company's solutions are designed to detect, respond to, and mitigate cyber threats in real time. *Tools:*

- **Darktrace Antigena:** An AI response tool that can react to in-progress cyber threats, slowing or stopping them as required.

5. CrowdStrike

Description: A cybersecurity technology company, CrowdStrike provides cloud-native endpoint security solutions powered by AI. They offer protection against cyber breaches. *Tools:*

- **CrowdStrike Falcon:** Offers endpoint protection, threat intelligence, and cyber attack response services. Uses AI to detect and respond to threats in real time.

6. Quantum Xchange

Description: As the name suggests, Quantum Xchange specializes in quantum-safe encryption methods, aiming to offer next-level data protection, especially against potential quantum computer threats. *Tools:*

- **Phio Trusted Xchange (TX):** A quantum-safe key management and distribution system designed to make cryptographic keys quantum-safe and to support the quantum key distribution.

7. RSA

Description: A name synonymous with cybersecurity, RSA offers a wide array of security products that range from authentication solutions to risk management. *Tools:*

- **RSA SecurID:** Renowned multi-factor authentication solution that ensures secure access.

- **RSA Archer:** GRC (governance, risk management, and compliance) solution, essential for enforcing AI-proof security guidelines and regulations.

8. Guardtime

Description: Guardtime specializes in blockchain-based solutions, focusing on ensuring data integrity at every step. *Tools:*

- **KSI Blockchain:** Guardtime s proprietary blockchain technology, focusing on ensuring data integrity without the need for consensus-based trust models. Relevant for providing an immutable record, which is crucial for AI-proof security.

9. Okta

Description: Okta is a frontrunner in identity management solutions, focusing on workforce and customer identity. *Tools:*

- **Okta Identity Cloud:** A suite that offers a range of identity services including multi-factor authentication and single sign-on, crucial for AI-proofing access.

10. Zscaler

Description: Operating in the cloud security space, Zscaler offers solutions for web security, firewall, and data protection. *Tools:*

- **Zscaler Internet Access:** A full security stack as a service, providing secure access to the internet and applications. Integrated AI for advanced threat detection and response.

11. Fortanix

Description: Fortanix focuses on runtime encryption, ensuring that data remains encrypted during its entire lifecycle, even during computation. *Tools:*

- **Runtime Encryption Platform:** Offers a unique approach by ensuring data remains encrypted not just at rest and in transit but also during execution.

12. Duo Security (a Cisco company)

Description: Duo Security, now part of Cisco, specializes in multi-factor authentication, making sure that users are who they say they are. *Tools:*

- **Duo MFA:** An easy-to-use, scalable, and flexible multi-factor authentication solution.

13. Yubico

Description: Yubico specializes in hardware authentication devices, providing a physical layer of security. *Tools:*

- **YubiKey:** A hardware-based multi-factor authentication solution that can effectively combat AI-driven breaches that exploit weak or compromised passwords.

14. IBM

Description: A global tech giant, IBM has a wide array of cybersecurity solutions under its belt, many of which employ AI for enhanced protection. *Tools:*

- **IBM Watson for Cyber Security:** Uses AI to analyze vast amounts of security research and real-time cyber threat data.

- **IBM Quantum Experience:** While still in its nascent stages, IBM is pioneering quantum computing that has implications for both AI-driven threats and quantum-proof encryption.

15.2. Acronym List

2FA: Two-Factor Authentication

5G: 5th Generation Mobile Network

AGI: Artificial General Intelligence

AI: Artificial Intelligence

ANN: Artificial Neural Network

APPI–Act on the Protection of Personal Information

API: Application Programming Interface

APT: Advanced Persistent Threat

AR: Augmented Reality

AR: Augmented Reality (also repeated from Section 10)

BC: Business Continuity

BI: Business Intelligence

BIA: Business Impact Analysis

CCPA: California Consumer Privacy Act

CISO: Chief Information Security Officer

CNN: Convolutional Neural Network

CPU: Central Processing Unit

DDoS: Distributed Denial of Service

DL: Deep Learning

DNN: Deep Neural Network

DPA: Data Protection Act

DR: Disaster Recovery

EDA: Exploratory Data Analysis

GAN: Generative Adversarial Network

GDPR: General Data Protection Regulation

GPU: Graphics Processing Unit

HIPAA: Health Insurance Portability and Accountability Act

IAM: Identity and Access Management

IDS: Intrusion Detection System

IoT: Internet of Things

IPS: Intrusion Prevention System

LGPD–General Data Protection Law (Lei Geral de Proteção de Dados)

MFA: Multi-Factor Authentication

MITM: Man-in-the-Middle

ML: Machine Learning

MLaaS: Machine Learning as a Service

NLP: Natural Language Processing

NoSQL: Not Only SQL (a type of database that doesn't use SQL)

OECD–Organization for Economic Co-operation and Development

PIPL: Personal Information Protection Law

PKI: Public Key Infrastructure

QKD: Quantum Key Distribution

RL: Reinforcement Learning

RNN: Recurrent Neural Network

ROI: Return on Investment

RPA: Robotic Process Automation

RPO: Recovery Point Objective

RTO: Recovery Time Objective

SQL: Structured Query Language

TPU: Tensor Processing Unit

TTP: Tactics, Techniques, and Procedures

UN–United Nations

VPN: Virtual Private Network

VR: Virtual Reality

15.3.   Resources and Further Reading

This section provides a curated list of resources, ranging from foundational texts to cutting-edge research papers, to help readers delve deeper into the subjects touched upon in this guide. These resources are ideal for board members, executives, and any professional interested in AI, data management, and their intersections with business strategy.

Books:

- **"Artificial Intelligence and Cybersecurity: Theory and Applications"** by Tuomo Sipola, Tero Kokkonen, and Mika Karjalainen (Springer, 2023). This book provides an introduction to the application of artificial intelligence (AI) in cybersecurity. It covers a wide range of topics, including threat detection, anomaly detection, and incident response.

- **"Artificial Intelligence (AI) Governance and Cyber-Security: A beginner's handbook on securing and governing AI systems"** by Taimur Ijlal (Independently published, 2023). This book provides an introduction to AI governance and cybersecurity. It covers a wide range of topics, including the risks of AI, the need for governance, and how to secure AI systems.

- **"Artificial Intelligence: A Guide to Intelligent Systems"** by Michael Negnevitsky: A comprehensive introduction to the principles and practices of artificial intelligence.

- **"The Master Algorithm"** by Pedro Domingos: This text explores the quest for the one algorithm that can derive all knowledge from data.

- **"Reinforcement Learning: An Introduction"** by Richard S. Sutton and Andrew G. Barto: A fundamental text on reinforcement learning, a type of machine learning.

- **"The Hundred-Page Machine Learning Book"** by Andriy Burkov: A concise guide to machine learning for professionals and enthusiasts alike.

- **"Life 3.0"** by Max Tegmark. Explores the three different tiers of life and the potential future of AI in transforming both software and hardware of life forms.

- **"Superintelligence: Paths, Dangers, Strategies"** by Nick Bostrom. Discusses the potential scenarios and risks associated with AI surpassing human intelligence.

- **"The Coming Wave"** by Mustafa Suleyman. Analyzes the impact of recent AI breakthroughs and the cyclical nature of technological advancements.

- **"Power and Progress"** by Simon Johnson and Daron Acemoglu. Examines the relationship between technology and societal progress, questioning the common belief that technological advancement inherently leads to societal benefits.

- **"Human Compatible: Artificial Intelligence and the Problem of Control"** by Stuart Russell. Focuses on designing intelligent machines that align with human objectives without causing harm.

- **"The Alignment Problem"** by Brian Christian. Explores the challenges in aligning AI systems with human values and ethics.

- **"AI Needs You: How We Can Change AI's Future and Save Our Own"**. Discusses the role of human agency in shaping the future of AI and navigating its challenges.

- **"Guardrails: Guiding Human Interaction with AI"**. Offers insights into establishing frameworks and guidelines to safely integrate AI into society.

- **"Artificial Intelligence: A Modern Approach"** by Stuart Russell and Peter Norvig. A comprehensive textbook providing a deep dive into the mechanisms and applications of AI.

- **"The Alignment Problem"** by Brian Christian (2020). Details the challenges and strategies for ensuring AI systems perform as intended without unintended consequences.

Papers and Journals:

- **"Playing Atari with Deep Reinforcement Learning"** by Volodymyr Mnih, Koray Kavukcuoglu, David Silver, et al.: A foundational paper from DeepMind on deep learning and reinforcement learning.

- **"Understanding Machine Learning: From Theory to Algorithms"** by Shai Shalev-Shwartz and Shai Ben-David: An in-depth dive into the theoretical underpinnings of machine learning.

Websites and Online Resources:

- **arXiv**: A free distribution service and an open-access archive for scholarly articles in various disciplines, including a vast number of AI research papers.

- **Google AI**: Google's AI research branch offers a plethora of articles, research papers, and tools related to AI.

- **OpenAI**: A research organization committed to ensuring that artificial general intelligence benefits all of humanity. Their site contains numerous research publications and resources on AI.

- **MIT Technology Review–AI Section**: A curated collection of articles focusing on the latest advancements and news in the AI sector.

Reports and Industry Publications:

- **"The State of AI in 2020"** by McKinsey & Company: An industry report providing insights on AI trends, adoption, and challenges.

- **"Artificial Intelligence—The Next Digital Frontier?"** by McKinsey Global Institute: This report discusses the potential impact of AI on the business world and economy.

- **"Global AI Survey: AI proves its worth, but few scale impact"** by McKinsey & Company: A survey that offers a global perspective on how organizations are capitalizing on AI.

Conferences and Forums:

- **NeurIPS**: The annual Neural Information Processing Systems conference, one of the most prestigious events in the AI research community.

- **ICML**: International Conference on Machine Learning.

- **AAAI**: The Association for the Advancement of Artificial Intelligence's annual conference.

- **World Summit AI**: A globally recognized event focusing on the broader implications and applications of AI in various sectors.

Courses and Training:

- **Coursera's "Machine Learning"** by Andrew Ng: A foundational course on machine learning, ideal for beginners.

- **edX's "Artificial Intelligence (AI)"** by Columbia University: A deep dive into AI for those looking for a more academic approach.

- **Udacity's "Artificial Intelligence for Trading"**: A niche course that combines AI with finance and trading.

- **MIT OpenCourseWare "Artificial Intelligence"**: Free course material from MIT's introductory course on artificial intelligence.

News Articles:

- **US military targets deepfakes, misinformation with AI-powered tool By Colin Demarest and Jaime Moore-Carrillo,** DefenseNews https://www.defensenews.com/information-warfare/2023/08/01/us-military-targets-deepfakes-misinformation-with-ai-powered-tool/

- **Ethical AI and Privacy Regulations to Know**–BDO USA

https://www.bdo.com/insights/advisory/ethical-ai-and-privacy-series-article-2-the-regulations

- **Biden Issues Executive Order to Create A.I. Safeguards**–The New York Times. https://www.nytimes.com/2023/10/30/us/politics/biden-ai-regulation.html

- **The privacy paradox with AI**–Reuters. https://www.reuters.com/legal/legalindustry/privacy-paradox-with-ai-2023-10-31/

- **'Substantial progress' made on Biden's AI executive order**–NY1. https://ny1.com/nyc/all-boroughs/politics/2024/01/29/progress-president-joe-biden-artificial-intelligence-ai-executive-order

- **Biden signs ambitious executive order addressing AI**–AP News. https://apnews.com/article/biden-ai-artificial-intelligence-executive-order-cb86162000d894f238f28ac029005059

- **Biden's executive order on AI: Where to go from here**–Federal News Network. https://federalnewsnetwork.com/commentary/2024/02/bidens-executive-order-on-ai-where-to-go-from-here/

- **US lawmakers double down on AI, privacy correlation**–IAPP. https://iapp.org/news/a/us-lawmakers-double-down-on-ai-privacy-correlation/

- **Twitter taught Microsoft's AI chatbot to be a racist asshole in less than a day**–The Verge. https://www.theverge.com/2016/3/24/11297050/tay-microsoft-chatbot-racist

- **Tay: Microsoft issues apology over racist chatbot fiasco**–BBC News. https://www.bbc.com/news/technology-35902104

- **Deepfakes a 'Weapon Against Journalism,' Analyst Says**–VOA News. https://www.voanews.com/a/deepfakes-a-weapon-against-journalism-analyst-says-/7442897.html

- **Three things privacy pros should know about AI and data privacy**–Google Blog. https://blog.google/technology/ai/google-checks-data-privacy-ai-update/

- **In 2016, Microsoft's Racist Chatbot Revealed the Dangers of Online Conversation**–IEEE Spectrum. https://spectrum.ieee.org/in-2016-microsofts-racist-chatbot-revealed-the-dangers-of-online-conversation

- **What Biden's executive order on AI does and means**–CBS News. https://www.cbsnews.com/news/biden-ai-artificial-intelligence-executive-order/

- **Deepfakes and Their Impact on Society**–CPI OpenFox. https://www.openfox.com/deepfakes-and-their-impact-on-society/

- **The campaign to take down the Biden AI executive order**–POLITICO. https://www.politico.com/news/2024/01/25/conservatives-prepare-attack-on-bidens-ai-order-00137935

- Do deepfake videos undermine our epistemic trust? A thematic analysis–PLOS ONE. https://journals.plos.org/plosone/article?id=10.1371%2Fjournal.pone.0291668

- 'Deepfakes' are here. These deceptive videos erode trust in all news media–The Washington Post. https://www.washingtonpost.com/politics/2020/05/28/deepfakes-are-here-these-deceptive-videos-erode-trust-all-news-media/

- Microsoft shuts down AI chatbot after it turned into a Nazi–CBS News. https://www.cbsnews.com/news/microsoft-shuts-down-ai-chatbot-after-it-turned-into-racist-nazi/

- Data Privacy and AI: What Should UK and EU Employers Look out for in 2024–Littler. https://www.littler.com/publication-press/publication/data-privacy-and-ai-what-should-uk-and-eu-employers-look-out-2024

- Tay, Microsoft's AI chatbot, gets a crash course in racism from Twitter–The Guardian. https://www.theguardian.com/technology/2016/mar/24/tay-microsofts-ai-chatbot-gets-a-crash-course-in-racism-from-twitter

This list is by no means exhaustive, but it should provide a robust starting point for further exploration. As the fields of AI and data management are rapidly evolving, staying updated through continuous learning is crucial.

15.4. Glossary

5G Technology: The fifth generation of cellular network technology, succeeding 4G, and provides faster and more reliable communication with ultra-low latency.

Activation Function: A mathematical function applied to a neural network neuron's output, helping the network learn complex patterns.

Adaptive Systems: Systems that change their behavior based on feedback.

Adversarial Attacks: Manipulations aimed at fooling AI models, especially deep learning models, by providing deceptive input to get the model to produce an incorrect output.

Adversarial Machine Learning: A technique used in the field of machine learning that attempts to fool models by feeding them malicious input.

AGI (Artificial General Intelligence): Artificial intelligence that can understand, learn, and apply knowledge across a wide range of tasks at a level comparable to human intelligence.

AI (Artificial Intelligence): The capability of machines to mimic human intelligence, encompassing everything from simple automated tasks to complex problem solving.

AI Biases: Systematic and repeatable errors in the AI system that create unfair outcomes, such as privileging one arbitrary group of users over others.

AI Competency: The level of knowledge, expertise, and skill in AI technologies.

AI Crisis Management: Strategies and processes designed to manage, address, and mitigate crises or major failures related to the deployment or use of AI technologies.

AI Ethics: A multidisciplinary field of study that examines the moral implications and responsibilities that come with the creation and use of artificial intelligence.

AI Governance Frameworks: Guidelines, rules, and best practices set by an organization to ensure the responsible development and use of AI technologies.

AI Governance: A framework that provides a clear structure for how AI, and related data, should be used, managed, and monitored in an organization, often entailing policies, procedures, and standards.

AI Literacy: The ability to understand and be informed about the strengths, weaknesses, and nuances of AI technologies.

AI Regulatory Bodies: Organizations or agencies that set standards, rules, and guidelines for the development, deployment, and use of AI technologies.

AI Training Data: Data used to train machine learning models. The quality and quantity of this data play a significant role in the success of the AI model.

AI Transparency: The clarity and openness provided by AI developers regarding how their AI models operate, make decisions, or derive conclusions.

AI-Enhanced Malware: Malware that uses AI techniques to improve its efficiency in penetration, adaptability, and evasion of detection.

AI-First Strategy: An approach to business strategy and design where AI is considered the primary driver or central component for products, services, or solutions.

AI-Powered Cyberattacks: Cyberattacks that use artificial intelligence to improve the efficiency and effectiveness of their malicious activities.

AI-Powered Defense Mechanisms: Solutions that utilize artificial intelligence to predict, monitor, and counteract cyber threats.

AI-Proof: Refers to strategies or solutions that are designed to withstand the challenges, threats, or complexities introduced by evolving AI technologies.

Algorithm: A set of steps or procedures used to solve a specific problem or accomplish a certain task. In AI, algorithms often determine the logic for machine learning models.

Algorithmic Bias: When an algorithm produces results that are systematically prejudiced due to erroneous assumptions in the machine learning process.

Algorithmic Efficiency: Refers to the performance of an algorithm in terms of its resource usage (like time and memory) for a given input size.

Anomaly Detection: The process of identifying items, events, or observations that do not conform to an expected pattern in a dataset.

AR (Augmented Reality): A technology that superimposes a computer-generated image or data onto a user's view of the real world.

Attention Mechanism (in Deep Learning): A mechanism in a neural network that allows it to focus on certain parts of its input, leading to more accurate models for tasks like machine translation.

Attribute-based Encryption (ABE): A cryptographic method that uses attributes for the user's private key and the data item's ciphertext to define who has access to a specific piece of data.

Augmented Reality (AR): A technology that superimposes a computer-generated image, sound, or other sensory enhancements over a user's view of the real world.

Automated Decision Systems (ADS): Systems that use technologies, including machine learning, to make determinations without human intervention.

AutoML (Automated Machine Learning): The process of automating the end-to-end process of applying machine learning to real-world problems.

Autonomous Systems: Machines or systems that can perform tasks without human intervention, such as self-driving cars or drones.

Backpropagation: A supervised learning algorithm for training artificial neural networks, used in conjunction with an optimization method such as gradient descent.

Backup and Recovery: The process of creating copies of data to restore the original in the event of data loss.

Bayesian Networks: A type of statistical model that represents a set of variables and their conditional dependencies in a directed acyclic graph.

Behavioral Biometrics: A method of verifying individuals based on unique patterns of physical or behavioral traits, like keystroke dynamics or mouse movement patterns.

Bias (in Machine Learning): A model's error due to incorrect assumptions in the learning algorithm.

Bias in AI: Refers to algorithms that systematically and unfairly discriminate against certain groups of people. This can arise from various factors, including but not limited to, biased training data or prejudices in algorithm development.

Bioinformatics: An interdisciplinary field that develops methods and software tools for understanding biological data, especially when large-scale datasets are involved.

Blockchain: A decentralized ledger of all transactions across a network, which can be used to record transactions across many computers so that any involved record cannot be altered without the alteration of all subsequent blocks.

Botnet: A network of private computers, infected with malicious software and controlled as a group without the owners' knowledge to send spam or launch attacks.

Botnets: A network of private computers infected with malicious software and controlled as a group without the owners' knowledge.

Chatbots: AI-powered conversational agents designed to simulate human-like interactions and provide answers to user queries in natural language.

Cloud Storage: A cloud computing model in which data is stored on remote servers accessed from the internet, or "cloud," managed by a cloud provider.

Cognitive Computing: Systems and applications that simulate human thought processes and mimic the functions of the human brain through self-learning algorithms using data mining, pattern recognition, and natural language processing.

Computer Vision: An interdisciplinary field that teaches machines to interpret and act on visual data, similar to the way humans use their sight.

Convolutional Neural Network (CNN): A deep learning algorithm that can recognize patterns directly from pixel images with minimal preprocessing. They have proven effective in various perceptual tasks, such as computer vision.

Cryptography: The practice and study of techniques for secure communication, protecting information from adversaries.

Cyber Hygiene: The practices and steps users take to maintain system health and improve online security.

Cyber Insurance: A form of coverage designed to protect businesses from internet-based risks, such as data breaches or cyberattacks. Some policies may also cover losses caused by AI-related failures.

Data: Data is a representation of facts, concepts, or instructions in a formalized manner suitable for communication, interpretation, or processing by human beings or by automatic means. Source: Data Management Body of Knowledge(DMBoK)

Data Augmentation: The process of artificially increasing the size of your training dataset by creating modified versions of existing data.

Data Availability: Ensuring that data remains accessible when and where it is needed without compromise to its security.

Data Breach: An incident in which sensitive, protected, or confidential data is copied, transmitted, viewed, stolen, or used by an individual unauthorized to do so.

Data Dictionary: A collection of descriptions of the data objects or items in a data model for the benefit of programmers and others who need to refer to them. A list or inventory of data, with metadata that describes its contents, context, and structure, including the definition of data elements and their inter-relationships. Source = Data Management Body of Knowledge (DMBoK)

Data Element: Atomic unit of data considered in context, including data items as defined in data dictionaries, directories, or catalogs. A data element represents a single, indivisible unit of data that is considered within a particular context. It could refer to a single piece of information, such as a customer's name, a product code, or a date of birth, and is typically defined within a data dictionary or similar repository of metadata. Source = ISO 11179 Metadata Standard

Data Governance: The exercise of authority and control (planning, monitoring, and enforcement) over the management of data assets. It requires a cultural shift in the organization, reinforced by leadership, and facilitated by appropriate tools, techniques, and training. Source = Data Management Body of Knowledge (DMBoK)

Data Encryption: The process of converting data into a code to prevent unauthorized access. The process of converting plain text or data into an unreadable format, known as ciphertext, using an algorithm and an encryption key. This cryptographic technique ensures that only authorized parties with the corresponding decryption key can access and read the original data.

Data Ethics: The branch of ethics that evaluates data handling practices with respect to the moral dimensions they encompass, including privacy, fairness, and respect for the rights of individuals.

Data Federation: A technique that involves collecting data from disparate sources and making it available in a unified manner, irrespective of the original location or format of the data.

Data Integration: The process of combining data from different sources and providing users with a unified view of it.

Data Integrity: Ensuring the accuracy and consistency of data over its entire life cycle. It is a critical aspect to the design and implementation of any system which stores, processes, or retrieves data.

Data Lake: Large storage repositories and processing engines that allow businesses to store structured and unstructured data at any scale and analyze it using different analytics and machine learning tools. A storage repository that holds a vast amount of raw data in its native format until it is needed. This definition emphasizes the central concept of a data lake as a storage solution for various types of data, including structured, semi-structured, and unstructured data, without the need for prior transformation. The data is stored in its original format until it's required for analysis or processing. This approach contrasts with traditional data warehousing methods, where data is typically structured and transformed before being stored. Source: Bill Inmon, often regarded as the "father of data warehousing"

Data Lakehouse: A unified data platform that combines the scalability and flexibility of data lakes with the structure, governance, and query capabilities of data warehouses. It aims to address some of the limitations and challenges associated with traditional data warehousing and data lakes. Source: Bill Inmon, often regarded as the "father of data warehousing"

Data Lifecycle: The sequence of stages that a particular unit of data goes through from its initial generation or capture to its eventual archival and/or deletion. The Data

Management Body of Knowledge (DMBOK), published by DAMA International, outlines the data life cycle.

Data Acquisition/Capture: This stage involves the collection of raw data from various sources, such as databases, sensors, files, or external systems. Data may be acquired through manual input, automated processes, or integration with other systems.

Data Storage: Once data is acquired, it needs to be stored in a secure and organized manner. This stage involves decisions about where and how to store data, including considerations such as storage technologies, data formats, and access controls.

Data Processing/Transformation: Data often requires processing or transformation to make it usable for analysis, reporting, or other purposes. This stage involves activities such as cleaning, filtering, aggregating, and enriching data to improve its quality and relevance.

Data Analysis/Usage: In this stage, data is analyzed to extract insights, identify patterns, and make informed decisions. This may involve various analytical techniques, such as descriptive, diagnostic, predictive, or prescriptive analytics, depending on the organization's goals and requirements.

Data Archiving/Retention: Over time, data may become less frequently accessed or needed for operational purposes. This stage involves archiving or retaining data for compliance, historical reference, or other purposes. Data retention policies and practices are established to ensure data is stored appropriately and securely.

Data Disposal/Deletion: Eventually, data may reach the end of its useful life or become obsolete. This stage involves securely disposing of or deleting data in compliance with legal, regulatory, and organizational requirements. Proper data disposal practices help mitigate risks associated with data breaches or unauthorized access.

These stages represent a high-level overview of the data life cycle, highlighting the key activities and processes involved in managing data from acquisition to disposal. Effective data management practices ensure that data is accurate, accessible, secure, and compliant throughout its life cycle.

Data Lineage: A visual representation of data's lifecycle, highlighting how data is sourced, processed, stored, and utilized in its environment.

Data Management: The process of ingesting, storing, organizing, and maintaining the data created and collected by an organization.

Data Masking: A method for creating a sanitized version of data by obscuring individual data items within a database, making the data anonymous but retaining its authenticity for testing or development purposes.

Data Mining: The process of discovering patterns and knowledge from vast amounts of data. It involves extracting information from data and transforming it into an understandable and usable structure.

Data Monetization: The process by which businesses earn revenue from their data assets.

Data Processing: Collection and manipulation of data to produce meaningful information.

Data Provenance: Information about the origin and lineage of a dataset.

Data Redundancy: Storing the same data in more than one place, which can be intentional (for backup or performance reasons) or unintentional, leading to inconsistencies.

Data Replication: The process of copying data from one location to another, ensuring consistency between redundant resources to improve reliability, fault tolerance, or accessibility.

Data Retention Policy: A policy that governs the duration for which a company's data should be stored and when it should be discarded.

Data Silos: Separate databases or repositories of data that are kept apart from a business's main data processing and storage systems and aren't easily accessible or integrated into the business's main data infrastructure.

Data Sovereignty: The concept that digital data is subject to the laws of the country in which it is located.

Data Stewardship: The management and oversight of an organization's data assets to ensure that data is accessible, reliable, and maintained, and that its users are held accountable for its use and protection.

Data Tampering: The deliberate modification of data in an unauthorized manner, often for malicious purposes.

Data Warehouse: Large central repositories of integrated data from one or more disparate sources. An architectural structure that supports the management of data that is: A collection of integrated subject-oriented databases designed to support the Data Decision Support function, where each unit of data is relevant to some moment in time. The data warehouse contains atomic data and lightly summarized data.[298]

Data Warehousing: A system used for reporting and analyzing data, where data is uploaded from operational systems and undergoes processing to ensure its quality, relevancy, and accuracy.

Database Management System (DBMS): Software that handles the storage, retrieval, and updating of data in a computer system.

DataOps: An automated and process-oriented methodology used by analytic and data teams to improve the quality and reduce the cycle time of data analytics.

DDoS Attack (Distributed Denial of Service): A malicious attempt to disrupt the normal traffic of a targeted server, service, or network by overwhelming the target with a flood of internet traffic.

Decentralized Data Systems: Systems where data is stored across a network of personal computers rather than in a central database.

---

[298] Source = Bill Inmon, often regarded as the "father of data warehousing."

Decentralized Systems: Systems where components, data, or processes are distributed across multiple locations or platforms rather than being controlled from a single centralized point.

Decryption: The process of converting encrypted data back into its original form.

Deep Learning: A subfield of machine learning that uses neural networks with many layers (hence "deep") to analyze various factors of data.

Deepfake: AI-driven technology that creates hyper-realistic but entirely fake content, often used to produce videos that appear real. A deepfake refers to a manipulated or synthesized media, typically video or audio, that appears to be real but is actually fabricated using advanced AI techniques, particularly deep learning algorithms.

Differential Privacy: A system that allows organizations to share aggregate information about a dataset by describing patterns of groups within the dataset while withholding information about individual participants.

Digital Forensics: The process of uncovering and interpreting electronic data for investigative purposes.

Digital Signature: A mathematical scheme for demonstrating the authenticity of a digital message or document, offering proof of origin, identity, and status of an electronic document.

Digital Transformation: The integration of digital technology into all areas of a business, resulting in fundamental changes to how businesses operate and how they deliver value to customers.

Digital Twin: A digital replica of a physical entity, process, or system. It acts as a bridge between the physical and digital worlds by using sensors to collect real-time data about a physical item.

Distributed Computing: A model in which components of a software system are shared among multiple computers to improve efficiency and performance.

Edge Computing: A distributed computing framework that brings data storage and processing closer to the location where it's needed to improve response times and save bandwidth.

Encryption At Rest: Refers to the encryption of data that is stored in a database, file, or certain applications, ensuring that it is unreadable if an unauthorized party tries to access it.

Encryption: The process of converting information or data into code to prevent unauthorized access.

Endpoint Security: The approach of protecting a corporate network when accessed via remote devices like laptops or other wireless devices. It ensures security for all endpoints that connect to the network.

Ensemble Learning: Machine learning methods that combine several models to produce one predictive model, often to reduce overfitting.

Ethical AI: The practice of designing, developing, and deploying AI in a manner that aligns with accepted human values and norms, prioritizing fairness, accountability, and transparency.

Explainable AI (XAI): An area in AI focused on creating techniques and models that make the decision-making process transparent and understandable.

Feature Engineering: The process of selecting and transforming variables when creating a predictive model using machine learning.

Federated Learning: A machine learning approach where the training process occurs across multiple devices or servers holding local data samples without exchanging the actual data. This helps preserve privacy and reduce communication costs.

Feedback Loop: In the context of machine learning, it refers to the process of feeding the model's predictions back into the model for further training and refinement.

Few-shot Learning: Training a model on a very small dataset—challenging due to the increased chance of overfitting.

Firewall: A network security device that monitors and filters incoming and outgoing network traffic based on an organization's security policies.

GAN (Generative Adversarial Network): A class of artificial intelligence algorithms that consists of two networks, the generator and the discriminator, which are trained together. The generator tries to produce data, while the discriminator tries to distinguish real data from fake data.

GDPR (General Data Protection Regulation): A regulation in EU law on data protection and privacy for all individuals within the European Union.

Generalization: The ability of an AI model to perform well on new, unseen data.

Generative Models: A type of machine learning model that's used to generate new, synthetic instances of data that can pass for real data.

Genomic Data: Information related to genes and their functions, often used to identify genetic disorders and predict disease risks.

Governance Framework: A structured approach to governing, typically comprising a set of rules, practices, and processes used to direct and manage an organization.

Gradient Descent: An optimization algorithm used to minimize the function representing the model error.

Hashing: A process that transforms input data of any size into a fixed-size value, typically used for verifying data integrity.

Homomorphic Encryption: A cryptographic method that allows computation on ciphertexts, generating an encrypted result which, when decrypted, matches the result of the operations as if they had been performed on the plain text.

Honeypot: A security mechanism set up as a decoy to lure cyber attackers and detect, deflect, or study hacking attempts.

Hyperautomation: The application of advanced technologies, including AI and machine learning, to increasingly automate processes and augment humans.

Immutable Data Storage: Data storage systems where data, once written, cannot be changed or deleted.

Inference Engines: Components of a system that apply logical rules to the knowledge base to deduce new information.

Insider Threat: Refers to risks posed by individuals within the organization, such as employees, contractors, or business associates, who have inside information concerning security practices, data, and computer systems.

Intrusion Detection System (IDS): A system or software application that monitors network or system activities for malicious activities.

Intrusion Detection Systems (IDS): Devices or software applications that monitor networks or systems for malicious activity or policy violations.

IoT (Internet of Things): Refers to the network of physical devices, vehicles, home appliances, and other items embedded with sensors and software for connecting and exchanging data with other devices and systems over the Internet.

Knowledge Graph: A knowledge base that uses a graph-structured data model or topology to integrate data from different sources and represent information as entities and the relationships between them.

Latent Variables: Variables in statistical models that are not directly observed but are inferred from observed data.

Long Short-Term Memory (LSTM): A type of RNN designed to recognize patterns over long intervals of time.

Machine Learning (ML): A subset of AI that involves the use of algorithms and statistical models to enable machines to improve their performance on a task through experience.

Machine Learning as a Service (MLaaS): Cloud services from providers that offer machine learning tools as part of cloud computing services.

Machine Learning Models: Algorithms that give computers the ability to learn from and make decisions based on data without being explicitly programmed for a specific task.

Machine Vision: The capability of a computer to perceive, interpret, and make decisions based on visual inputs (like identifying defects on a production line or recognizing faces).

Malware: Malicious software specifically designed to disrupt, damage, or gain unauthorized access to computer systems.

Model Inversion: An attack that aims to extract details or secrets from a machine learning model by querying it.

Model Optimization: The process of adjusting a machine learning model to improve its accuracy, efficiency, or both.

Model Poisoning: The introduction of harmful data into a machine learning model's training set to corrupt its outcomes.

Multi-factor Authentication (MFA): A security system that requires more than one method of authentication from independent categories of credentials to verify the user's identity.

Multimodal Learning: Machine learning models designed to process and relate information from multiple different data sources, like text and images together.

Natural Language Processing (NLP): A branch of AI that focuses on the interaction between computers and humans through natural language, aiming to enable machines to understand and respond to human language inputs.

Neural Architecture Search (NAS): An automated method for finding the best-fitting neural network architecture for a specific dataset and task.

Neural Network: A series of algorithms that attempt to recognize underlying relationships in a set of data through a process that mimics the way the human brain operates.

Neuroevolution: A form of artificial intelligence that uses evolutionary algorithms to generate artificial neural networks, optimized for a particular task.

Neuromorphic Computing: A branch of computing that aims to mimic the neural structure of the human brain, creating hardware that can simulate neurons and synapses.

NLP (Natural Language Processing): A field of artificial intelligence that gives computers the ability to understand, interpret, and generate human language in a meaningful way.

NoSQL Database: A class of database management systems that do not use the traditional tabular relational database model, often more scalable and flexible than relational databases.

On-Premises Computing: Computing infrastructure that is located physically at an organization's premises, rather than being hosted by third-party services.

One-hot Encoding: A process of converting categorical data variables so they can be provided to machine learning algorithms to improve predictions.

Overfitting: A modeling error in machine learning when a model is too closely tailored to the training data and performs poorly on new data.

Phishing: A method used by cybercriminals to deceive individuals into providing sensitive data by pretending to be a trustworthy entity, usually via email.

Post-Quantum Cryptography: Refers to cryptographic algorithms that are secure against the potential threats posed by quantum computers.

Predictive Analytics: Techniques that use statistical algorithms and machine learning techniques to identify the likelihood of future outcomes based on historical data.

Prescriptive Analytics: A type of data analytics that uses machine learning to offer suggestions for ways to handle potential future scenarios.

Public Key Infrastructure (PKI): A combination of hardware, software, policies, and standards that work together to provide a framework to assist in preventing unauthorized access to information.

Q-learning: A model-free reinforcement learning algorithm used to find the best action to take given the current state.

Quantum Computing: An area of study centered on the development of computer-based technologies centered around the principles of quantum theory. Quantum computers use quantum bits or qubits, which can be both a 0 and a 1 simultaneously, enabling them to perform multiple calculations at once.

Quantum Encryption: A method of encoding data in such a way that it can only be deciphered by using the principles of quantum mechanics, promising potentially unbreakable encryption.

Quantum Key Distribution (QKD): A technique that uses quantum mechanics to securely exchange cryptographic keys between two parties, preventing any eavesdropping attempts.

Random Forest: An ensemble learning method that fits multiple decision tree classifiers or regressors on various sub-samples of the dataset and uses averaging to improve predictive accuracy and control overfitting.

Ransomware: Malicious software that blocks access to a computer system or data, usually by encrypting it, until a sum of money is paid.

Recurrent Neural Network (RNN): A type of neural network well-suited for sequential data like time series or natural language.

Redundancy: The duplication of critical components or functions of a system with the intention of increasing the reliability of the system.

Reinforcement Learning: A type of machine learning where agents learn how to behave in an environment by taking actions and receiving rewards or penalties based on those actions.

Robotics Process Automation (RPA): Technology that allows anyone to configure computer software, or a "robot," to emulate and integrate the actions of a human interacting within digital systems to execute a business process.

Robust AI: Artificial intelligence systems that are designed to operate effectively under different conditions, including adversarial attacks or when faced with unfamiliar inputs.

Robustness (in AI): The ability of an algorithm to continue functioning accurately even when faced with problematic or unexpected input.

ROI (Return on Investment): A metric used to measure the profitability of an investment.

Sandboxing: A security mechanism used to run an application in a restricted environment to prevent it from affecting other parts of the system.

Secure Sockets Layer (SSL): A protocol for establishing secure links between two devices, typically a web server and a browser.

Semantic Analysis: A process that determines the meaning of a sequence of words in a sentence or document. In AI, this helps machines "understand" and respond to user queries in a more human-like manner.

Semi-supervised Learning: A middle ground between supervised and unsupervised learning, where the model is trained using a combination of labeled and unlabeled data.

Sequence-to-Sequence Models: Models that convert sequences from one domain (e.g., sentences in English) into sequences in another domain (e.g., the same sentences translated to Spanish).

Smart City: An urban area that uses various types of electronic methods and sensors to collect data, with insights gained from that data used to manage assets, resources, and services efficiently.

Stakeholder: Any person, group, or organization that has an interest in or impact on an organization's objectives and operations.

Supervised Learning: A type of machine learning where the algorithm is trained on labeled data, meaning the data is paired with the correct answer.

Swarm Intelligence: A form of artificial intelligence inspired by the behavior of social insects, like ants and bees, that emphasizes the collective behaviors of decentralized and self-organized systems.

Synthetic Data: Data not obtained from real-world events but artificially created, often used for training machine learning models when real data is scarce.

Tokenization: The process of replacing sensitive data with unique identification symbols that retain all the essential information about the data without compromising its security.

Transfer Learning: A machine learning method where a model developed for a task is reused as the starting point for a model on a second task. It's essentially a method of transferring learned features from one application to another.

Transparency in AI: The clarity and understandability of AI decision-making processes.

Transparent AI: AI models and operations that are clear and understandable, typically to aid humans in understanding how decisions or predictions are made.

Tuple: A segment, record, or group of data elements. Represented as a row of data in a two-dimensional (flat) file.

Turing Test: A measure of a machine's ability to demonstrate human-like intelligence. If a machine can converse with a human without the human knowing it's a machine, it passes the test.

Two-factor Authentication (2FA): An extra layer of security used to ensure people can't easily gain unauthorized access to an account, typically requiring not only a password and username but also something that only the user knows or possesses.

Underfitting: When a model is too simple to capture the underlying structure of the data, leading to poor performance.

Unsupervised Learning: A type of machine learning where the algorithm is trained on unlabeled data, detecting patterns and relationships in the data without any pre-defined classifications.

Validation Data: A subset of data used to assess the performance of a machine learning model, but not involved in the actual training of the model.

Virtual Reality (VR): A simulated experience that can be similar to or entirely different from the real world, typically requiring users to wear headsets.

Virtualization: The act of creating a virtual version of something, including virtual computer hardware platforms, storage devices, and computer network resources.

VR (Virtual Reality): A simulated experience that can be similar or completely different from the real world.

Word Embeddings: The representation of words or phrases in vectors of real numbers, often used in NLP tasks.

Zero-Day Exploit: An attack that targets a software vulnerability unknown to the software's maker and typically has no available fixes at the time of the attack.

Zero-Day Vulnerability: A software security flaw unknown to the software's creator, and thus they have had no time ("zero days") to address and patch it.

Zero-Knowledge Proofs: A cryptographic method by which one party (the prover) can prove to another party (the verifier) that they know a value X, without conveying any information apart from the fact that they know the value X.

Zero-shot Learning: Training a model to handle tasks it hasn't seen before during training.

Zero Trust Architecture: A security model that assumes that threats could be both external and internal, and thus, no entity inside or outside the network should be trusted by default.

Index

www.ingramcontent.com/pod-product-compliance
Lightning Source LLC
Chambersburg PA
CBHW051749200326
41597CB00025B/4496